RO
MASSE

A Life in Foot
and a Coach to the

ROY MASSEY

A Life in Football
and a Coach to the Stars

With Mark Metcalf

First published by Pitch Publishing, 2023

Pitch Publishing
9 Donnington Park,
85 Birdham Road,
Chichester,
West Sussex,
PO20 7AJ
www.pitchpublishing.co.uk
info@pitchpublishing.co.uk

ISBN 978 1 80150 434 8

Typesetting and origination by Pitch Publishing
Printed and bound in Great Britain by TJ Books, Padstow

Contents

Acknowledgements

MANY THANKS to John Bottomley, Julia, Liam Brady, Gary Bray, Rob Dipple, Jim Fox, who sadly died before this book was published, Steve Gordos, Chuka and Alex Iwobi, Andy Kelly, Graham Lloyd, Paul Massey, Ritchie Piggford, Charles, Matthew, Chris and Joe Willock, Sue Shipp, Paul Nevard, Jonathan Clark, Carl Fletcher, Daria Maria Koukoleva and all at Pitch Publishing for making this book possible.

Foreword by Liam Brady

I TOOK over as head of youth development at Arsenal in 1996. When Howard Wilkinson became the FA's technical director, overseeing coaching at all levels of the game, he began to dramatically change youth and schoolboy football through the academy system.

Clubs could now seek to sign children from the age of eight upwards. I needed a department at Arsenal dedicated to the younger schoolboys. Roy had come to my attention quite a lot with the work he was doing for Norwich City. He had set up a centre in London for Norwich and he was getting a lot of good young players for Norwich who Arsenal, Spurs or West Ham should have been recruiting.

I thought he would be a good asset to the academy in recruiting the younger element and I made a great choice as he was absolutely brilliant in running and coaching and managing the eight-to-12-year-old groups in the academy. Roy created great relationships with the boys.

Roy created a team of scouts – including some who had been with Norwich – and coaches. Roy was also very strong with parents and they got on well with him. Roy would take children on tours and the parents would love it. There was a great atmosphere around the academy and that was because of Roy.

His success was tremendous. We won the FA Youth Cup three times in those 16 years with many of the boys who Roy had recruited at nine, ten and 11 years of age. Quite a lot went on to play for the first team and/or be sold for a lot of money. Roy's work really paid dividends for the academy.

Introduction

Roy Massey – a lifelong football man and coach to the stars

IN 1998 the biggest change yet in the history of the development of young footballers transformed Roy Massey's life. Inspired by Howard Wilkinson, one of Massey's opponents as a player, the FA agreed to facilitate the creation of an academy system that would allow clubs to attract and train children from eight years old upwards.

Chosen to oversee this radical initiative at Highbury, club legend and head of youth development Liam Brady was quick to choose Massey as his assistant academy manager.

In these pages we learn how the structure was designed from scratch and plans laid, and later refined, to discover and help develop a rich vein of young talent capable of making it to the first team at one of the world's greatest clubs.

In a highly competitive field, Massey explains why certain young players such as Jack Wilshere, Bukayo Saka and Alex Iwobi made it at Arsenal and why he, wrongly as it transpired on occasions, allowed others to leave. There are also heartbreaking stories of youngsters who had their lives as players snatched from them by career-ending injuries.

Roy Massey's own story is that of a dedicated and lifelong football man whose 50 years in the professional game spanned the full gamut of the sport's dramatic and evolutionary change.

Here is a man, unlucky with injuries throughout his whole career as a player, but always respected enough for his knowledge and experience to ensure that he was never short of an important role in the game he would always love.

Massey scored goals for his hometown club Rotherham United, followed by spells at Leyton Orient and Colchester United, before another serious injury brought his playing career to an early end at an age at which most players are nearing their peak.

He then combined working as a PE teacher and managing in non-league football with behind-the-scenes work to discover and nurture young talent at Colchester.

Massey, who was brought up on tales of great games by his grandfather Jimmy, an FA Cup winner with Sheffield Wednesday in 1896, recalls what it was like playing in the lower leagues just after the end of the maximum wage and in a decade when England won the World Cup. He explains why he turned down the opportunity to sign a professional contract with, among others, Arsenal and Aston Villa, in the early 1960s. He also recalls the inspiration he felt when Colchester manager Dick Graham asked him to revive the Essex club's youth system and how his eye for talent, organisation, training methods and motivational skills aided the development of many youngsters into successful players.

Little wonder then, in the wake of the launch of the Premier League in 1992, that Norwich City asked Massey to join them as they moved to revolutionise their own youth programme.

His success at Carrow Road didn't go unnoticed and when Liam Brady asked Massey to join him at Arsenal it was the start of a flourishing 16-year partnership. Even after leaving the Gunners in 2014, Massey remained in football well into his 70s, with spells scouting for three Premier League clubs.

Throughout the book, Massey's love for football is never far from the surface, as from an early age it was always, like most of us, what he dreamed he would do for a living.

Chapter 1

Finally signing for Arsenal

IN FEBRUARY 1998 I was appointed assistant academy manager at Arsenal. My role was to establish a recruitment and development programme for boys aged eight to 12.

I started work there on 1 March 1998; it was one of the most exciting days of my life. The drive down the road to Highbury, Arsenal's north London home for 85 years, was a great thrill. The white East Stand frontage lay ahead of me with 'Arsenal Stadium' set proudly in big red letters over the imposing main entrance which brought awestruck visitors to the famous Art Deco marble halls with its terrazzo floors.

The entrance was intended to impress and indeed would serve as a monument to the club's permanence in the top flight of the English game. Its status as a Grade II listed building meant it survived the demolition of the stadium itself, being incorporated into the design for the apartments built on the site. But I had no time to linger; I had an appointment with Liam Brady.

Dublin-born Liam, or 'Chippy' as he was best known, was an Arsenal and Juventus legend who had made more than 600 club and international appearances. This included close to 300 for the Gunners. He won the FA Cup with the club in 1979, when he was selected by his peers as the Professional Footballers' Association Players' Player of the Year.

Liam later captured successive Italian league titles with Juventus, a remarkable feat, but he came 'home' in July 1996 to take up the post of Arsenal's head of youth development and was also the academy director.

From 1991 I had been working for the Norwich City youth department. This was initially on a part-time basis. I also ran coaching sessions in Colchester and at a centre I established at Potters Bar in Hertfordshire.

At the time, professional clubs had schools of excellence to which they sought to attract players who were aged at least 13 years old. But junior football was changing. When I became full-time with Norwich in the 1994/95 season, I was asked to look for talent as young as eight. And at the start of 1997/98, Liam, aware of the radical changes imminent under Howard Wilkinson, asked Arsenal's scouts to follow suit. These talent spotters began watching district school football in north London but when they approached the better players they found that I had already got there first and signed many of them.

Liam soon got in touch to ask me if Norwich's under-nines, under-tens and under-11s would play against their Arsenal counterparts at Potters Bar. The Norwich boys had been training and playing with us for some time. Unsurprisingly, they won these games fairly comfortably. A few weeks later, we received a letter from Liam stating that he would be approaching six of the Norwich boys he had watched to offer them trials with Arsenal.

Norwich later played Arsenal in an under-14 match, putting Ross Flitney – a trialist goalkeeper from Potters Bar – in their goal. Ross had a very good game and the following day I rang his father saying I was pleased to offer his son schoolboy forms on the strength of his performance against Arsenal.

There was an embarrassed silence at the end of the telephone. Eventually, Mr Flitney said that an Arsenal scout had been to his house that morning and Ross had signed for the club. It was apparent that the hunt for young talent was suddenly becoming even more of a cut-throat business.

Clearly impressed by the work I had been undertaking on behalf of Norwich, Liam approached me at the start of 1998 to ask if I would consider becoming the assistant manager at the developing Arsenal academy.

Brady's assistant head of youth development was David Court, who had signed for Arsenal as an amateur in 1959 before turning professional and making close to 200 first-team appearances. Both men greeted me fondly, as did Sue Shipp, the academy secretary appointed just a few weeks before me. I did not know then that I was embarking on a 16-year adventure with one of the greatest football clubs in the world.

Arsenal had actually come calling for me before, 34 years earlier, when I was just 20 and had, with great reluctance, only recently turned down opportunities to sign as a professional for several clubs.

In 1962 I had started studying for a Physical Education certificate at St Paul's College, Cheltenham, now part of the University of Gloucester. I knew that attaining that qualification could guarantee me job security for life and after doing so I hoped to play professional football until becoming a teacher in later life. But in my first term at college, I was accepted for trials with Arsenal.

These were to take place over Christmas 1962 but a bleak, icy winter saw them cancelled for months. I did not make my debut until 23 February 1963. This was in the Metropolitan League as an amateur for the Gunners' A team at Guildford City's ground. We won 3-0 and I scored twice. I later played four more league matches and in the semi-final of the League Cup and scored five goals. I also made my reserve-team debut in a 4-1 victory against Leicester City. I scored once and did the same in another reserve match when Peterborough were beaten 2-1. This gave me a record of nine goals in eight matches.

My team-mates included Peter Simpson, Peter Storey, John Sammels, David Court and George Armstrong, all of whom later became regular Arsenal first-team players.

Former Arsenal and England full-back George Male, the Gunners' youth development officer, then contacted me to discuss my availability for games. I could only play for Arsenal when the college did not have a game as it was a course requirement that I prioritised college fixtures over playing, at any level, for anyone else. I did not envisage that more than 30 years later I would be doing George Male's job.

Arsenal won the Metropolitan League in 1962/63, collecting 54 points from 32 games, scoring 107 goals and conceding 29. Oxford United's reserves came second and West Ham A finished fifth.

The Arsenal A team was created in 1929 to give opportunities to younger players. In 1931/32 they won the London Professional Mid-Week League. With football suspended during the Second World War it was not until the 1948/49 season that the A team was resurrected.

In 1958 they joined the Metropolitan League. The venture was initially successful – with title wins in 1958/59, 1960/61 and 1962/63 – but Arsenal later left after the 1968/69 season, mainly because strong amateur teams were proving tough opposition for the youngsters. Arsenal had finished that season in 13th place out of 16 teams.

In the lead-up to the start of 1963/64, I accepted an invitation to train with the Arsenal reserve squad. I enjoyed sharing digs during this time with John Radford, who, like me, was a Yorkshireman. Clearly those in charge felt that with our broad Yorkshire accents we would have one person each we could understand!

On the first training day, John said he was going to take part in every practice session using his left foot only. John went on to have a fine career and gained legendary status at Arsenal. Despite being a young man in 1963, John did not need a coach to help him improve a weakness in his game. He identified a problem and fixed it himself.

I enjoyed training with Arsenal and I especially recall a pre-season friendly against Cambridge United that was due to be played at Highbury. The heavy non-stop rain had left the pitch flooded and the game was moved to the training pitch at London Colney. I scored two headers in a 3-0 victory. That was now 11 goals in nine appearances for Arsenal.

I remember the following day a small article in a local paper which stated that the first-team's centre-forward Joe Baker, who was Billy Wright's first signing in July 1962 from Hibernian, should look over his shoulder as college boy Roy Massey appeared to be a big prospect. In September 1963 I scored five goals in two Metropolitan League matches against West Ham and Kettering Town.

The Arsenal reserve team was first set up when the club played South of the Thames in Plumstead and was known as Royal Arsenal. After the First World War, Arsenal reserves played in the London Football Combination, and in 1999 they joined the newly formed Premier Reserve League. The reserves later became an under-21 team with three over-age outfield players and one goalkeeper permitted in matchday squads.

There were generally a couple of thousand spectators at the reserve games in the early 1960s. I was always delighted to pull on the iconic Arsenal kit with its red shirts and contrasting white sleeves. The design, introduced by Herbert Chapman in 1933, made the team instantly and forever recognisable.

On 2 November 1963 I scored once in a 5-0 victory against Colchester United reserves. The Arsenal forward line was Skirton, Court, Massey, Sammels and Gould.

I was then unable to play any more games for Arsenal until the Christmas holidays when I scored once against Rainham Town for the A team in a 4-3 victory. On 28 December 1963 I played what proved to be my final appearance in an Arsenal shirt and it proved a difficult afternoon as Tottenham reserves beat us 4-0. My overall record for Arsenal was 18 goals in 14 appearances.

Towards the end of the 1963/64 season, Arsenal manager Billy Wright, the legendary Wolves and England half-back, called me into his office to offer me a professional contract. At the time the club had the best overall record in the Football League with seven title wins, one more than Aston Villa and Sunderland. Arsenal had won the FA Cup three times.

This offer presented me with a very difficult decision. Do I sign as a professional footballer for Arsenal? Doing so would require terminating my college course; I had already completed two of the three years.

Clearly, such are the sums of money involved today in signing a professional contract with one of the biggest clubs in the land it would be a much more difficult decision to remain at college, as a young player can become rich very quickly.

In the end I decided to decline the offer as it would have meant not completing my PE certificate. In the long term this was to prove a wise decision.

But if I had played for Arsenal in the first team, I would have followed in the footsteps of another footballer from Mexborough, my hometown. Lionel Smith was born in 1920. During the Second World War he served as a sapper and was badly injured. He made his league debut at left-back in May 1948, aged by then 28. He was still good enough to go on to make 162 league appearances plus 18 in the FA Cup including the final in 1952 which Arsenal lost 2-0 against Newcastle United. Lionel, who was a brilliant passer, good in the air, quick in recovery and swift to clear his lines, was a league champion in 1953 and he was capped six times for England. He later played for Watford.

I had returned to Arsenal just as they were about to complete one of the greatest seasons in their proud history. They beat

Newcastle at Wembley to lift the FA Cup for the seventh time and also won their 11th league title, their first in the new Premier League era. Only Liverpool had won the title on more occasions. For the second time Arsenal completed the Double of winning the league and FA Cup in the same season, a feat they first achieved in 1970/71.

The decision by the Arsenal board to appoint their first overseas manager in Frenchman Arsène Wenger in 1996 had paid dividends. Vice-chairman David Dein had wanted Arsène to become manager in 1995 but he was overruled by other board members who preferred Bruce Rioch, the Bolton Wanderers boss and a former Scottish international. Rioch lasted one season at Highbury with Arsenal finishing fifth in the Premier League.

Dein finally got his man when the board backed his judgement. Dein and Wenger were to forge a magnificent partnership and the manager built a success level that seems unlikely to be replicated anytime soon. Silverware was to become the norm and it was won thanks to a brand of exciting, fast, stylish, attractive football.

Nevertheless, appointing Wenger in 1996 was a bold move by Arsenal. Dutch legend Johan Cruyff, three times a European Cup winner with Ajax in the 1970s, was the favourite to take over but was overlooked in favour of Wenger who on his appointment said, 'I love English football, the roots of the game are here. I like the spirit round the game and at Arsenal I like the spirit of the club and its potential.' Many pundits had not heard of Wenger – 'Arsène who?' – and queried whether he could bring success to the north London club.

Wenger's playing career had not been a major one but he had played professionally, appearing twice for RC Strasbourg in France when they won Ligue 1 in 1978/79. As a manager he inspired Monaco to the title in 1987/88 and the Coupe de France in 1990/91 before enjoying cup success with Japanese side Nagoya Grampus Eight in 1995 and 1996. Wenger was a deep thinker and had strong ideas about team building.

The Arsenal side Wenger selected to face Newcastle in the 1998 FA Cup Final was Seaman, Dixon, Winterburn, Vieira, Keown, Adams (captain), Parlour, Anelka, Petit, Wreh and Overmars. The substitutes were Platt, Manninger, Bould, Wright and Grimandi. Ray Parlour and Tony Adams were the only two of the 16 to have come up through the Arsenal ranks. By setting up the academy the aim was to bring through more homegrown talent, which now would be drawn from across the world.

In my 16 years with the academy, Arsène was the only first-team manager I worked with. He was in charge until 2018, bringing great success with four Premier League championships and seven FA Cup victories plus losing appearances in the Champions League and UEFA Cup finals of 2006 and 2000 respectively.

Before Wenger arrived, Arsenal had a reputation for boring football; many games were low-scoring and while 1-0 wins were pleasing for the fans it was not particularly entertaining.

What those results did show was that the defending was first class. The names of Lee Dixon, Tony Adams, Martin Keown, Steve Bould, Nigel Winterburn and the goalkeeper, David Seaman, remain legendary at the club.

Wenger built his first successful side on this defence. He combined this with his extensive knowledge of top players in France such as Patrick Vieira, Emmanuel Petit, Robert Pires and Thierry Henry to turn Arsenal into a great side. Arsène was also fortunate to have Dennis Bergkamp and Ray Parlour at the club when he arrived. Over the following years he also led the way for Premier League clubs to search for world-class talent in Europe and South America. Such an approach often included spending heavily in order to attract players such as Vieira – who had been with AC Milan in Italy – from other top clubs.

Wenger never interfered with the running of the youth department, leaving it in the capable hands of Liam Brady. Don Howe was the under-18 team coach. Only once during my 16 years with the club did Wenger visit the academy, when we opened a sports centre at the newly built premises in Walthamstow. Clearly he believed that Liam had the experience and knowledge to take care of youth development.

As a young assistant first-team coach, Wenger had a year at Ligue 2 side AS Cannes, where he also set up the training academy, recruited young players from the age of five upwards, carried out trials and rethought the training sessions. Youngsters trained between 8.30am and 10am and then from 2pm to 4pm.

On my first visit to the training ground at London Colney, I was introduced to Wenger by his assistant Pat Rice who explained to him that I had been appointed to recruit and develop young players. The new boss laughed that he and Pat would be watching from the stands with their walking sticks by the time some of these players were ready for the first team.

It was not just an age factor. Wenger already had a great team and he had the resources – only, of course, if spent wisely – to compete in the transfer market against other top clubs for the best players. Wenger's success in leading Arsenal to their greatest-ever period over the next decade undoubtedly meant it would be difficult to produce players from the academy good enough to become first-team regulars. How do you develop youngsters to fill the boots of the likes of Henry, Seaman, Vieira, Adams and Petit?

What Wenger was prepared to do was give opportunities for any youngster who impressed him when doing well in training with the first team. While some had their careers cut short by injuries, many others did not quite show the consistency of performance required to play at the top level of the Premier League and in the Champions League.

Arsène was always willing to help out if we wanted to sign a young player for the academy. On occasions I would take boys and their parents to the training ground to meet some of the first-team players.

Don Howe had a wonderful playing career as a full-back with West Bromwich Albion and England. He established himself as a coach with England and he was the first-team manager at West Brom, Galatasaray in Turkey, Arsenal, Queens Park Rangers and Coventry City. He was a lovely man as he always had time for people and he gained success through his knowledge of the game and encouragement rather than criticism.

When I joined the Arsenal academy, George Armstrong was the reserve-team coach. When I was training and playing for the A team and reserves at the club in the early 1960s, George, a direct winger who made 621 appearances for Arsenal, was establishing himself in the first team at the age of 19. George was an ever-present in the Double-winning 1970/71 side. His testimonial against Barcelona at Highbury in March 1974 attracted 36,000 fans.

George would visit the academy; he took a great interest in the young footballers. George was very popular among the young reserve players and everyone at the club was devastated when he suddenly collapsed during training after suffering a brain haemorrhage in October 2000. He died in the early hours of the following day. George was a wonderful footballer and an outstanding human being. A pitch at the London Colney training ground is named after him.

Developing the right facilities

For the first two years of academy football, from 1998 to 2000, the under-nine to under-12 squads played their home matches at weekends at the historic Brentwood School in Essex, which dates back to the 16th century. I later discovered that it was the site of the execution in 1555 of Catholic martyr William Hunter. Nothing quite so sinister took place when I was there!

Every Monday we trained on the floodlit Astroturf pitch. The development of floodlights in the 1950s and Astroturf a decade later proved to be a great combination for football coaching. Astroturf was first used in 1966 at the Houston Astrodome. Not only could it help overcome the cost of laying and maintaining natural grass, it could also be used in bad weather. The facilities – as we'll get to later on – were not the best, however.

Liam Brady and club director Richard Carr were soon searching for somewhere to buy so that the academy could have its own facility. A suitable venue was found in west London but it was felt that it was too far from the Arsenal catchment area that took in the East End and Essex from which many notable players had emerged over the years, including West Ham United's Bobby Moore, Geoff Hurst, Martin Peters and Trevor Brooking.

As the academies developed, West Ham had a tremendous array of talent with most of their young players coming from Essex and east London, although they did venture into north London, notably to take Joe Cole from Somers Town, Camden, from under the noses of the staff at Arsenal. However, Arsenal had their own talent from Essex in the Romford-born duo Tony Adams and Ray Parlour, who between them made more than 1,000 first-team appearances for the club.

Driving through Walthamstow, Liam and Richard noticed a 'for sale' sign on a site in Hale End containing playing fields, a pavilion, changing rooms and tennis courts. It belonged to the Royal London Hospital, the facility having long been used by hospital staff. It was just in the right place being next to the Crooked Billet roundabout, where the A406 and A172 met. It would be easily accessible for parents driving their boys to training and it was also a short bus journey from the Blackhorse Road tube station. Highams Park tube was also nearby.

Arsenal had no hesitation in buying the ground, which formally became the Arsenal Football Club Youth Academy, more commonly known as Hale End. Money was spent on the dressing rooms and the pitches. Groundsmen were instructed to mark out three pitches for 11 v 11 matches and a similar number for eight-a-side games.

The tennis courts, which had been kept in pristine condition under the tender care of the two groundsmen – Phil Howard, a Spurs fan, and John Stewart – had to go. They were replaced by a floodlight Astroturf pitch. This dismayed John and Phil, the latter having worked on these courts for 30 years, but they soon came to terms with the fact that Hale End was being used to develop footballers instead of future tennis players. Their relief was reinforced when Liam told them their jobs were safe. Phil even swapped sides to become a Gunner and loved going to watch games at Highbury and later the Emirates Stadium.

Like all of us, he was especially thrilled to watch young players who had come through Hale End make their first-team debuts. Phil and John, whose wife Moira did the cleaning and made the numerous refreshments at Hale End for the players and coaching staff, spent well over a decade working for Arsenal. Both men retired, like myself, in 2014.

In the 2000/01 pre-season we started preparing the training ground and within two years a first sports hall was built on one of the pitches. I had my own office and it was with some pride that I went to work each day and heard the opinion that with up-to-date facilities we could not fail to develop players who might one day play for Arsenal in the Premier League. Our facilities were the envy of the other London clubs, all of whom were a long way from matching our progress.

Chelsea was sharing pitches with Fulham and Wimbledon, and it was not until 2004 that the Stamford Bridge club started construction of their own training centre at Cobham where the facilities are now excellent.

Tottenham had sold their academy training ground and were renting pitches from a local club. This unsatisfactory state of affairs only changed when their new training ground at Hotspur Way, Enfield was finished in 2012.

The Chelsea and Spurs youth academy systems have developed several youngsters who have played for the first teams and internationally, and competition between the top London clubs to find youngsters who might make the grade is now understandably fierce. Any promising player fortunate enough to have several top clubs chasing him might be swayed to opt for the club with the best facilities.

I retired in September 2014 along with Liam Brady, who was replaced with Andries Jonker – who had been assistant to Louis van Gaal at the 2014 World Cup held in Brazil where they took the Netherlands to third place.

In his first year in charge of the academy, Andries persuaded the directors to invest in a complete overhaul of the facilities. The process took two years to complete. There is not an inch of the old academy that I now recognise. This includes a rightly much-improved security system which means that all cars are checked before entering the site and visitors have to complete a registration form. In the early years at Hale End, it had proved possible for two thieves to get on to the site and enter the changing rooms before taking Gordon Lawrence's car keys and then stealing his car.

The radical transformation is for the better, and Arsenal can compete in terms of facilities with Chelsea and Tottenham to sign the best young players in the London area.

There are far more people employed today at the academy than when I started. Back then, Steve Leonard and I, plus the three groundsmen, were the only full-time staff but we did have very enthusiastic, reliable part-time people helping us out.

Tunde Adeshokan, Gordon Lawrence, Rob Dipple and Ossie Aibangee were the first coaches I appointed to work with the under-nine to under-12 age groups. I came across Rob when I went to watch his under-ten team play. He was a young man in his early 20s. I could see that he was passionate and had loads of enthusiasm for the game. I noted one of his players who was head and shoulders above the rest.

Ossie subsequently went on to work for Tottenham before becoming manager of Brentford's academy where he recruited good staff and, together, they built up the standard of the players the Bees were attracting.

Tunde has given great service to Arsenal as a coach since he started with the Gunners in 1999 and subsequently as a scout, a role he was still undertaking on a part-time basis at the time of writing.

It was my job as assistant academy manager to ensure that coaches treated all the players the same. They might have a liking for some of their players, often because they are the best in the squad, or even a dislike because of their attitude, but it was extremely important that this like or dislike was never felt by any of the boys.

The four coaches and others who followed them attended training two nights each week and gave up their Sundays for the games programme. Gordon travelled in from Great Bentley, an Essex village 67 miles away from the academy. The coaches very rarely missed a session. Money was not their motivation; it was just a real desire to help the boys reach their full potential.

Arsenal and Highbury

The club was formed by David Danskin, who became Arsenal's first captain, and his friends in 1886. They all worked at the local ammunition factory, hence the club nickname of Gunners, at Royal Arsenal in Woolwich.

Highbury was originally built in 1913 when Woolwich Arsenal moved from south-east London to north London. The new ground was an opportunity for the club to attract more fans. The stadium was rebuilt in the 1930s when the famous Art Deco East and West Stands, designed by architect Claude Waterlow Ferrier, were erected. The immaculately kept pitch, on which over the years some of the best players in world football had performed, ran from north to south. Ferrier died in 1935 but his design for the West Stand was used to construct the East Stand under the supervision of partners in his company.

Highbury's record gate of 73,295 was for a First Division battle against title rivals Sunderland on 9 March 1935. Arsenal ended the campaign by winning the league for a third consecutive season. The famous team, which thus equalled Huddersfield Town's record of three consecutive championships in the 1920s, had been built by former Huddersfield manager Herbert Chapman, who died in 1934 aged just 55.

When I played at Highbury in the 1960s it had three covered stands. The open terracing to the left of the East Stand tunnel that led to the pitch had a huge 45-minute clock at the top of it – it became known as the Clock End. To the right of the East Stand was the terraced North Bank, which in 1936 saw a roof erected. This was subsequently replaced in 1954 after it was destroyed by the Luftwaffe during the London Blitz.

Chapter 2

A whole new ball game

MY FIRST tasks at Arsenal in March 1998 were threefold: assess the youngsters already at the academy; develop a coaching programme ready for the following season; and assemble a team of eight-year-olds good enough to play for the academy. I had around three months.

I was eight in 1951. The idea that professional football clubs would one day want to sign anyone so young would have been looked on with amazement. I did not play team football until I was nine when I was selected to play for the school team. I realised I had a talent to score goals and it was the best feeling in the world to see the ball sailing past the goalkeeper; so many goals were scored during my school days for St John's Primary School, Mexborough Secondary School, Mexborough Technical School, Don and Dearne Boys and Yorkshire Grammar Schools.

I remember my excitement when I played that first school game. Previously I had only played in knockabouts in the school playground. We had to walk a mile to the pitch – it was called the Red Rose, although it was not as pretty as its name. When we arrived, the farmer was removing the cows and I suppose my dribbling skills in part come from avoiding the cowpats when running with the ball.

Our shirts were Aston Villa colours of maroon and blue with short sleeves. They were not the shirts youngsters wear today; they had been lovingly knitted by one of the school dinner ladies. The boots were different too, with hard leather toe caps, but they did give us ankle protection, unlike some of the boots worn today.

The studs were leather and my dad had to nail them into the soles. Sometimes it felt as though I was running on a bed of nails. We drew that first game 1-1 and I scored our goal. However, the ball didn't actually hit the back of the net – we didn't have any. Our luxury was my mum giving out the sliced oranges at half-time.

As we were only a small Church of England school, selection wasn't easy and we did not win a game throughout that first season. But this didn't bother us; it was taking part in the match that mattered. I think it made me more competitive because I had to try harder in order to win a game. I had a passion for football because I just loved playing, but I never thought then of becoming a professional.

If I was on my own with a ball, I would spend hours, kicking it against the outside wall, doubtless much to the annoyance of the neighbours. I did not think that doing this would improve my control and passing skills; I was just enjoying kicking the ball against the wall and controlling it when it returned to me. If a friend was with me, we would pass to each other, and if there was four in our group we would play two-a-side with our jackets on the ground as goalposts. If there were ten of us we would play five-a-side, and if there were 20 we would play ten-a-side with all age groups mixed in.

I never had a coaching session at school. Football lessons always meant a game, sometimes 15 versus 15. If you were the best player you had possession of the ball more, so looking back this helped my skill development.

My cousin Roger was a left-winger and my friend Alan a goalkeeper. I was always centre-forward. We spent many hours on the local playing field with Roger crossing the ball with his left foot for me to strike or head the ball past Alan. This heading and shooting activity later helped me score many of my Football League goals.

In 1997, Howard Wilkinson, in his role as the FA's technical director, produced the FA document 'Charter for Quality' which overhauled youth development.

Two years earlier the FA had let it be known that clubs could consider altering their scouting and coaching systems to recruit children from as young as eight years old. There were only five clubs enlightened enough to take on board these proposals.

One of these was Norwich City, who I had been working part-time for since 1991 in developing the talents of 12- and 13-year-old players in the Colchester and London areas. In 1995, Norwich asked me to go full-time in my post. I gladly accepted and so 24 years after I was forced to finish as a professional player due to injury, I returned to working full-time in football. My efforts as a non-league manager, scout and coach for young players had finally paid off.

The 1997 FA document by Wilkinson, who I knew well, recommended selecting good, young players from representative school and youth-club football and establishing academies at professional clubs.

Previously, the rule was that boys were signed at 13 and trained at their local club's school of excellence, then those with potential could be signed on schoolboy forms when they reached aged 14.

Before Howard introduced the idea of academies, coaches and scouts at their various clubs were loath to look at boys as young as eight. They could not see the point of recruiting at such an early age.

In March 1998, how was I going to find sufficient players aged eight who were good enough to represent Arsenal in a little over three months?

I decided to contact the managers of the top Sunday clubs in London who ran teams of seven- and eight-year-olds. I asked if they would be prepared to send their two best players to our training ground at Potters Bar for a weekend of trials and assessments. Initially I was very pleased with the response and almost 60 boys attended.

But as the trials progressed, I became slightly disappointed with the overall standard of the boys' ability. Examining their surnames, I noticed many matched those of the team managers. I had been duped. Managers had not sent their best players, preferring instead to send their own sons to the trials. Maybe they were looking at their own boys through rose-tinted glasses and genuinely felt that they were the best players in their team.

Parents can get carried away with the anticipation of their son becoming a famous footballer. I have often told parents that having the best nine-year-old in London really means nothing. However, if he is the best 19-year-old in London then they may well have a top player on his hands.

The first under-nine team to represent the Arsenal academy held its own against the other London professional clubs we played. But it only produced one professional player, in Gavin Hoyte, born in Leytonstone in June 1990, who signed full terms for Arsenal in September 2007.

Gavin featured for Arsenal's under-18 and reserve teams, captaining both at times. He made three first-team appearances in the League Cup and played 30 minutes as a substitute in a Premier League match against Manchester City in November 2008. Gavin was released by Arsenal in May 2012 and has since played for numerous clubs in the Football League and National League, also winning three international caps for Trinidad and Tobago.

Back in 1998 I was very keen to make a good start and enhance the talent that was already at the academy. A parent from Enfield rang me and asked if I would have a look at his boy, who he said was a useful footballer. I was told he was 12 years old, that his name was Bonti and he had come over from Africa in order to settle in the north London area.

Bonti took part in a training session. My first impression was that he was certainly good enough to be invited back, despite the fact that he was slightly bigger and stronger than most 12-year-olds. I spoke to his dad and arranged for Bonti to play against Watford. The father said that he had another son who was younger and he was also a good footballer. The younger brother came down to train with the under-11s the next evening. He proved to be a very strong and quick player, and I was quite excited at the thought of adding him to the youngsters already at the academy.

Bonti played very well against Watford so I invited him to take part in a tournament we were attending in Holland. I asked his dad to bring in Bonti's passport the following week. Feeling pleased with myself, I was in the office the following Monday morning when the telephone rang.

'Hello, Roy, it's Bonti's dad, can I come over to see you?'

'Of course,' I replied and arranged to meet him that afternoon. A rather sheepish dad came into the office and he told me that he had made a mistake bringing his boys to training.

'Bonti isn't 12,' he said.

'How old is he?' I replied.

'He is 15 years old,' said Dad.

'How old is your youngest son?' I asked.

'He is 13 years of age.'

The father was extremely sorry regarding this deceit and for wasting my time. He explained that he had brought his sons over from Africa two years earlier and had put them in a local school three years below their rightful age so that they could catch up on their education. This seemed a reasonable thing to do, but I told him that there was no way that I could sign them for the academy. We shook hands and I wished the boys well for their future.

Two days later I was in the office when the telephone rang. It was the headmistress from the Enfield school where Bonti was a pupil. She knew that he had been training with us and had heard that there had been a query regarding his age, so asked me if I could throw any light on the matter.

I was quite evasive as I did not want the young man to get into trouble. The headmistress picked up on my reluctance to divulge Bonti's age. She said that his education would not be affected but he had played for the school sports teams the previous year and through his efforts they had won the district football, basketball, cross-country and athletics competitions. It was felt that if the age rumours were true then the respective trophies should go back to the sports associations. I confirmed her suspicions, the trophies were returned and the boys continued their education.

This was a great lesson to me not to get too carried away if a boy came in for a trial who was bigger, stronger and more powerful than his team-mates, even if I knew for certain their age. Many boys reach puberty early and have almost realised their full potential in terms of their physical development. The boy who reaches puberty later in his teens also has a problem in that he struggles physically when he has to play on a full-sized pitch. Such boys can be discarded before their full potential becomes evident.

Coaches spend much time in developing the technical ability of the players, which is vitally important at a young age. Academies introduced small-sided games, which were eight v eight for the under-nine to under-12 age groups. I watched many of the small-sided games but wondered if they helped improve the technical ability of a player.

At the first team's Shenley training ground, I had the chance to pick the brains of Brazilian international Sylvinho who was the regular left-back for Arsenal from 1999 to 2001. I took the opportunity to ask him about the development of young players in his country. He informed me that boys between eight and 11 only played four v four for football.

Sylvinho's time at Arsenal ended when a problem with his passport meant that he had to leave the club. He went to play in Spain and he twice won the UEFA Champions League with Barcelona, in 2006 and 2009.

Four years after academies were introduced, the staff at Manchester United attempted to attract clubs to their way of developing young players. Their idea was also to play four v four games with a pitch divided into four areas. One game was with goals, another was to dribble the ball over the line, a further activity was to dribble the ball through cones set up at the corners of the pitch, and the fourth was a keep-ball session in which you counted how many passes you could make before the opposition intercepted and regained possession. The idea was sound, but failed to inspire other clubs as three of the games did not include shooting.

With the amenities of clubs today I am sure that clubs could improve the technical ability of the younger age groups by playing five v five games on a pitch divided into four areas with portable goals on each area and with each team consisting of a goalkeeper and four outfield players, who would line up in a diamond shape with a defender at the base, two midfield players and a forward at the tip of the diamond.

Although the diamond shape would change, the players would always be expected to be conscious of their position in relation to their team-mates. The most valuable players in football today are the goalscorers and these small-sided games would be invaluable for the development of centre-forward play and scoring. The centre-half and midfield players would always be looking to play the ball to the centre-forward who then has many decisions to make when he receives it. Does he lay the ball off for a give and go? Does he continue to shield it first? Does he turn and dribble past the centre-half to shoot?

In these games the centre-forwards would have many different types of goalscoring opportunities, standing them in good stead going forward to play 11 v 11 football. Likewise, the centre-half would have many opportunities to defend and the midfield players numerous opportunities to link up with their defender and centre-forward, as well as having many shots at goal. The keepers would be in constant action.

The players would have many more touches of the ball than if they were playing eight v eight football, plus they would need to make decisions themselves. Also, the parents would not get so excited about their team winning because with so many goals being scored, they would forget the result!

In my early years at Arsenal, I arranged under-nine, under-ten and under-11 games against Tottenham Hotspur on three consecutive days at Easter. On one occasion, the under-11s played on the Monday and I was shocked by the behaviour of both sets of parents. It was as if they were watching the first XI playing. They were dissatisfied with many refereeing decisions and reacted badly if a player mistimed a tackle. At the match's conclusion the parents' attitude was dictated by who had won.

The following day, prior to the under-tens match, I called all parents together and told them what had happened the previous afternoon. I was determined it would not be repeated. The penny seemed to drop when I said their sons were not Spurs or Arsenal players but were youngsters who happened to be wearing an Arsenal or Spurs shirt.

Of course every parent wants the best for their boys, but football does seem to bring out a passion unlike any other sport.

During my many years as a PE teacher I arranged basketball, rugby, cricket and hockey matches. Parents watch their youngsters play and they cheer and clap but these sports do not generate the intensity regarding the need to win the game. Of course, contracts from top clubs are being given to youth players of 18 years of age that will make them millionaires by the time they are 21. So perhaps it is no wonder that adults can be anxious if their boys look as though they are not going to make the grade. But some parents put too much pressure on the boys to achieve success. This can be detrimental to their development.

The story of a dad making breakfast for his teenage son puts everything into perspective. When he is frying the eggs his son bursts into the kitchen and says, 'Careful, careful! Put in some more butter! Oh, my goodness! You are cooking too many at once. Too many! Turn them now! We need more butter! Oh my, where are we going to get more butter? They are going to stick! Careful, careful I said! You never listen to me when you are cooking! NEVER! Turn them! Hurry up! Are you crazy? Have you lost your mind? Don't forget to salt them. You know you always forget to salt them. Use the salt. USE THE SALT!'

The dad stares at his son, 'What's wrong with you? Do you think I don't know how to fry a couple of eggs?'

The son calmly replies, 'I just wanted to show you what it feels like when I'm trying to play football.'

Unfortunately, academies are tailor-made and highly appealing to the talented young footballer who is brought up in a caring, middle-class environment. Father is very keen to help and he takes his son into the garden to see if the boy enjoys kicking a ball. When the child shows some technique, his dad or mum takes his lad to the local grassroots football club. There he is coached and plays in small-sided games.

The boy is starting to look to have some ability and a scout from the local professional club watches him play in a game and is impressed enough to ask the parent to bring his son along for a coaching session with the academy at under-nine-year age level following which he is offered a chance to sign academy forms. Mam or dad have no idea of the commitment that is required of them or their son, especially if the boy is retained by the academy for the next eight years.

First, Mum and Dad need a reliable car in order to take their son to training two or three times a week. Every Sunday is taken up transporting the lad to matches, some of which could be two hours from their home.

Younger boys are not allowed to travel more than one hour to training, so if they live in East Anglia the only clubs they can sign for are Norwich, Ipswich, Cambridge and Peterborough. They all have very good youth policies, but if a family live in London they have got far more clubs to choose from, including many who are in the Premier League. Few clubs pay travel expenses and so this naturally makes it more difficult for boys from disadvantaged backgrounds whose parents might not be able to afford for them to join an academy, particularly at an early age.

When academy football was first thrust upon professional clubs for the 1998/99 season, we had to adapt very quickly at Arsenal in devising a coaching programme for boys under the age of ten.

Decades earlier, Ajax and other professional clubs in the Netherlands were developing their own youngsters at this age. Ajax were exceptional in developing world-class players from their academy. They built their philosophy from the acronyms SPIT and TIPS.

When scouts were looking at young players in their local league, they were asked to look at Speed, Personality, Intelligence and Technique in this order. The assumption was that, after being coached over so many years, Technique would be the priority, followed by Intelligence (decision-making), Personality, then Speed, it being assumed that a young footballer who is a quick runner over a certain distance will always have pace as he gets older.

Boys who did not show great running ability were never given the chance to play for an academy. Today we know that many boys can develop strength and speed after puberty, with such as Harry Kane illustrating the flaw in the original belief.

We based our coaching on skill development, helping boys to be confident with their right and left feet and have the ability to receive the ball with a good first touch.

Football intelligence is essential for the development of any young player. This means making the right decisions when in possession of the ball and the right movements when looking to receive a pass from a team-mate. In order to develop football intelligence and decision-making, opposition players must be involved in the coaching session. Practising without opposition can help with technique development, but introducing an opponent into the session makes it more real, forcing players to make the correct decisions or they will lose possession of the ball. I did not want players to become robotic, I wanted them to think for themselves and improvise.

I went on several FA coaching courses. One day in the late 1970s stands out in my memory. It was at Lilleshall, near Telford, the FA development centre before it was transferred to St George's Park.

Wiel Coerver played professionally in the Netherlands, winning the Dutch league in 1956 with his local side Rapid JC. When he retired from playing, Coerver managed several clubs including Feyenoord Rotterdam with whom he won the UEFA Cup and the league title in 1974. He also developed a new structured coaching method, later named after him, which many coaches throughout the world subsequently embraced.

On this day at Lilleshall, 50 coaches went on to the field to see Coerver. He was standing with the ball at his feet with the England under-15 squad spread out behind him, each also with a ball in front of them. He introduced himself and then proceeded to demonstrate various dribbling skills and movements with the ball, with the schoolboys practising the same movements.

A game was started where the players were encouraged to use these dribbling skills whenever appropriate. Many years later when coaching at the Arsenal academy, my thoughts went back to that session when our parents were moaning at one of our under-13 players, Alex Zahavi, for losing the ball when trying out one of his own skills.

Coerver drew in some new ideas regarding deceiving and dribbling past an opponent. His work has been passed on by the coaches of today so that young academy players can entertain with great skill when they become professionals.

Skill alone is not enough to earn a living from professional football. The physical and mental side is just as important. In the initial academy days, the coach had the full responsibility for developing fitness as well as skills and football intelligence. The coach would start every session with a 15-minute warm-up, jogging around the pitch and doing exercises along the way. At the end of each session he would finish off with some sprints.

Nowadays that individual only has to deal with the coaching as new jobs have been created for sports scientists, whose role is to devise and look after the fitness requirements of each young player. Facilities have improved over the years and top-class clubs have established indoor fitness gymnasiums for the sports scientist to use and devise fitness routines for each age group.

Regarding mental strength, once again, in the early stages of academies the coach was responsible for the development of each squad player regarding their behaviour and attitude. Our motto was 'talent+attitude=success'.

Boys in a squad come from different backgrounds. Some have overbearing parents who are desperate for their boy to make the grade; others have parents who put no pressure on their son regarding his football ability. Some youngsters may be over-confident in their ability and others could be lacking in belief. The coach must analyse each individual's character in order to help them reach their full potential.

At the same time, other new roles have removed the full responsibility for the progress and development of young players from the coach.

There are now education and welfare officers, psychologists, parents' relation officers, video technicians, tour operators, chefs and kit men. All are appointed on a full-time basis. This means progress of the players can be monitored by professional people who are educated in their particular field of child development.

The old coach with his many skills has thus been pushed into the background and new ways of working introduced that are considered better. However, I think these changes have reduced the opportunity for a coach to develop excellent personal relationships with the boys in their teams. I feel that this is a great pity both for the coaches and the players under their direction.

When I was appointed at the Arsenal academy, Dermot Drummy became coach with the under-14 squad. Dermot had been an apprentice at Arsenal during the period when Liam Brady was playing for the first team. He also had the responsibility for collecting some of the under-16 players early each morning and transporting them to Highams Park School for their education.

Dermot was a great character and he loved winding up his colleagues. At one of our weekly Monday meetings for all full-time coaching staff, Liam was reviewing the work done over the season and he was somewhat critical of the standard of keepers at the academy. He was probably right but I thought this was a personal criticism of my work and we had a heated discussion regarding the quality of the goalkeepers in our squads.

I was later sitting at my desk somewhat disgruntled when the telephone rang. The voice at the end of the phone said that he was an agent and that he had a very good goalkeeper who he wanted to bring to the academy. The boy was 15, 6ft 2in tall, had great spring, excellent ball-handling skills and was as brave as a lion. I was getting very excited at the prospect of bringing in an outstanding young goalkeeper and proving Liam wrong.

'When can you bring the lad in?' I asked eagerly.

There was a pause and the voice at the end of the line said, 'There is only one slight problem.'

'What is that?' I asked.

'He has only got one arm,' the caller replied.

I knew then that I had been 'Drummied'. Dermot was brilliant at disguising his voice. He played many such pranks on the staff but I was probably the guy who fell for them most.

One Monday morning Dermot was in the office after he had dropped off some of the boys at school. The phone on my desk rang and Dermot answered it. My good friend Albert Birbeck was on the other end of the line. The day before, Albert had been at Hale End to watch the academy boys play and welcome the opposition when they arrived, escorting them to their dressing room and generally making sure that they had all that they wanted. When he got home on the Sunday afternoon, Albert realised that he had left his mobile phone on my desk. He had rung Hale End early on the following morning to make sure that his phone was still there.

'Who is that speaking?' Albert said.

Dermot knew that Albert was asking the question. 'It is Carlos the cleaner,' said Dermot in a Spanish accent.

'Carlos, is there a mobile phone on the desk?'

Dermot, still pretending to be Carlos, confirmed that the phone was on the desk and told Albert that he had it now in his hand.

'Oops, oh dear. I am sorry but I have just dropped the phone in the bucket of water.'

Albert was seething and asked Carlos to get the phone out of the water quickly. Heated exchanges followed between Albert and Carlos, and eventually Dermot realised that the prank had gone too far. 'Albert, it's Dermot.'

'Dermot,' said Albert, 'would you please tell Carlos to get my phone out of his bucket of water.' It took several seconds for Albert to realise that he had been a victim of one of Dermot's many wind-ups.

I first met Albert when he attended a coaching course I was conducting in Colchester during the summer of 1974. He was head of the welding department at the Colchester Institute. I was impressed with his coaching and at the end of the course I asked him if he would like to assist me at Clacton Town, where I was player-manager. He later accompanied me when I moved back to Colchester United in a scouting and coaching capacity and then on to Norwich City in similar roles. He was delighted when I asked him to work with me at Arsenal, particularly as he was a keen supporter.

When we left Norwich we were leaving a club that had just opened up their new training ground, purchased from funds generated by Chris Sutton's transfer to Blackburn Rovers. The facilities were first class with goals and lush green pitches expertly marked out for eight v eight and 11 v 11 games by the full-time ground staff. I told Albert that we would be leaving to work with even better facilities at the Arsenal. How wrong could I be.

In September 1998, Arsenal did not have a venue to play under-nine to under-12 matches. Thanks to the agreement of Brentwood Private School, which had extensive playing fields, I was able to obtain some pitches to play academy games on Sundays.

The school staff were very co-operative and told me that I could use the field on the opposite side of the road from the school. This was a great start for us except that there were no goals or football pitches marked out for eight v eight games. One 11 v 11 pitch was available for under-12 matches.

Liam Brady gave me permission to buy three sets of portable goals and cones to mark out the pitches. On our first day of academy football at Brentwood, Albert and I arrived at 8am to assemble the portable goals, fix the nets, mark out three pitches with cones, then carry the goalposts to the pitches and firmly fix them to the ground with the pegs provided. While we were getting everything prepared for a very exciting, historic morning of junior football, it started to rain heavily. Albert and myself were soaked. I reminded Albert of the time I told him we were going to a club with better facilities than Norwich. He grinned, but we were happy.

This was our routine for two seasons but we eventually did, as featured in Chapter 1, get great facilities when Arsenal purchased the facility at Hale End in Walthamstow.

I am always pleased to see boys I once taught do well. Not long after I began working for Arsenal, I received a phone call from a young man in his early 20s, John Cook. I had been John's teacher at Thomas Lord Audley School in Colchester. My former student had just successfully completed his physiotherapy degree and he wanted to know if there were any vacancies where I worked. There weren't, but I told him that we needed a physio on Sunday mornings for the under-nine and under-12s matches that were played on adjacent pitches at our home venue at Brentwood. This meant he could easily deal with any injuries.

John had a long journey to travel on Sundays from his Colchester home. After the games I gave him £10 for his petrol which only just covered his fuel bill. However, his dedication paid off because after two years he was offered a full-time job at Arsenal where he subsequently worked for 15 years as the academy and youth-team physiotherapist until he left to develop his own practice.

* * *

I spoke earlier in the chapter about knowing Howard Wilkinson well. Our paths crossed many times during our careers in football.

In 1983 the Massey family decided to donate grandad Jimmy's 1896 FA Cup winners' medal to Sheffield Wednesday, thus enabling it to go on display in the museum at Hillsborough. The Owls' manager then was Howard. My dad, uncle John and I went to hand over the medal to Howard, who was looking forward to holding it. However, it slipped out of his hand and fell under the table. Howard and myself were both on our hands and knees looking for this precious medal. We eventually found it and had a laugh about what had happened.

I had played for Leyton Orient in the late 1960s against a Brighton & Hove Albion side containing Howard. My home debut in September 1967 was against Brighton, when he was at number seven for the Seagulls and I opened the scoring when I hooked the ball high into the net. Brighton, however, came back to win 2-1.

It was a game of incidents, not all of them connected with football. For a start, Brighton were four minutes late getting on to the field. When they were awarded a dubious penalty for hands against Tom Anderson a few minutes before half-time, Brian Tawse equalised which prompted a fan to rush on to the pitch and charge towards the referee, Mr Wallace. Fortunately he was arrested by three policemen before he got to the official.

Just as the second half began, a firework was thrown on to the pitch and Mr Wallace thus issued a warning over the tannoy system to the crowd that he would abandon the game if there were any more disturbances. Then, on 56 minutes, Ray Goddard made a good save to deny Charlie Livesey but Kit Napier fired again from the rebound and his shot was deflected home by a defender. That is the sort of luck you get when you are bottom of the table which Orient were after seven games.

The sides met again just over a year later and this time Orient beat Brighton 3-2 at Brisbane Road. Another game with plenty of action saw Brighton have skipper Nobby Lawton sent off with about 25 minutes to go after he clashed with Vic Halom. The referee Ray Johnson also awarded us a penalty and Terry Mancini, who later played for Arsenal, duly fired home his second goal of the game to make it 3-1. Brighton did not give up and Kit Napier got a late goal to make the closing minutes a bit nervy.

Howard had signed for Brighton after he had been let go by Sheffield Wednesday, then of the First Division, after playing 22 times for the Owls between 1962 and 1966. He was to make over 100 first-team appearances for the Seagulls over the next five years before he dropped down into non-league football with Boston United.

Howard managed Sheffield Wednesday between 1983 and 1988 and he afterwards went on to take over at Leeds United. He brought back former glories to Elland Road in 1991/92 by winning the title in what proved to be the final season of First Division football before England's top flight broke away from the Football League to form the Premier League. Leeds, who Howard had taken to promotion from the Second Division just two seasons earlier, overcame a strong challenge from Manchester United under Alex Ferguson, whose time would come.

Howard left Leeds in late 1996. In January 1997 when he began work for the Football Association as the technical director, overseeing coaching and other training programmes across all levels of the game, I thought it was a good appointment. Howard later began the National Football Centre project that resulted in the opening in 2012 of St George's Park. He also twice acted as caretaker manager for the England national team.

Chapter 3

Success stories

THE ARSENAL academy has helped many youngsters to fulfil their dreams of becoming top-class professionals watched by millions. These players, many still playing today, are very much the lucky ones as for every academy graduate who makes the grade there are 99 who do not.

There are 12,000 academy players on the books of professional clubs at any one time. But, even of those taken on as scholars at 16 under a two-year programme of full-time football and education, only one in six remains in football five years later. There are an estimated 500 to 600 scholars at clubs annually.

In March 2021, former Everton starlet John Paul Kissock told the *Daily Telegraph* about the 'culture shock' he experienced when he was released by the Toffees in 2009, not long after being considered good enough to be on the bench for a Merseyside derby. Kissock has admitted he broke down in tears when shown the door by the club he supported all his life but he soon had to face up to more practical concerns, not least a sudden slump in income when he became a taxi driver. Kissock contends that academies should do more to help young players to learn a trade from aged 16 onwards.

Kissock really struggled football-wise after Everton, even going down to the West Cheshire League before flirting with a couple of EFL clubs later.

Jack Wilshere was a little lad but from the off he took your breath away. I had settled into my role at Arsenal when club scout Shaun O'Connor rang me early one morning. I could hear the excitement in his voice. He was working for Barnet whose under-nine side had played Luton Town's under-nines the previous evening with the Hatters team containing what Shaun regarded as an outstanding player who hailed from Stevenage.

I immediately contacted Dean Rastrick, the academy manager at Kenilworth Road, who agreed to allow Jack to have a trial with Arsenal. I felt immediately that this young boy had as good a chance of becoming a top-class footballer as any I had ever seen. He could control the ball, run with it, and no one could stop him.

We invited Jack and his dad to meet us in the dressing room and sought to persuade them that Arsenal was his future. Sure enough, he signed for us. We subsequently paid Luton a compensation fee to sign Jack as a schoolboy player.

Jack's first game for Arsenal's under-tens was at Norwich. I was overseeing the under-14 match at the same time but I was eager to find out how Jack had fared. I asked our coach Gordon Lawrence if he had witnessed anything special. He asked me how much I had paid out and when I replied it was £2,000 he told me I had wasted my money.

After his mediocre start, Jack developed into an outstanding footballer with a very competitive edge. He was included in the under-12 squad to play in a prestigious tournament, featuring many top European clubs, at Bierbeek in Belgium.

We reached the semi-finals and were set to play against Feyenoord. One of the competition's officials told me that Jack was in line to be named the player of the tournament. I was absolutely delighted to hear this as, though it was very satisfactory to win the trophy, it would be extra special to see one of our players grab the award for being the best player. After all, the main task of youth development coaches is to develop individual talent rather than winning teams.

Before the big match I took Jack to see the trophy room and asked him if he would like to take the biggest trophy in the cabinet home with him. I told him that he needed to have a good match against Feyenoord and it would be his. He was naturally delighted and I felt that if he played well, then we had enough good players around him to progress to the final. He went off into the dressing room beaming at the thought of what he might win.

I was sitting at the back of the stand with my colleagues Steve Leonard and Gordon Lawrence, the coaches for the under-12s team, on the touchline.

When the game kicked off, the ball was played out by Feyenoord to their left wing. Jack was playing in midfield and he ran directly towards the left-winger. He was sprinting towards the ball as it advanced towards the Feyenoord player. I was saying to myself, 'Slow down, Jack!' Just as the ball reached the opposing winger, Jack lunged towards him and in doing so his momentum took him into the Feyenoord lad who was bundled over the touchline and into the crowd, among whom were some who made it clear that they were unhappy with what they had just witnessed.

Reaching towards his pocket, the referee dashed towards Jack and just as I thought it would be a yellow card, I could see the official brandishing a red. The game had been going for less than 30 seconds and Jack was sent off without ever touching the ball. So much for being named player of the tournament, and as for winning the fair play trophy – forget it. To make things even more disappointing, we lost the semi-final 2-1.

Jack was naturally upset in the dressing room after the match. He had to be consoled by the staff. But even as a youngster Jack was mentally strong enough – and too good a player – not to overcome the disappointments that come with playing football professionally. He became Arsenal's youngest-ever league debutant at the age of

16 years and 256 days when he came on as a substitute against Blackburn Rovers at Ewood Park in September 2008. He later played for England.

Jack had the potential to be one of the great players of English football. He did twice win the FA Cup with Arsenal but, unfortunately, repeated injuries, many sustained from late challenges by less-talented defenders, proved to be major handicaps.

Jack is the current head coach of the Arsenal under-18s. I am sure he will do a fine job.

Henri Lansbury was undoubtedly one of the most talented boys at the Arsenal academy. I first saw him when he was aged just six, playing in an under-eights game at Potters Bar, when I was working for Norwich City. Henri, with his parents' approval, was happy to come along and train with the Norwich youngsters and two years later, in 1999, I asked him to join the Arsenal academy's under-eights. He has gone on to have a fine career and after making a handful of first-team Arsenal appearances he moved to Nottingham Forest in 2012, before signing for Aston Villa in 2017. He later had a spell with Bristol City and signed for Luton Town in 2021.

Alex Iwobi, born in May 1996, played regularly for the Arsenal first team for two years before joining Everton for a fee approaching £30m in August 2019. Alex was a choirboy. He never missed a training session but as a youngster he needed to assert himself more. He had good ability when in possession of the ball but needed to address his running style and athleticism. Arsenal offered him a scholarship which he accepted even though he was aware that other boys in his age group were being offered professional contracts.

In other words, it looked as though the club felt that these players showed more potential than Alex. Many parents in this position would kick up a fuss and complain that their boy was also deserving of a professional contract. This was not the way Alex's dad, Chuka, looked at the offer.

The other boys who were offered professional contracts have not been able to reach the heights Alex has achieved. As with the case of the talented nine-year-old who has all the adulation, the same can apply to the 16-year-old who is offered professional forms. Maybe he is in a comfort zone and then loses the desire and determination to work hard and develop his ability in order to cope with the greater demands of playing regularly in the real world of professional football. Alex was not the best player in his group but he had the desire to overtake his team-mates. Although I am an England fan, I was delighted for him when he scored against England for Nigeria at Wembley in June 2018.

Ainsley Maitland-Niles, born in August 1997, showed ability with the ball at a young age but like Alex Iwobi he seemed to lack some drive and competitive edge. He would drift in and out of games without making a great impression. Then he would suddenly receive the ball and produce a piece of skill that no one else on the pitch could reproduce. With this ability, it was up to the coaches to help him develop a competitive instinct.

Ainsley was well down the pecking order in terms of influencing a match in his academy team because being born in late August meant he was the youngest member of his year group.

The club was very patient with Ainsley before Liam Brady offered him a scholarship at the age of 16. He continued maturing as a player and as a person and was rewarded with a professional contract. Many of Ainsley's former academy team-mates had shown more potential and they may well wonder how he has left them standing, to play Premier League and international football as well as collecting an FA Cup winners' medal.

The time of the year a player was born always gave me a problem when deciding which eight-year-olds should be signed for the academy. Each year we arranged trials and coaching sessions for as many as 40 boys selected throughout the London area by scouts, who worked tirelessly to get the best young players to train with us.

Part of my role was to select the best 15 players for the under-nine squad. The age groups were for boys born from 1 September to the following 31 August, the same as age groups at school. A boy born in September competing against a boy born in July or August, like Ainsley, is usually going to be bigger, stronger and quicker. Physical qualities will always be an advantage when playing football and so it is no surprise that far more boys attached to academies are born between September and December.

In my early years of youth development work, when we could sign boys as young as eight, I felt persuaded to sign too many players based on their physical qualities. I wrongly assumed that such boys would always maintain the physical element of the game while believing that good coaching would enhance their ability on the ball.

Matthew Connolly was a ten-year-old centre-forward training with the Arsenal youngsters during my first year at the club. He was there before the academy rules had been put in place.

His mum, Margaret, put me on the spot after a training session and asked if I was intending to sign Matthew. I was undecided. We had a game against Chelsea under-tens the following day and I told her that I would make a decision after that.

As it turned out, we were short of defenders. Matthew was asked to play centre-half and he excelled, prompting me to sign him for the under-11 squad. Matthew continued as a defender for the rest of his career at Arsenal. He played with the academy until he was 16 when he was offered a scholarship.

Matthew was not the top player in his age group by any means; he was a young man who did not seek attention, always attended training sessions and gave his best in fitness and skill training at all times. As he grew it was obvious that he was going to be tall enough to play as a centre-half at senior level. Matthew was a quiet, confident young player and he did well enough at academy level to be offered a professional contract. He became the youngest-ever captain of the Arsenal reserve side.

The highlight in his mum's eyes was going to be his Premier League debut on 1 May 2006, a night match at Sunderland. Margaret had taken her son to every game since he started playing, plus every training session. What dedication parents must show for many years by transporting their boys to matches and training. The ultimate goal for them all is to see their son making his debut for the first team and so it was with Mrs Connolly.

She was determined to be there and drove all the way from London to Sunderland. The excitement was immense when she took her place in the stand with a packed stadium of more than 44,000 supporters including many Arsenal fans. Expectation quickly turned to despair when Matthew pulled up in the warm-up and was unable to take his place in the team. Such is football's rollercoaster of ups and downs.

But this disappointment was all long forgotten a few months later when she saw Matthew play in the opening fixture at the Emirates Stadium, Dennis Bergkamp's testimonial against Ajax, watched by 54,000 fans. Suddenly, all the many years of travelling to games and to training sessions was worth it.

Just like the club's relocation to north London in 1913, the move to a new ground was deemed necessary to allow more fans to attend matches. The tragedies on the terraces at Heysel in 1985 and again at Hillsborough four years later had led to major stadiums in Britain becoming all-seated in 1993.

Even grounds in the lower leagues that were allowed to retain some terracing had their capacities severely cut. Two of my former clubs, Rotherham United and Colchester United, both eventually moved to newly built stadiums.

The capacity at Highbury fell in 1993 to 38,000. It was full for every match. Options for further expansion were severely restricted as all the stands were hemmed in by housing and any expansion was certain to be very expensive. Only moving to a new venue would allow Arsenal to meet modern demands.

Matthew made his competitive first-team debut in a League Cup victory against West Bromwich Albion on 24 October 2006, and he also appeared as a substitute in the 6-3 victory over Liverpool at Anfield in the quarter-final of the competition.

Although Matthew did not become a regular member of Arsène Wenger's magnificent squad, he has subsequently gone on to play with distinction with clubs in the Football League Championship and Premier League.

By 2020, he had won promotion to the Premier League with Queens Park Rangers in 2011, Reading in 2012, Cardiff in 2013, Watford on loan in 2015 and Cardiff again in 2018. This must be a record. He has also played for the England under-21 team.

Matthew's mum is very proud of his achievements and she epitomises the love and dedication that parents have which enables their sons to reach their full potential. Of course, many boys who sign academy forms do not go on to become professional footballers and as a coach my aim was to make sure that the boys and their parents had fond memories of their period at the Arsenal academy.

Fabrice Muamba was another player we released – but fortunately we brought him back. He lived over the road and he came in and asked for a trial at aged 14. He was big and we could not turn down someone who had the audacity to come in and ask for a trial at Arsenal. He was not great on the ball but we felt he could become a big, strong centre-half and we agreed to allow him to train at the academy. However, after four training sessions he took part in a trial game in which his team were beaten 3-0 and played poorly.

Liam told me to tell Fabrice that he wasn't at the standard we required. After I did so I informed him that as he lived in Walthamstow I would recommend him to his nearest professional club, Leyton Orient, my former team. As Fabrice did not have access to transport for training and the games this would also be a suitable place to play football. The following day I was in my room when a knock came on the door and Fabrice poked his head round to ask when I was going to contact Orient and set up a trial for him.

Such enthusiasm and attitude are just what any young player needs. I asked him what he was doing the following Wednesday evening and when the answer was nothing, I told him that before I would recommend him to Orient, I would like him to play in one more Arsenal academy game.

I was short of a centre-half for a match against Norwich's under-14s. It was an end-of-season fixture at Highbury. We beat Norwich 5-0 and Fabrice had a good game, so much so that I invited him to come back for pre-season training. This meant we could have another look at him. After two weeks of training, Fabrice was playing in a practice match. Liam was watching with Steve Leonard and was taken aback to see Fabrice in the team.

I had gone against his wishes in giving Fabrice another chance but after watching the lad again Liam immediately told Steve to go to his house and get his parents to sign forms before he moved elsewhere. Ironically this proved not as easy as I anticipated. Fabrice's dad was very doubtful about him becoming a footballer as he wanted him instead to become a doctor or a lawyer. Steve did eventually get him to sign the forms.

Fabrice had the enthusiasm to become a professional. In their final year as under-16s at the academy, Steve would ask the boys to write down their thoughts by answering a simple questionnaire which asked them where they hoped to be, from when they started their scholarship to them turning 21. Steve recalls that Fabrice and Joe Willock were spot on with their predictions of playing for England's under-18s and under-21s and for the Arsenal first team.

As both players were offered a two-year scholarship, rather than the more lucrative scholarship plus a guaranteed professional contract, these were very optimistic predictions. But, to their credit, they achieved their aims.

Fabrice made two first-team Arsenal appearances in the League Cup before going on loan to Birmingham City and then being transferred to Bolton Wanderers, then of the Premier League, for £4m. Most fans will know about the tragic occurrence when Fabrice collapsed at White Hart Lane playing for Bolton against Tottenham. His heart even stopped beating in the ambulance on the way to the hospital. The medics at the scene were brilliant and their care played a key role in the fact that he pulled through. Everyone in football was delighted.

Mind you, there was one moment in his Arsenal career when he was not flavour of the month. He was playing in an FA Youth Cup tie against Brentford, whose side consisted of several local boys. They had a very strong team and having finished 2-2 after extra time, the game went to penalties.

Needing to score our fourth penalty to take us through to the next round, Fabrice chipped the ball towards the middle of the goal. Such a penalty looks spectacular when the goalkeeper dives to his right or left and the ball floats into the net where he was standing. Unfortunately, the Brentford goalkeeper, Sam Moore, who now does the video analyst job at the Arsenal academy, stayed where he was and made a very easy save. Brentford eventually won through to the next round.

I am not sure if any of their youngsters made it into the professional game but millions of pounds' worth of players were on the pitch for Arsenal that evening. Besides Fabrice, Alex Song, Nickolas Bendtner, Anthony Stokes, Jay Simpson and Henri Lansbury played. It is always disappointing to lose a game but coaches and staff in youth development should realise that their main task is to develop each individual youngster to their full potential and thus not get too upset if their team are defeated.

Josh Dasilva was another lad who really worked hard to impress. One of our scouts, Ryan Gordon, came into my office one day to say that a 12-year-old had attended his own private coaching school and showed some ability. Ryan wanted to know if it might be possible for the youngster to come over to the academy for a six-week trial. I agreed to this and Josh, who was a decent-sized lad, came in with his parents for his first coaching session.

It is always difficult for a young player to come into an academy on his first session, as was noted with Kevin De Bruyne, who had coaching sessions at Hale End when he was 12. Josh naturally did not know anybody and he was training with confident boys who had played for, and trained at, the academy for the past few seasons.

Josh did not particularly impress in his first sessions, but it was clear that he had some strength, had good running ability, was good on the ball and possessed decent football intelligence. We therefore gave him that trial where he eventually showed his ability in the games programme and he was deservedly offered an academy place.

Throughout his four seasons he was a model member showing a great attitude, attending all sessions and putting in maximum effort both in training and matches. He was never rated as one of the most outstanding young players in his age group, mainly due to his quiet personality, but he never had a bad game and you never said, 'Poor Josh, he was rubbish today.' He always held his own. He continued to show good all-round skills and throughout puberty he was developing a physical presence and some pace. When he was 16, he was offered a scholarship and gradually showed his potential both in the youth team and the under-23s.

By the time he was 20, Josh, like many young players at a Premier League club, had not shown he was ready for first-team action despite acquiring two years' experience with the under-23s. When Brentford, then of the Championship, made an enquiry about signing him, he was very keen to take up the challenge and was transferred in 2018 for a considerable sum. He has played a big part in Brentford's rise to the Premier League.

Kieran Agard was brought in by scout Gary Nott at the age of nine. The Newham-born lad was a lively young player, very competitive and a strong runner. He really wanted to be a footballer and his efforts and endeavours made you warm to him. I thought he would make a player at academy level and at times when you are judging a young player that is all you can calculate. You want to see what he is like as he gets older.

It did not quite work out for Kieran at Arsenal; he did not achieve his ambition of signing as a professional for the club. But his continuing hard work after he left in 2005 paid off when he later established himself with Yeovil Town. At my former club Rotherham United he scored 26 goals in all competitions during the 2013/14 season and was part of the winning side at Wembley against another of my former sides, Leyton Orient, in the League One play-off final. Kieran has made more than 300 Football League appearances.

Jay Emmanuel-Thomas was among the second intake of boys at the Arsenal academy in August 1999. He was very tall and it was felt he could make a fine centre-half as he had excellent ball control and a strong physical presence. Jay played as a centre-half throughout his school and youth career with Arsenal. He enjoyed great success, culminating in winning the FA Youth Cup, and also played at under-17 and under-19 level for England. He regularly scored goals when he went into the opponents' penalty area for dead-ball kicks.

Jay signed a professional contract and, despite Arsène Wenger saying he could be the club's next centre-half, he insisted he wanted to play as a centre-forward. He subsequently played in this position for the reserves and Arsène did give him an opportunity to play in his favourite position for the first team. He was not going to be the next Thierry Henry. After several loan spells, Jay moved to Ipswich Town and later Bristol City, where he had some success and scored goals regularly.

At the start of the 2021/22 season, Jay signed a contract for Aberdeen and while he has made a good career for himself, I wonder if he could have made his mark in the Premier League if it had been possible for him to have improved his knowledge of centre-forward play from the age of nine onwards.

Nicklas Bendtner joined the Arsenal academy despite great interest from Liverpool. Bobby Arber was a full-time scout with the Gunners, and I knew him some years earlier when I was playing at Orient when he was an apprentice there. His role at Arsenal was to identify talented young players in the under-15 and under-16 age groups both in England and abroad, and this brief certainly paid off when he attended an under-16 tournament in Portugal and noted a big centre-forward warming up to play for Danish club KB – the oldest club in the world outside Britain.

The young Bendtner handed his earring to his dad before the game started and then, besides his size and strength, showed good technique, so Bobby decided to approach his father about his availability. Nicklas was due to go to Liverpool the following week but Bobby persuaded him to visit Arsenal and he was soon offered an apprenticeship, at the age of 14. In December 2005, when he was 17, he signed as a professional. He subsequently went on to make more than 100 first-team appearances for Arsenal and played three times for his country at the 2010 World Cup finals, scoring once.

He went on to win 81 caps for Denmark and retired in June 2021.

Wojciech Szczęsny was another player Bobby spotted on his continental scouting trips; the Polish keeper, already big and strong, stood out in an under-16 international against France.

When Bobby approached Wojciech's parents they said he was due to go to Bolton Wanderers on trial. Bolton subsequently did not offer him a contract, so Arsenal were quick to invite him in for trials. He soon established himself as a goalkeeper with great potential, but his career was almost over before it began.

As a youth-team player, Wojciech was doing some training in the gym at Shenley, the first-team training ground. As he stooped to pick up the barbells, not realising how heavy the weights were, he broke both wrists.

Not many goalkeepers would make a comeback after such horrendous injuries and he subsequently went on loan to Brentford and Roma. Bobby would travel to Rome to watch him play and check that everything was well with him in Italy. Wojciech told Bobby that Roma had a young goalkeeper in the reserves who was outstanding. This was Hugo Lloris who went on to have a wonderful career with Tottenham Hotspur and France. Wojciech came back from Italy and established himself in the Arsenal first team, before being transferred to Juventus. He has played many games for the Polish national team.

Eddie Nketiah has made a name for himself scoring goals for the England under-21 side and gradually establishing himself with the Arsenal first team. He started his academy football with Chelsea as a young boy then came to the attention of the Arsenal academy when he played against them for Chelsea under-14s and had a very good game. Although very small for his age, he had speed and good technical ability.

After the game, Bobby was walking to the car park when he passed Chris and Joe Willock. He stopped to speak to them about the game and mentioned the little centre-forward.

'He is bad,' they said. Bobby initially thought they were referring to his character, then quickly realised that 'bad' meant good! The youngsters told him that Chelsea were releasing Eddie. This was music to Bobby's ears. He contacted Ian Gilmour, who recommended youngsters from the south London area. Ian spoke to Eddie and his parents and they agreed to him having trials with Arsenal. It did not take long for Eddie to be offered the opportunity to join the Gunners.

Emile Smith Rowe was actually recommended to the club by another academy player's mum. Young players come to the attention of clubs in many different ways and not always because a scout has seen them play.

George Phillips, a young south London keeper, signed for the Arsenal under-nine squad. Two years later his mum, who supported her son at all times by transporting him to training and matches, mentioned to the under-nine to under-12 academy coach Mark Ridgeway that Chelsea had just released an 11-year-old called Emile Smith Rowe, who attended the same school as her son. With this information Mark sent scout Alan Knowles to watch Emile play.

Alan recommended asking the boy to come in for a trial period. Although he was not outstanding, he did well enough to be offered a contract with the academy. After having a year on loan at Huddersfield, Emile is now a full England international and is establishing himself as a first-team player at the Emirates Stadium. George Phillips was later released by Arsenal and joined Colchester United at 18.

Ovie Ejaria arrived at the academy aged eight and showed wonderful ability. West Ham United were also very interested in him and we were all gutted when his dad rang to say that he was signing for the Hammers.

However, a year later, at the end of his under-nine season, his mum came into my office to say that Ovie would like to come over to play with the Arsenal academy. I was delighted.

Ovie was a pleasure to work with and showed great ability on the ball. When he was 16 and in his last school year, Liam Brady offered him a scholarship while other boys in his group were offered professional contracts. Ovie was disappointed and delayed signing his contract.

Liverpool offered him a professional deal and so we lost him to the Anfield club, for whom he subsequently made a handful of first-team appearances. He then went out on loan to Sunderland, Rangers – where he played under the direction of Liverpool legend Steve Gerrard – and Reading, who then signed him permanently in August 2020 for a £3m fee.

Bukayo Saka came to the academy aged eight thanks to Miguel Rios. Miguel was a young man who was introduced to the Arsenal academy staff when we took the under-13 squad to a tournament in Spain. He was employed by the competition organisers and as he spoke fluent English, he had the responsibility of looking after the Arsenal group. We returned the following year and Miguel again looked after us very well.

He was actually based in London and asked if he could come over to see me at the academy. I took the opportunity to ask him to do some scouting for us in west London. He accepted this role on a very part-time basis with great enthusiasm as he saw it as a potential opening to a full-time post. He brought in several youngsters but clearly the standout was Bukayo Saka, who has proved to be one of the most talented players produced by the Arsenal academy.

When Bukayo was still a schoolboy, Miguel left Arsenal and moved into a full-time role at Brentford. He grasped his opportunity with both hands. At the time of writing Miguel is the chief scout at Watford.

Bukayo had a very good left foot and he played on the left side of the defence. He showed composure on the ball. He had strength and pace but the slight concern was that as he got older his success would not be maintained once the other players could compete physically with him. However, Bukayo had a maturity beyond his early years and he showed great football intelligence, ability on the ball and a real desire to become a professional.

Bukayo earned himself a scholarship and then a full-time contract at 17 and soon he made his first-team debut in November 2018. Two years later he made his England international debut against Wales. No doubt taking a penalty against Italy in the European Championship Final at Wembley in July 2021 was a daunting experience for him. The fact that the goalkeeper saved his spot kick, allowing Italy to win the tournament, did not faze Bukayo as he went on to play superbly for England at the World Cup in Qatar.

Our scout in the north London and Hertfordshire region, Brian Stapleton, spotted a young player named **Nathan Tella** in an under-eights tournament. Although smaller than the other boys he was playing with and against, Nathan's enthusiasm, pace and ability on the ball impressed Brian.

When he came to Arsenal for trials, Nathan did well enough to be selected to sign academy forms. He gladly accepted and for the next eight years he did well enough each year to be retained for the following season. Although not one of the outstanding players in his group in terms of contributions to the games, Nathan was a credit to the academy, displaying a maturity beyond his years. He was a quiet boy with an inner strength and a desire to improve his game through hard work in coaching sessions.

Arsenal offered Nathan a scholarship when he left school at 16. However, at the end of his scholarship he moved on to

Southampton, signing a professional contract, and he eventually earned a place in the first-team squad. In early September 2022, I noted on the TV results service that a Tella had scored two goals for Burnley. Not aware of any other professional player by the surname Tella, I assumed that the Burnley hero was Nathan and that he must have been transferred on loan from Southampton.

Two days later, Nathan's dad, Harry, a lovely man, rang to tell me that his son was on loan at Burnley for the 2022/23 season and, hopefully, playing on a regular basis will give him the opportunity and experience to develop his game in order for him to command a regular first-team place in the Premier League.

Reiss Nelson was brought in for training at the age of eight by scout Alan Knowles. He had already been spotted by Tottenham Hotspur, with whom he was training. Alan had been driving home after watching a district schoolboy game and as he passed a park he noticed a group of young footballers enjoying a game between themselves.

Alan stopped to take a look and after a while he saw a little boy receive the ball before dribbling past three opponents. As the keeper came out to stop his shot the young player feinted to shoot and, as the keeper dived to anticipate the shot, the boy dribbled round him before calmly slotting the ball into the goal. Alan was impressed. The boy was Reiss Nelson and Alan asked the eight-year-old to come and train at the Arsenal academy, where he subsequently stayed for many years before signing professionally for the Gunners. Reiss was a member of the squad that captured the FA Cup in 2020 and at aged 23 he still has the finest years in football ahead of him.

Tommie Hoban was signed at the age of eight. He was a quiet and polite boy with good skills but he lacked tenacity and was released seven years later. He was taken on by Watford and successfully went on to make almost 60 first-team appearances as a defender for the Hornets and also represented Republic of Ireland at under-21 level. He later played for Blackburn Rovers, Aberdeen and Crewe Alexandra before unfortunately being forced to retire early due to injury.

Chukwuemeka Ademola Amachi 'Chuks' Aneke was in the same age group as Benik Afobe and Harry Kane and he was taller and stronger than his team-mates even at the age of nine. He had great physique, good skill on the ball and was very competitive. He signed as a professional in the summer of 2010 and came on as a last-minute substitute in a League Cup match against Shrewsbury Town in September 2011.

A lack of pace meant Chuks did not start a first-team game for Arsenal and he was loaned to Stevenage, Preston North End and Crewe before joining Belgium side Zulte Waregem and then moving to Milton Keynes Dons, where he averaged a goal every three games in close to 100 appearances. At the time of writing, he is in his second spell at Charlton Athletic and has made over 300 senior appearances in a fine career that, at age 29, still has a few years remaining.

Isaac Haydon had played against Arsenal for Southend United on several occasions and always impressed, so much so that Steve Leonard recommended him to Liam Brady and Isaac eventually signed at the age of 13. After playing two League Cup games he joined Hull City on loan and he later showed his mental strength and football skills by playing well enough to earn a five-year contract with Newcastle United. At the time of his departure from London he said, 'Being at Arsenal was a great experience, I learned a lot there and have a lot to thank them for, but I needed to move on and so when Newcastle came in for me, I jumped at the chance.' He has forged a great career with over 150 appearances for the St

James' Park club. At the start of the 2022/23 season, Isaac joined Norwich City on a season-long loan.

When I was working for Norwich City, eight-year-old **Jay Simpson** came over to our training ground at Potters Bar and immediately impressed with his pace, and ability to shoot whenever the opportunity came his way, which helped him to score many goals. Along with Henri Lansbury, I invited him to follow me to Arsenal when it became clear that Norwich would have to close down their centres in the London area due to the new academy rules restricting signings, in his case, to living within an hour of the city.

Jay was an outstanding member of his academy team. Liam Brady offered him a scholarship and professional contract which Jay and his parents were delighted about. Jay progressed to playing for the reserves and made it into the first team on occasions but did not impress enough to become a regular performer with Arsène Wenger's team. He moved to Hull City and my old club Leyton Orient before having a loan spell with Philadelphia.

Chuba Akpom came to Arsenal when eight years old. Sean O'Connor, a full-time Arsenal scout for many years, brought him and Alex Iwobi for trials and both played impressively for several years at the academy. At aged 16, Chuba was offered a scholarship with a professional contract and he had all the trademarks of being a very fine centre-forward. He progressed to the first-team squad but – unsurprisingly – found it difficult to convince Arsène Wenger that he was the one to replace Thierry Henry. After various loans, he went to PAOK Salonica in Greece where he was very successful, tempting Middlesbrough to pay £2.75m to sign him in September 2020.

Stephy Mavididi played against the Arsenal academy under-12s with Southend United. He was the outstanding player and after some negotiations he signed for Arsenal as a schoolboy player, then an amazing opportunity came along when Arsenal released him to join Liam Brady's former club Juventus. This must have been a great experience for him. Although Stephy did not make the first team often in Italy, it must have given him confidence to move on and score goals for Montpellier in Ligue 1.

Daniel Bentley was brought by his mum to the Arsenal academy for a trial when he was 14. He had good skills but it is difficult with goalkeepers because you really are looking to see if they will also grow to a great height as even 6ft tall is not quite what you require now. You are looking to see how tall their parents are and so signing a keeper is often a bit more of a gamble. We didn't have a lot of good goalkeepers coming through but after discussing this with my colleagues it was felt that Daniel, although slightly too quiet at this time, would take the opportunity as he was confident and brave, qualities which I knew from sitting as a child on my grandfather Jimmy's knee are essential to making it as a goalkeeper.

After a productive training session with Alex Welch, Daniel was invited back as Alex could see some potential in him. After some weeks settling in I decided to take him to the Nike Cup, held at Warwick University. This was an annual competition for Premier League under-14 teams and the winners went on to play in the world competition. After the tournament, Liam thought that Danny was not quite up to the standard to become a professional with a Premier League club.

When I spoke to Daniel and his mum to tell him the disappointing news, I said that I did not want to lose him altogether so I suggested that he came to the academy two nights each week in order to have coaching sessions with Alex. I further advised him to sign for a club in the Brentwood area where he lived, suggesting it should be a club near the bottom of the league as this would mean he would be in constant action in dealing with shots and crosses.

Daniel did this and continued training with Alex for the next two years until he was due to leave school. We recommended him to Southend United who were very pleased to offer him a scholarship. Daniel went on to play in the first team at Southend and was then transferred to Brentford in the Championship for £1m. A £4m move came for him when he went to Bristol City and he has established himself as one of the best goalkeepers in the Championship.

Daniel has proved to be another case of a boy dreaming of being a professional who had to cope with being rejected at an early age in his football development. He was a keen, enthusiastic young footballer even when playing for his Sunday league team but his mental and physical development, allied to his bravery, has helped him carve out a very successful career.

* * *

It was the bravery and enthusiasm of a keeper who inspired my love of football. As a lad I was brought up on tales of great matches; I was lucky because my grandfather Jimmy played in many of them! The biggest was the 1896 FA Cup Final which back then ranked alongside England v Scotland as the biggest game in the world.

On that famous day my grandfather was in goal for the Wednesday – as they were then – against Wolverhampton Wanderers as they battled it out at Crystal Palace before a then-record crowd of 48,836. The Owls won 2-1 and my grandfather played an important role in the success as he made plenty of fine saves, especially towards the end of the match as Wolves pushed for an equaliser.

To collect a winners' medal in this era was everything and Jimmy thereafter always wore his medal on his waistcoat. He lived until he was 91 and I would visit him every Sunday and sit in the armchair in front of the living-room fire listening to his tales. I recall he told me that in his first game for Wednesday he had gone to catch the ball and was knocked over the line with it in his hands by the centre-forward. A goal was awarded but the next time in a similar situation he tipped the ball over the bar and then crouched down and flipped the forward over him and into the post where he suffered a broken arm.

Keepers are a breed apart and to be a good one you have to be mentally tough but from reading about him he was also very brave, handled the ball well, had good reflexes and was physically strong. In terms of training, I understand he did a lot of shot-stopping with the players shooting at him. He was clearly a good player but he made it apparent to me that Tommy Crawshaw and Fred Spiksley were the best players in the team that won the FA Cup. He really admired both of them. Spiksley scored both of Wednesday's goals on that day, including one that is arguably the quickest-ever FA Cup Final goal as some match reports contend that it was ten seconds quicker than Louis Saha's 25-second strike for Everton in 2009. I guess we will never know for certain.

Spiksley's second goal was hit so hard that when the ball hit the net it rebounded back on to the pitch. Wolves keeper Billy Tennant was so confused at seeing the ball in front of him that he just kicked it back up the field. He was under the impression that it was still in play and, amid all the excitement, he then failed to see his side restart the game by kicking off again. At the end, Tennant went up to the Wednesday hardman Mick Langley to shake his hand and ask when the replay would be. But there was no need to play again as the Yorkshire side had won 2-1.

Tennant had to be satisfied with a runners-up medal. At least he got one, unlike Bob Ferrier who despite being the 12th man did not get one. The unlucky Wednesday player had been informed on the Friday that if the overnight weather was rainy then with the pitch turning soft he would play. If there was no overnight rain and the pitch was in good condition then Langley would play – which is what happened. Langley later commented that it would always be best if players knew the day beforehand if they were playing as this gave them time to relax and concentrate on the task ahead.

The Wednesday were the first club from Yorkshire to win the FA Cup and such was the turnout to welcome them on their return to Sheffield that a planned parade through the streets had to be hastily abandoned. Even in its infancy, football created a passion and loyalty among club supporters that no other sport can touch even today.

In recent years I have been left thrilled by the publication of a book on the life of Spiksley, which is now being used as the background to a documentary film on the early years of football from 1870 to just after the Second World War. I was interviewed on camera talking about my grandfather and how the development of young talent within football has radically altered since Spiksley's day. He became a globetrotting coach and was the first man to coach on three continents.

Like myself, Spiksley was very keen to use coaching to help improve the skill levels across football at all ages. In 1929 he helped make the first training film – for Pathé News, including sound. Even before then, Spiksley had put forward the idea that professional clubs should open up football schools – or academies as we would call them today – where young players could be properly coached.

When Spiksley played for Gainsborough Trinity and the Wednesday at Arsenal in the 1880s, he was nicknamed by the Gunners supporters as 'The Wind' – this was because he was the quickest player of his day. Even when he reached his 50s, Spiksley ran professionally for a living.

He was even brave enough to contend that Herbert Chapman, the legendary Huddersfield Town and Arsenal manager, had ruined football by removing the finer points of the game as a result of dropping the centre-half into a defensive position after 1925, when the offside law was changed. The adjusted law meant an attacker now needed only two players, rather than three, between them and the goal to avoid being offside. Spiksley also believed the role of the inside-forward was changed to a more defensive one.

Tommy Crawshaw, whose great grandson Tom is also in the documentary film, was a great centre-half and captain. He was almost unbeatable in the air. He played ten times for England and won two First Division titles and two FA Cups while with Wednesday. The book has also allowed me to find out much more about my grandfather, who first played for Denaby United, Mexborough and then another non-league side, Doncaster Rovers, where he must have been good because he was selected to play for the All-Sheffield XI in 1892 against the Glasgow XI in a game that ended 3-3.

After signing for the Wednesday in 1894, it took a bit of time for Jimmy to replace Bill Allan in goal. In the first round of the 1896 FA Cup, he came into the side after Allan had been injured in a league match. My grandfather played well, as they won at Southampton St Mary's, and stayed in the team for the rest of the run – wins over league champions Sunderland, before what was a record crowd at Olive Grove, where Wednesday played between 1887 and 1899, of 28,000, then Everton and Bolton after a replay in the semi-final. In the final he made a great save in the last minute against his hometown club.

The following season he played every league and FA Cup match and also featured in a thrilling game that saw Wednesday draw 4-4 in Fred Spiksley's testimonial against the famous amateur side Corinthians. In 1897/98 he only missed one match and he was a member of the Wednesday side that overcame Sunderland 1-0 in a rough FA Cup tie at Newcastle Road that saw him assaulted by the home forwards. Such was the Sunderland fans' disappointment with their defeat that they rioted afterwards and Jimmy and the other members of the team had to be smuggled out of the area.

In 1898/99 he again only missed one match but it was a terrible season for him and the club. In one match he conceded nine goals as Derby County's Steve Bloomer ran riot and notched six himself. Match reports indicate that Jimmy actually played well and prevented his side from a heavier defeat, but Wednesday were relegated at the end of the season.

The 1899/1900 season saw the opening of the famous Hillsborough and Jimmy was in the opening-day 11 as Wednesday beat Chesterfield 5-1 with Spiksley scoring their first goal on their new home ground, Hillsborough. That season Wednesday won every home match as promotion was secured at the first attempt. Just 22 goals were conceded in 34 league games, of which Jimmy missed just one. He had a great understanding during this season with the full-backs Willie Layton, who had replaced Jack Earp, and Ambrose Langley, who was a real hard case and was hated by fans of opposing sides. Layton's great-grandson is Michael Knighton, the former Manchester United director and Carlisle United owner, and he is very proud of Willie's achievements in winning one FA Cup in 1907 and two league titles in 1902/03 and 1903/04.

Midway through the 1900/01, Jimmy lost his place to Frank Stubbs. His final Wednesday game was on 9 February 1901 in a 1-0 FA Cup defeat to Bury, who were the great FA Cup side at the start of the 20th century with victories in 1900 and 1903.

My grandfather made 173 starts – 75 wins, 36 draws and 62 defeats – for Wednesday and collected an FA Cup and Second Division winners' medals. He told me of the great comradeship between the players and of how they were treated like kings by Sheffielders when they returned with the FA Cup in 1896. He said it was a close game and he was proud he had made a couple of good saves late on to keep Wednesday in the lead. At home matches he said that Wednesday often attracted big crowds who were rarely abusive, as is so often the case today, and who would be very happy if Wednesday won.

When he finished at Hillsborough, Jimmy moved back to play for Denaby United as an amateur and found paid work down the pit. Although players were not paid anything like the sums they are today, it must still have been a difficult transformation for him to make as he moved from working outside in the open air as a footballer to toiling underground as a coal miner. He eventually had 11 children to feed and clothe. Life became particularly difficult when he lost an eye due to a workplace accident. His employer admitted responsibility for this injury and awarded him the princely sum of one shilling (5p) a week as compensation.

One of his sons, Tom, also worked at the pit. Playing for a local football team he broke his leg, which was placed in plaster. He was unable to work but when a worker saw him kicking a ball in a local field he told the pit deputy that he had seen Tom playing football. The fact that he still had his plaster on his leg was not reported and the pit deputy stopped Tom's injury money, claiming he should be at work. Jimmy visited the deputy and explained that his son was still in plaster. An argument escalated into a fight. With the deputy on the floor and Jimmy leaving the office, the deputy said, 'Massey, tha'll never work at a pit again in this area.' As a consequence, he was refused work at every pit in South Yorkshire.

To supplement money coming into the household, my grandma Fanny took over a fish and chip shop next to the Reasby Arms, a very popular pub in Denaby. The shop was really profitable but Fanny often felt sorry for her customers who did not have the money to pay for their food. 'Pay me next time you come in,' she would say, but many of them rarely bothered.

Jimmy had to be tough to play in goal when professional football was in its infancy. Goalkeepers had to be able to withstand the physical challenges that were allowed in the 1890s.

He died when I was aged 17 and never saw me become a professional footballer.

Chapter 4

Liam Brady, master of mind games

BY 2000 Liam Brady and David Court were settled in at the new first-team training ground at London Colney, where the scholarship boys would have their training and education and play in under-18 matches on Saturdays. Neil Banfield was the under-16 coach and Don Howe coached the under-18s. I organised activities at Hale End and was ably assisted by Steve Leonard who, like me, was required to undertake multiple roles as a coach, fitness mentor, child protection officer, parent liaison officer, education welfare officer and minibus driver. Unlike myself, Steve was also the kit man!

Dermot Drummy was a full-time coach with Paul Davis and Steve Bould, both legendary Arsenal players, adding their experiences as part-time coaches with the schoolboy teams. Paul went on to work for the FA and Steve was eventually appointed as full-time under-18 coach when Don retired. Steve was later Arsène Wenger's first-team assistant after Pat Rice retired.

Until the players reached 14 years old, it was my decision as to who was retained for another season. At 14 and in later years, Liam, who all the full-time coaches met and discussed the previous weekend's games with on Mondays, took the decisions on who to retain.

I always found it difficult to tell a young boy that he was being released. It caused me so much pain in my first year to see a nine-year-old so upset on being told the bad news that I decided that any child recruited aged eight would be guaranteed a minimum of two seasons. My relationship with the players was exactly how I approached my job as a PE teacher in that I sought to get to know them well as I wanted all of them to achieve their full potential.

Arsenal operated teams at under-nine, under-ten, under-11, under-12, under-13, under-14 and under-15s, who played on Wednesday evenings, along with teams for players aged 14 to 16 and then 16 to 18. That made nine teams in all and I would watch seven or eight games each week. At home matches I could stand on a balcony and see three matches at a time.

On one occasion, my wife Julia attended, and commented 'I couldn't believe it. After the games finished, Roy went down to greet each team and he would tell a particular player – on each team – who had impressed him or scored a great goal how thrilled he had been to witness his performance. He seemed to have three or four sets of eyes.'

At the end of each season, players who had represented the under-10s, under-11s, under-12s and under-13s and who were not considered good enough were released on an annual basis. At 14, players were offered a two-year extension or released. Then at 16 they were either offered a two-year scholarship, released, or offered a two-year scholarship with a professional contract.

I found Liam to be an intelligent, astute person who was able to motivate and get the best out of his staff. And although not trained as one, Liam was a very good psychologist.

Mark Randall from Milton Keynes came to my attention when he was 13 and at Northampton Town. He played well in a trial match and I decided to sign him. Over the next two years he developed into a very good midfielder. At the end of his under-15 season he was included in the squad for a tournament in Andorra, and several sets of parents, including Mark's, journeyed out to watch the games. After we had lost in the final to Inter Milan,

Mark's father thanked me for all the efforts the club had put in to helping his son become a footballer. Mark had enjoyed the tournament and his dad said that he would look forward to seeing me when pre-season started.

The day before training resumed, I had a phone call saying that Mr Randall had passed away. This, of course, was a great shock and it took me back to when my own son Richard lost his mum Christine at the tender age of 13.

I did not expect to see Mark at training the following day. But there he was; his uncle had brought him. I can't imagine how difficult this must have been but it showed great character and mental strength to be with all his team-mates. Over the following months Mark continued to develop his game and no doubt his efforts helped him, in part, take his mind off the devastation of losing his father at such a young age.

Towards the end of the season, Mark was sent a letter confirming he had been offered a scholarship. The normal process would be for the player or parents to confirm in writing that the youngster wished to accept. But instead, Liam came into my office and he was fuming. Mark, via his uncle, had let us know that he wished to see if other clubs were interested in signing him before accepting the Arsenal offer.

Liam acted quickly, inviting Mark, his mother and his uncle to the first-team training ground for a meeting. Liam also asked me and David Court to attend.

The Randall family were met by Arsène Wenger who was very good and spoke about giving youngsters a chance in the first team if they were viewed as good enough.

Liam then began the meeting by saying he was aware that Manchester United had shown interest in Mark. This was denied by the family, clearly uncomfortable with this suggestion.

Liam asked Mark to consider a scenario when he got older and was happily married with a nice house. Suppose that directly over the road was a single woman and Mark felt that he might like to live with her to see if his life was better. 'What do you think your wife might say, Mark?' He then replied, 'She'd say don't come back.'

'Precisely,' said Liam, who then told Mark he was going to write down his offer on a piece of paper. As he gave it to Mark, he said, 'If you go to Manchester United to take a look round then don't come back to Arsenal.' After a five-minute discussion with the family, Mark walked out of Liam's office as a professional Arsenal player.

Mark began his career well and, in his first year as a professional, Arsène was as good as his word and gave him his chance in the first team. He came on as a substitute for the opening game at the Emirates Stadium – the Dennis Bergkamp testimonial, then he went on tour with the first team in the summer of 2006 and made his first-team debut in a League Cup third-round match at West Bromwich Albion in October before being picked again for the fourth-round tie at Everton. He was rewarded with a longer contract the following summer and continued to play in the FA Cup and League Cup, showing good composure on the ball and fine passing ability. But it gradually became clear that the pace of the Premier League was going to be too fast for him. After loan spells with Burnley, his local club Milton Keynes Dons, and Rotherham United he eventually signed for Chesterfield in 2013.

Mark was still playing with Larne Town in Northern Ireland as recently as 2022.

Liam also used his undoubted skills at mind games when he faced an argument between feuding parents. Sanchez Watt and Alex Zahavi were playing for the under-12 side and were among the best players at the academy at the time. But there was a rivalry brewing between their fathers.

It threatened to boil over when both boys were training on the floodlit Astroturf pitch at Hale End. The parents were watching the training from the heated viewing room. Maybe one of the boys didn't pass to the other and one of the parents moaned that his son should have received the pass. An argument took place and I had to step in to calm these grown men down. Liam arranged to meet both parents in his office the next day. He asked me to attend the meeting, during which Alex and Sanchez waited in the main hall at Hale End.

The meeting started with both parents trying to defend themselves about their roles in the argument, which then restarted. After five minutes of listening to them arguing, Liam suddenly asked them to leave his office, take the boys with them and never come back to the academy. He said he would send their release papers the very next day. The parents were shocked and protested but Liam was adamant that he did not want them at the academy any more.

Both fathers walked out of the room feeling somewhat humiliated and took the boys to their cars to go home. I was also disappointed and went to my room to consider the consequences of Liam's decision. Two outstanding young footballers who the coaches had worked with over the years, and who were thought to have great potential, were to be released without compensation. The scouts who brought these boys to the club would also be disappointed.

Liam came into my office but before we could discuss the situation there was a knock on the door. Mr Zahavi walked in and said that his boy was in tears as he did not want to leave Arsenal.

After a moment, Liam said that if Mr Zahavi could settle his differences with Mr Watt then he would consider letting the boys stay. Mr Zahavi went out of the room and within minutes both parents came back arm in arm, singing and dancing and saying that they were the best of friends. Liam had, of course, wanted the boys to stay all along.

Within two years Alex had an offer to go to Barcelona which he and his family accepted but he never fulfilled his playing potential. His uncle is the famous agent Pini Zahavi and I understand Alex is now working in the agency business. Pini was involved in the changes of ownership at both Portsmouth and Chelsea and was agent to Rio Ferdinand at the time of his record-breaking transfer in 2000 for £18m from West Ham United to Leeds United. The central defender was then sold in 2002 to Manchester United for £30m, out of which Zahavi was paid £1.3m for arranging the deal.

Liam's approach to parents who did not want to co-operate with academy rules almost came unstuck with Charles and Sarah Willock who had three boys – Matthew, Chris and Joe – training with us.

Our scout Shaun O'Connor, who also worked for Barnet at senior level, brought in Chris Willock when he was six. I had organised a tournament at the JVC Centre, adjacent to the indoor sports hall at Highbury. Shaun invited the under-sevens of Interwood Soccer School to the event. This north London junior club was very well run by Trevor Bailey and his brother Danny and very active in signing the best players in the area. Interwood produced several youngsters who went on to become professional players, such as Bradley Johnson, who we signed as a nine-year-old and later released. He went on to have a very successful career at Leeds United, Norwich City and Derby County.

Chris showed such unbelievable talent at the tournament that I invited him to some training sessions at the academy and to play for the under-eights. He was too young to sign academy forms but it was my way of keeping him attached to Arsenal and he was easily capable at the age of six of playing under-eight football.

The youngest of the three brothers was Joe. When I met him, he was only five. His mum Sarah and dad Charles brought him to Saturday morning training to watch Chris in the sports hall.

Throughout the session Joe cried his eyes out and pleaded to play. There was no pacifying him until I invited him on to the playing area so that he could kick a ball about. Suddenly he stopped crying and a smile came to his face. When Joe was seven, he was playing for the pre-academy team against Watford. Coach Rodney Clements had a wonderful way with the boys. In this game, Joe ran through the defence and with the goal at his mercy he hit the ball wide of the post. Rodney took off his glasses and said, 'Joe, do you want these?' Joe laughed and got on with his game before going on to score a hat-trick.

Having taken on his younger brothers, I signed Matthew from West Ham when he was ten.

All three Willock boys signed for the Arsenal academy for several years and lived only half a mile from the training ground. They were all very talented but Chris was the one to show the most potential.

As I had approached Chris to play under-eight football when he was a year younger, he continued to play at this higher age group until he was in the under-12 team. Liam, in his wisdom, then thought that Chris should now play in his own age group rather than play with the under-13 age group. At the same time, Liam put another player from the under-12s up to the under-13s. He was a strong, physical player who might benefit from playing with the under-13 squad, whereas Chris was small for his age and might do better in his own year group.

Letters about this were sent to both parents. Almost as soon as the letter arrived on Charles Willock's doorstep, he telephoned me to say that Chris was in tears as he was to leave his friends and team-mates and it was an insult to put him down particularly as he was able to hold his own when playing with boys a year older.

A meeting was held between Liam, David Court and myself and Mr and Mrs Willock. I put the view that Chris, being small for his age, would be better off now playing in his own age group. Liam said that it was policy for boys to play in the main within their age groups.

Mrs Willock, a strong woman, pointed out that Liam had put another player from the under-12s up to the under-13s. After views had been expressed, Mr and Mrs Willock understood that Liam was not going to change his mind and so they decided to walk out of the meeting. Liam said that if they were unhappy, they could remove their sons from the academy.

We started our pre-season without the Willocks and after a few weeks I enquired with Steve Leonard if the boys had been fixed up with another academy. I was informed that Chelsea wanted to sign Chris and that they had been to Tottenham but did not want to play for Spurs as the boys were Arsenal fans. I spoke to Steve and said we should go to their house to see how the boys were getting on and see if they had been fixed up with another club. We hoped not.

When we arrived and knocked on the door there was no answer. We called for Sarah to come out and see us. When she did, we were informed that none of the three boys had signed for any club and they were missing going to the Arsenal academy. This was music to our ears.

The next day we spoke to Liam about the boys coming back to the club. He wasn't too keen. Steve had an idea that if he gave Liam's mobile number to Mr Willock, he could ring him to ask if his boys could come back to the academy. Steve was going to ring Mr Willock to tell him to speak to Liam when he was in a good mood.

This is precisely what happened and it was agreed that all three of us would meet Mr Willock. At the meeting Liam said that he would think about bringing the boys back but there was no guarantee. A week later Mr Willock rang me to say that Liam had not contacted him. I spoke to Liam about his decision and he told me to ring Mr Willock to say that the boys could rejoin. The Willocks were delighted.

When Chris returned to the academy, he had to agree to play in his own age group and soon settled in to play with his new team-mates. Liam's decision proved to be correct as Chris continued to show his ability. He moved up over the next three seasons with the under-12, under-13 and under-14 teams. At the beginning of the under-15 season, which is year ten at school, Chris left his school in Walthamstow to join the newly formed education system at the academy where teachers from the local Highams Park School would come along to take ten of the gifted academy under-15 players through their GCSE programme for the next two years. The boys would train every day and have meals provided for them.

As I was then with the boys every day, it was easier to observe the character of each young player. Chris lived within walking distance of the academy and, although the education lesson started at 9am, he would stroll in just in time or even be a few minutes late. After a telling-off he would make an effort to be on time for a while. He often did not succeed. I was having doubts as to whether Chris would reach his true potential in years to come due to his casual approach to life.

He wasn't interested in his academic studies and would give in too easily if he experienced any difficulty in his GCSE subjects. However, his application for his football was still high on his agenda. His talent and performances in the games were still of high quality but he was somewhat limited in terms of his physique and pace. When he was 16 and leaving the education programme at the academy, he accepted an offer of a scholarship for two years at London Colney.

During his scholarship he showed his ability to become a professional footballer, and made his first-team debut against Nottingham Forest in the League Cup in September 2016.

Having signed professional forms with Arsenal, Chris still knew his first-team chances would be limited and, at the age of 19, he made the bold decision to take his boots to Portugal. In June 2017 he signed for Benfica and made his reserve-team debut two months later.

In recent times, other youngsters appear to be making a move to European clubs either on loans or in a permanent transfer in order to gain more experience to further their careers. Initially the thought of a move abroad sounds exciting, but in many cases the boys become homesick and miss their family and friends. Life cannot be much fun if you are also struggling to get into the first team. Chris was thrown a lifeline when West Bromwich Albion offered him a season-long loan in August 2019. At the time of writing, Chris is playing for QPR and has established himself in the first team and now has the chance to develop to his full potential.

Matthew Willock, who was a very quiet and conscientious player, was not offered a scholarship. He went on to Manchester United and after his scholarship there he was given a professional contract. Following loans in Europe, Scotland and at Crawley Town, plus a spell with Gillingham, Matthew signed for Salford City at the start of the 2021/22 season. He was released in the summer of 2022.

Joe also showed little interest in the education programme but he was very enthusiastic when training and playing. He probably showed less potential than his older brothers but it did not prevent him making his Premier League debut in midfield against Newcastle United in April 2018. He was just 18 and he became the fourth player born after Arsène Wenger took charge at Arsenal to play for the club. Joe also became the 56th teenager to represent Arsenal during the Premier League era – more than any other club. Jack Wilshere was the youngest at 16 years and eight months. Joe played the last 15 minutes of the 2019 UEFA Cup Final and collected a runners-up medal as Arsenal were heavily beaten 4-1 by Chelsea. He did, though, receive a 2020 FA Cup winners' medal as an unused substitute, when Arsenal beat Chelsea 2-1 in the final, after also playing in previous rounds.

At the start of the 2021/22 season, Joe was signed for a fee of £22m by Newcastle. I think Steve Leonard and myself were right to persuade Liam to change his mind those many years ago.

Mr and Mrs Willock must be pleased that all three sons are earning a living as professional footballers. For something similar, I can only think of the five Clarke brothers who all played professional football. Allan Clarke was the most successful and played a large part in the rise of Leeds United under the guidance of Don Revie. Derek, Allan, Wayne – who won the League title with Everton in 1987 – and Kelvin all played at one time for Walsall while Frank played for many clubs including QPR and Ipswich Town.

Daniel Ballard's story to succeed as a professional footballer is one of sheer guts, determination and desire.

Daniel was eight years old when he signed for the Arsenal academy after a successful trial that was initiated by Brian Stapleton, a scout in the north London area, who had watched him play for his local club in Stevenage.

Throughout the next four seasons, Daniel played in defence and, although lacking some agility and pace, his competitive nature and commitment to training helped him gradually overcome some of his deficiencies. He was a very polite and likeable young boy who had a soft centre and he would find it difficult to control his emotions when he and/or his team were going through a difficult time. I was responsible for deciding on which youngsters aged nine to 12 to retain at the end of each season and I was happy to keep Daniel at the club.

Liam made it his responsibility to make the decisions on the players who represented the under-15 to under-16 age groups. At the end of his under-14 season, Daniel and his parents were in the office with Liam to go through his end-of-season report. Liam had decided to release Daniel, who sensed that this was to be the outcome of the meeting and he started to cry so much that Liam looked at this young boy sobbing his heart out at the thought of being released that he calmly said, 'Daniel, I am going to give you another two years with the academy.'

Daniel continued to enjoy and develop his football over the next two years and as he approached the end of the under-16 season, we had to make a decision on whether to release him, offer him a scholarship only or one with a professional contract attached. Daniel must have found it very stressful in the weeks leading up to this.

Andries Jonker, the recently appointed academy manager, asked Steve Morrow, the recruitment officer, if he had any centre-backs likely to come from other clubs to add to the under-16 squad. As there were two due to be signed from abroad, Andries told Daniel he was being released. The youngster now faced the prospect of contacting other clubs to try and set up trials and prove himself in a totally different environment.

Daniel was allowed to continue training at Arsenal and then he broke his ankle during a training session. After his recovery he attended trials at Stevenage, who were preparing to offer him a scholarship when Andries was informed that the two overseas centre-backs had gone elsewhere.

Andries was set to take the squad to play Bayern Munich away and he was without a centre-half. He decided to ring Daniel to see if he would take the opportunity to play in Germany. Daniel accepted the offer and thus risked losing out on signing for Stevenage. The decision paid off for Daniel as Andries was so impressed with his performance that he offered him a scholarship, which was accepted. After completing the scholarship, Daniel was offered a professional contract and after highly successful loans spells at Blackpool and Millwall he signed for Sunderland.

Chapter 5

Young guns triumph in the toughest of tests

WHEN I had worked for the youth departments at Colchester United and Norwich City, few opportunities came along to take our squads to play in tournaments abroad. Not so at Arsenal where we had many invitations as tournament organisers knew we would prove a big attraction. I thought it was invaluable experience for the young Gunners to play against some of the top European clubs.

When academies play Sunday games against each other, the game time for each squad member is important and developing their ability is the main aim. The result is not particularly important (although to some coaches with an ego, winning is very important).

However, tournament football is very different. We would want to win the competition so as to give the boys a competitive edge, to feel the elation of winning games and also feel the disappointment of losing. It was also good for our coaches to compare the talent of our players with those from Europe.

In my second year at Arsenal we received an invitation to play in an under-11 tournament in Belgium. Our group had only just been assembled but they were the pick of the London area and we felt they were capable of giving a good account of themselves.

We won the group stage and felt confident that we could progress to the final four as we were drawn to play against Genk, a small Belgium professional club, in the quarter-finals.

We were representing Arsenal, one of the biggest and most successful clubs in Europe, and we assumed that putting on the Arsenal shirt to play against a small club from Belgium would mean our team would coast into the next stage of the tournament.

Our boys took time to settle and Genk were keeping possession. That will soon change, we thought. It didn't. Genk continued to produce a wonderful display of possession football and won 4-0.

When I congratulated the opposition manager, I asked him how often his boys trained. They attended training five nights a week and they had been doing so together since they were eight.

This was a lesson to all our staff that dedication combined with effort plus talent will lead to success. It does not guarantee a career at the top level but it does help a player to reach his full potential. The Genk youngsters could travel to their training ground five days a week as they lived locally. Some of them would even cycle there.

At Arsenal, parents had to make an enormous commitment to bring their sons to training two evenings a week. Travelling time could be up to one hour and there were also often delays due to traffic jams.

One particular invitation that caught my eye was a seven-a-side tournament in Majorca for the under-11 squad. I gladly accepted it knowing that one of the clubs taking part was Ajax, masters at developing young talent stretching back to Johan Cruyff, Johan Neeskens and Johnny Rep in the 1970s.

Some years earlier I had taken the Colchester youth team to a tournament in the Netherlands. The venue was next to Ajax's training ground, and we were invited to watch the Ajax under-tens play. We spotted Cruyff watching his son Jordi; Ajax were coaching under-nine youngsters upwards long before it was even considered in England.

One of the Arsenal squad for the Majorca trip was Joe Willock. For the Ajax match he was joined on the pitch by Reiss Nelson, Ebere Eze, now at Crystal Palace, and Nathan Tella, who spent the 2022/23 season on loan at Burnley from Southampton. In the present-day market these players total around £74m of talent.

The Ajax side contained Matthijs de Ligt, who left Juventus for Bayern Munich in 2022 for around £59m, Donyell Malen, now at Borussia Dortmund and worth £27m, and Justin Kluivert who has had various loan spells since signing for Roma in 2018 and is valued at £19m, making a combined total value of £105m in today's market. They beat us 5-1.

For many years the academy pre-season programme included a tournament for the under-12s and under-14s in the Netherlands hosted by the Dutch club Willem II Tilburg. Our first visit was very exciting as I had just started with Arsenal and was just getting to know other staff members.

We travelled by coach and were settling into the hotel when Liam Brady arrived and he introduced me to Clem, who I thought must be the kit man. I later asked Clem how long he had been doing the job and he explained he wasn't but Liam was his friend and so he helped at the academy whenever he could. This, of course, was at a time when few people were employed at academy level. Clem was also a massive Arsenal fan. I asked him what he did for a living and was left totally embarrassed when he said he was Clem Cattini, a world-class drummer who helped found Johnny Kidd & the Pirates before being one of the main drivers behind the Tornados in 1961, and playing on their international number-one hit 'Telstar'. We were all ears when he told us that the Beatles approached him before Ringo Starr and that he had been on tour with both Lulu and Billy Fury.

There were eight teams, including four Netherlands clubs, in each age group. In our third tournament we reached the under-12s final where we played the host team on the first-team pitch, which was a great experience for all the players.

Sanchez Watt put Arsenal in front in the first half but Willem II equalised after the break. With two minutes remaining, Sanchez waltzed around the opposing centre-half before scoring the winning goal. Parents enjoyed travelling abroad to watch their sons play for Arsenal and it was amusing to see some of them doing the conga in the stand to celebrate winning the tournament. And the name of the opposing centre-half? Virgil van Dijk, now a legend at Liverpool who was voted both the PFA Players' Player of the Year and Premier League Player of the Season in 2018/19.

Barcelona attended the tournament in Tilburg on a regular basis and one player in their under-14 squad stood out. He was Cesc Fàbregas. Two years later, aged 16, he signed for Arsenal and it did not take him long to establish himself in Arsène Wenger's first team.

A very small boy was in the dugout as a substitute for Barcelona. He came on at half-time and wowed the crowd with his extraordinary talent. His name was Lionel Messi.

But it wasn't always pure footballing skills which made an impression. Other youngsters revealed a mental maturity which belied their years.

During one tournament in Spain, 12-year-old Arsenal starlet Jeffrey Monakana proved he was already a winner at mind games.

After beating Atlético Madrid 1-0 in the semi-final, we needed to beat a top Russian side to win the tournament. The game ended 2-2 and went to penalties.

Our opponents had their under-14 and under-16 teams sitting behind the goal where the penalties were to be taken. In a marathon affair, the spot kicks were all successful until the Russians missed the ninth.

Taking the tenth, Jeffrey knew that the destiny of the tournament was in his hands. The Russian party were jeering and booing him. For any 12-year-old this would be a daunting position to be in. But, after calmly placing the ball on the spot, Jeffrey thumped it into the top corner of the net. What joy! Our players cheered and jumped on Jeffrey with delight.

On the bus from the stadium to the airport, I asked Jeffrey what he was thinking as he walked to the penalty spot with the opposition supporters jeering him. He said, 'I just pretended to myself that they were cheering me.'

What words of wisdom! Jeffrey has become a professional with spells as a midfielder at several clubs, including Preston North End and Aberdeen.

We went back to Spain to defend the trophy the following year. We reached the semi-finals and beat Barcelona 1-0 with the final against Real Madrid the next day. But after the match one player was missing from the dressing room. Ramone Agdomar was being attended to by our physiotherapist Dave Jude.

Dave said that Ramone, who had headed many balls out of defence during the game, had concussion. Back at the hotel we had to call for a doctor, who asked the youngster his name and where he lived. A dazed Ramone said he could not remember.

'He needs to go to hospital,' the doctor said. An ambulance was called. My colleague Michael Verguizas, who fortunately spoke Spanish, and I agreed to accompany Ramone as he sought urgent medical attention.

We would miss the final, our two remaining colleagues would look after the boys and we would all meet up at the airport after the final. Ramone's condition had to be our priority.

On the way to the hospital, I again asked Ramone his name and where he lived. This time he remembered.

Ramone had a very peaceful sleep while Michael and I dozed in the hospital chairs. Ramone was as fit as a fiddle the following day.

We met the party at the airport and discovered that Real Madrid had won the final 2-1. Tommie Hoban, part of the Arsenal youth system from the age of seven to 14, had a penalty awarded against him, which gave Madrid the trophy. But even the Spaniards in the 3,000 crowd thought this was a mistake by the referee and booed the official repeatedly, which was not really fair to him.

Tommie has gone on to play for several clubs including helping Watford to the Premier League. Ramone was unable to secure a professional contract with Arsenal but went on to play semi-professionally for such as Hitchin Town.

Top-class players can expect to spend a considerable amount of time travelling. It is something they need to accept as part of the job and they must not get frustrated when things don't go exactly to plan. Travelling to overseas tournaments thus helped our young players gain experience of what might lay ahead. And some memorable experiences did indeed lie ahead.

An under-tens squad bound for a tournament in Guernsey was split up when a bad accident blocked the M25. Our half of the party was diverted anticlockwise round the motorway where further delay meant we knew we would miss the flight. The other boys arrived in time but we had all the passports! The airport staff were magnificent, accommodating us on a later flight after allowing the boys already at the airport to travel on the pre-booked flight without needing to show passports. It was normal to collect all passports beforehand in case some boys forgot them but eyebrows were still raised at security when we checked in with twice as many passports as we needed. We went on to lose on penalties in the semi-final.

The trip home was the problem after an under-tens tournament in Brittany when we arrived at the airport to find it closed because of strike action. We were in a remote part of France with 25 young boys on board. But help was at hand. The tournament organisers arranged a coach to take us to Paris, where we booked into a hotel and travelled home by Eurostar the following morning.

I also took the under-13s to a tournament in Genk when I forgot the train and ferry tickets! We were able to rely on the goodwill of staff at Victoria Station but in Dover we drew a blank with the major ferry companies. There was another company half a mile along the seafront so we trudged there with our kitbags, battling against a storm brewing at sea. We were delighted to be booked on the next ferry. But another problem soon emerged. Benik Afobe, a very talented 12-year-old, had a Congo passport which allowed him to travel to Belgium but we were going via France and he couldn't travel there. A border force officer told me to wait while he called Calais. It seemed an eternity before he returned to say that Benik would be allowed through. First, though, was a rough sea crossing. The boat rocked and rolled with winds whipping up the waves. Most of our boys were sick. It was a relief to get off the ship and board the coach for Genk.

Benik made his England under-16 debut in the annual Victory Shield tournament in 2008, which involved the home nations. England won all their games, with Benik scoring in each one. The day after the first match I walked into my office and saw an England shirt on my desk. It was Benik's first one and he had given it to me as a thank you for all that I had done for him over the years. I didn't need any thanks but am still proud to say it sits framed in the hallway of our house.

Benik failed to establish himself as an Arsenal player, largely due to hip and cruciate ligament injuries which sidelined him for two years. He was loaned out several times before signing for Wolverhampton Wanderers who sold him to Bournemouth for £10m. The Bees then later recouped their money by selling Benik back to Wolves before he moved to Stoke City in January 2019. In the 2022/23 season Benik was playing for Millwall.

Chapter 6

The day the dreams are destroyed

INJURIES ARE part and parcel of any sport, especially football where speed and physical contact is part of the game. At Arsenal, several young players failed to reach their potential due to an injury. My own bitter experience means I know exactly how they felt.

Emmanuel Frimpong entered the Arsenal academy aged 11. He was born in Ghana in January 1992 but moved to Tottenham at an early age. He lived with his mum who did not have the time, the finances or the transport means to take him to a local club. It was only when he was nine and playing for his school that his teacher could see his talent and he sent him to the district trials, where he did well. One of our scouts at Arsenal, Clasford Stirling, saw him play and brought him to Hale End for a training session. Emmanuel was so impressive that we immediately signed him on academy forms and Clasford soon arranged transport for him to attend games and training.

Clasford had a great physical presence and a strong, deep voice you took notice of. He lived on the Broadwater Farm estate in Tottenham and was the community officer in charge of the sports centre where he ran football teams for all ages. Local boys respected him and he would bring his teams in the community minibus to play trial games at the academy. His son, Jude Stirling, became a professional footballer, firstly with Luton Town, playing with particular success at MK Dons between 2007 and 2011.

Emmanuel continued to train and play at the academy until he was 16 and he then went on to the first-team training ground for two years as a scholar. During those years he played for the Arsenal youth team that won the 2008/09 FA Youth Cup, beating Liverpool 6-2 on aggregate in the final. A professional contract was offered to him and he soon came to the attention of Arsène Wenger. He was selected to play alongside another academy product, Jack Wilshere, in the 2010 pre-season Emirates Cup which involved the home club, Celtic, AC Milan and Lyon. Both players, now aged 18, played extremely well. Emmanuel was praised by Arsène, 'Frimpong is a bit less of a dribbler [than Wilshere] but he is a winner.'

I went home thinking that the Arsenal midfield was secured for the next 12 years. How wrong could I be! The following week Emmanuel received a late challenge in a training game and the injury resulted in an operation where the damaged anterior cruciate knee ligament was operated on.

Emmanuel was out for much of the rest of the 2010/11 season, but with lots of hard work in the gym, fitness running and physiotherapy he was ready to start a new campaign. He came on as a second-half substitute for Tomáš Rosický to make his Premier League debut against Newcastle United in August 2011, and was then sent off the following weekend while making his full debut against Liverpool.

On New Year's Day 2012, Arsenal loaned Emmanuel to Wolverhampton Wanderers where he started well and became a crowd favourite. Playing at Queens Park Rangers he was hit with a late challenge by Joey Barton which saw Emmanuel twist on his good knee with his weight on this leg, damaging a cruciate ligament again. After a year's rehabilitation with Arsenal, it was clear that Emmanuel was not going to reach the heights everyone had hoped. He joined Charlton Athletic and after a season-long loan at Fulham he moved permanently to Barnsley, where, following the Tykes' relegation from the Championship at the end of the 2013/14 season, he was released.

Emmanuel later went to Moscow to play for FC Ufa but this period, which saw him racially abused in a local derby match by Spartak Moscow fans, went badly. He was released from his contract in April 2016 and, following short spells with another Russian club, Arsenal Tula, Sweden's AFC Eskilstuna and Cypriot side Ermis Aradippou, he retired due to injury in March 2019 at just 27.

Two other outstanding young players I signed also had their careers ruined through injury. **Ryan Smith** and **Conor Henderson** were both signed aged eight and gained scholarships before signing professional forms at 18. I sat in the stands at the old Highbury stadium to see Ryan make his debut as a 16-year-old in a League Cup tie against my old club Rotherham United in October 2003. The game went to extra time and penalties. Ryan played well and scored his penalty to make it 6-6, with Arsenal eventually winning through 9-8. I was so proud.

For someone so young he showed extreme calmness and confidence under pressure and all the signs were that with his excellent control and ability to dribble past defenders he could become a regular first-team player. He went on to make five more League Cup appearances for the Gunners, the last on 9 November 2004. A week later, he was playing in a reserve match at Ipswich where the opposing left-back was a trialist who was clearly determined to make sure that Ryan would not dribble past him.

Just before half-time, Ryan received the ball and the defender lunged into him and caught him on the knee. Ryan had his full weight on this leg and his cruciate ligament was damaged. He was out for a year after his operation.

The damage was done though and he never regained his original sharpness. He was loaned out to Leicester City for the 2005/06 season and then sold to Championship side Derby County but he struggled at Pride Park and moved on to Millwall in March 2007 before short spells at Southampton and Crystal Palace.

Ryan later tried to make a career in the US and Greece. He had some success but came back home to London after his career had finished. A few years later I saw him at a first-team game at the Emirates and I asked him how his knee was. It still gave him problems.

Conor, born in 1991, found himself in a similar situation to Ryan. Conor was an outstanding young player with the academy and played in the same team as Jack Wilshere. As a young professional, he was called over from the reserves to train with the first team and play in a practice game at left-back. Arsène Wenger was most impressed with Conor's displays and he was included on the bench for first-team away games towards the end of the 2009/10 season, and he made his debut against Leyton Orient in an FA Cup replay on 2 March 2011. Arsène said he thought Henderson would be a future first-team player.

Unfortunately, in pre-season training for 2011/12, Conor twisted his knee as he tried to turn quickly. A damaged cruciate ligament was the diagnosis, so another young player had to have a major knee operation. Conor had to go through the hard work of rehabilitation and the following year his efforts were rewarded as he began pre-season with some style.

He went on loan to Coventry City and, on his return, he was included with the first-team squad for a friendly match in Germany. He was doing well playing at left-back but when he was faced with turning suddenly after the opposing winger sought to go past him then his studs did not give in the ground. Again, the knee ligament was torn. Conor was released at the end of 2012/13 and then struggled badly at Hull City and a host of lower-league clubs before he moved to play in Bulgaria and Romania.

Emmanuel, Ryan and Conor are just three young players whose careers were ended or hindered through injury. It is a situation faced by many youngsters when, after going successfully through the academy programme, they are on the cusp of starting to play league football and then an injury ruins all their dreams. It is very hard to take because, while they may eventually accomplish many rewarding things in life, they will always be left with the question, 'I wonder, how good might I have been?'

It is a question I have also considered. Because, while I did have a career stretching to more than 100 Football League, FA Cup and League Cup appearances, scoring several goals including a League Cup hat-trick, my own chances were restricted by a series by injuries. It led to me quitting playing professional football at aged 27 and starting a long journey through the lower levels before returning full-time to the game at Norwich City in 1995.

But it wasn't all bad news. One player who overcame an adverse injury at an early age was **Hal Robson-Kanu**. I signed Hal for Arsenal when he was nine, and when he reached the under-14 age group it was decided to release him. Although he possessed good skills, he lacked some physical qualities and he was a very quiet young man who failed to assert himself in games.

His dad Ritchie took the decision very well but did say that his own older brother was a good size and this had convinced him that Hal could also be a late developer physically.

Hal joined the Reading academy and was offered a scholarship when he left school. At 18 he signed a professional contract there, but then in a youth match he sustained a knee injury, tearing his cruciate ligament, resulting in an operation. He worked tremendously hard in the gym to build up his strength and after six months out he was able to play again and he started to put in good performances for the reserve team. However, his progress came to a halt when another late tackle left him writhing in agony when the same ligament injury was torn again.

Hal and his dad waited for the verdict after the injury was assessed. Another operation was going to be needed and the specialist gave the shattering news that he did not think that Hal would play senior football ever again. But, with his dad's support, he set out to prove the specialist wrong.

Throughout the year following the second operation, Hal was first in the gym every day, working to build up his strength, particularly the quadriceps around the knee. When he was able to jog and then run, he worked tirelessly to improve his stamina, speed and turning technique. Ritchie was constantly involved in his son's recovery. Every morning he gave Hal a turmeric drink and he is convinced this helped the recovery process. Hal went on to score goals for Reading before being transferred to West Bromwich Albion. He also had a magnificent series of performances for Wales at the European Championships in 2016, his goals helping Wales reach the semi-finals.

Hal and Ritchie are now in partnership and have set up their own turmeric company providing energy drinks to various sports clubs and supermarket chains.

Chapter 7

You can't be right all the time

IF WE could see into the future, some decisions we make would be different. When I began at Arsenal there was a ten-year-old boy there called **Dwight Gayle,** who had a wonderful talent and an eye for scoring goals. As the format for the games was seven v seven on small pitches, he had great success for the next three years. When he played for the under-13s, the games, 11 v 11, were played on the bigger pitches.

Unfortunately, Dwight was very small, and against boys who seemed twice his size he struggled to score goals; he was released at the end of his under-14 season. I felt very disappointed for him but could not argue against the decision as his impact in games had been limited.

Three years later, Steve Leonard and I saw Dwight with some of his friends. We said hello, asked how he was getting on and enquired in particular about his football. He looked somewhat sheepish, said that he had packed in playing and was on a plumbing course. As we walked away, I felt quite downbeat that a talented young player with so much promise had believed it wasn't worth his while to continue playing, even just for fun.

I was therefore delighted when I heard a few months later that Dwight had started playing for Stansted in the Essex Senior League, where I had earlier managed Tiptree United.

After scoring a good number of goals with Stansted he moved to Dagenham & Redbridge, then of League Two (the old Fourth Division), before having a very successful loan spell with Bishop's Stortford. Then one January Saturday afternoon I was sitting in my front room watching *Soccer Saturday* on Sky Sports. Jeff Stelling, the presenter, announced that Dwight, on loan from Dagenham, had scored twice for Peterborough United against Middlesbrough.

Dwight signed permanently for Peterborough in January 2013, and in March he scored a hat-trick in a 3-2 win at Blackburn Rovers. These goals helped keep the Posh in the Championship.

His next move was to the Premier League when Crystal Palace paid more than £5m that summer. In a successful spell at Selhurst Park, Dwight collected an FA Cup runners-up medal in 2016 before this 'Roy of the Rovers' story was completed when Palace sold him to Newcastle United for £10m in July 2016.

I have told Dwight's story to many youngsters who have ambitions in football but whose careers are faltering. They won't all reach the heights of Dwight but with continued perseverance – and enjoyment of the game – they should reach their full potential.

On 7 February 2015 I watched the match between Spurs and Arsenal on TV. **Harry Kane** had just scored twice, including a late winner. He lifted up his shirt to reveal a T-shirt with a slogan which read 'That's for you Roy'. No, it wasn't intended for me! It was a clear message to Roy Hodgson, the England manager. Kane made his England debut at Wembley against Lithuania the following month.

I signed Harry for the Arsenal academy when he was eight. Gary Nott, a first-class scout, brought him to the club. Gary worked with me for four years and some of my best moments were on Saturday and Sunday mornings when the two of us went off to watch youngsters play at grassroots level.

Gary and Steve Leonard had gone to watch a six-a-side under-eights tournament organised by local Sunday league side Ridgeway Rovers. Gary was interested in two talented boys playing for Barking Celts and asked Steve to take a look at Ridgeway. Ten minutes into the game, two boys were already standing out, one showing some outstanding skills and another, playing up front, also doing well.

The Ridgeway manager Dave Bicknell, a Tottenham scout, asked Steve who had caught his eye. Dave told him that the two players were Nico Yennaris and Harry Kane. As Dave was a Spurs scout, it was only polite for Steve to ask him if it was fine to approach the parents of the two young boys and ask them if they would like to come along for a trial. Dave was very helpful, saying that both boys were Arsenal fans, and he introduced Steve to Nico's dad and Harry's mum.

Both boys subsequently did well enough in the trial to sign for Arsenal. Nico's mum was Chinese and his dad, Harry, was English. Harrry was very involved in the Essex Referees' Association and I asked him if he would provide referees and linesmen for the academy home games. He was delighted and he has done a wonderful job in doing that for more than two decades.

Harry Kane was one of those boys who showed good skills and football intelligence at a young age. He was quiet, extremely polite and well behaved and often overshadowed by the more boisterous young players. He was with the academy for four years when I decided to release him, feeling that his running and athletic ability would let him down eventually.

Nobody on the staff argued that I was making a mistake in releasing him. In fact, his dad told me that Harry would like to be a goalkeeper. I approached Alex Welch, the best goalkeeper coach in the business, asking him to take Harry on for a few weeks during which his potential as a keeper could be assessed.

Some sessions later Alex came over to me and said that Harry would never be a goalkeeper. Years later though, in October 2014 when the Tottenham goalkeeper Hugo Lloris was sent off in a 5-1 Europa League victory over Asteras Tripolis, it was Harry, who had earlier scored his first treble for Spurs, who was called upon to take over and he proved Alex right by failing to prevent a routine free kick slipping through his arms and over the line for the Asteras goal.

After leaving Arsenal, Harry subsequently had a trial at Tottenham but was not successful. He played for Spurs against Arsenal's under-12s. He was delighted to open the scoring against his former team-mates early in the game, but it finished 7-1 to Arsenal. Little did anyone know that the lone Spurs scorer that day would go on to become one of the best strikers in the world.

Harry was released by Tottenham and returned to Sunday league football. However, this would help him develop his skills as he could play without the pressure of being at a professional club.

He then later joined the Watford academy but after playing well in a match against Tottenham he began training with the north London club and soon signed a scholarship contract, turning professional in July 2010 at 17 and making his first-team debut in August 2011. Loan spells at Leyton Orient, Millwall, Norwich City and Leicester City helped him gain experience.

By the time of the Asteras tie, Harry was 21 and only just starting to establish himself in the Spurs team. In the summer of 2014, Mauricio Pochettino, twice winner of Spain's Copa del Rey as a player with Espanyol, had taken over as manager at White Hart Lane. Harry blossomed under the Argentinian and in the following season, his first as a regular, he notched 31 goals in all competitions. He has gone on to have a great career with, hopefully, many more years ahead.

The late development of players such as Harry and Dwight show what a difficult job youth assessors have in deciding which boys to release at the end of each season.

Jonjo Shelvey was another eight-year-old we signed for the Arsenal academy. He had marvellous skills, as he possessed great passing ability, read the game very well and he could jink past people.

After four years, his dad wanted him to leave because Jonjo could not get on with his coach, who would ask him to do press-ups if he made a mistake in training. I was disappointed but agreed to this request as I could not envisage Jonjo becoming the player he is today. He has kept the ability that was so clear even at a young age but has also added his charging tackles, yelling at top-class players in his own side as well as the opposition. Who can forget his lack of respect for Sir Alex Ferguson after he was sent off when playing for Liverpool against Manchester United?

Jonjo has played regularly in the Premier League for many seasons. Like Harry Kane, he was 12 when we allowed him to leave the academy. Jonjo had also been spotted by Gary Nott, who is still not best pleased with my decisions to release two of his players who were destined for great things in the Premier League.

Andros Townsend came to our training ground for a trial when he was nine. His mum, a lovely lady, was so keen for her son to do well. I agreed for him to spend a few weeks training with us before deciding if he was good enough to sign academy forms. Andros was competing with a very good under-nines team and eventually I told his mum that he wasn't quite up to the standard of the other boys in his group. She accepted the decision gracefully and took him home, no doubt both very disappointed.

Years later, after the academy had moved to new premises at Hale End, a lad was using our training ground to practise ball skills on his own. It was Andros. His garden backed on to our training pitch; he had signed for Tottenham and we allowed him to continue his own personal training on our pitches. He was not interfering with our training and was doing no harm.

Little did I realise that the Arsenal academy facilities would help a young boy reach the heights of playing for Tottenham and England.

When he was doing well for Tottenham, Andros was selected for the England squad for the 2014 World Cup in Brazil. A few weeks before this competition I was getting the staff lunch at the local Sainsbury's in Walthamstow. As I was getting in my car to return to the training ground, a voice behind me shouted, 'Roy!' As I turned to see who was calling me, I recognised Andros's mum. She had just finished her shopping and came running up to me, telling me, 'Roy, Andros has been selected to play for England in the World Cup.' I was pleased for both of them but felt somewhat disappointed at recalling the day I released him from Arsenal. She had a twinkle in her eye.

'Pity,' I said, 'we only had him in for a six-week trial.'

'Roy, he was training with you for six months.' Thanks for the reminder!

When Andros reached his under-18 age group and was playing with the Tottenham youth team, Arsenal were drawn to play Spurs in the quarter-finals of the FA Youth Cup at White Hart Lane. Just before kick-off I took my seat in the stand and was sitting next to Pat Rice, Arsène Wenger's assistant. Arsène was sitting in the next seat.

You could not wish to meet a more friendly person than Pat, and he was always interested in what was happening in the youth department. Pat had come through the youth system himself, signing as an apprentice with Arsenal in December 1964 before becoming a professional in May 1966.

He went on to make 829 appearances for the Gunners at various levels during a 16-year playing career. He was a brilliant overlapping full-back and a member of the famous 1971 Double-winning side, only the second of the 20th century. He also made 49 appearances for Northern Ireland.

Pat's loyalty to Arsenal was recognised when, following a short playing spell at Watford, he returned to Highbury as youth-team coach in 1984, taking the club's youngsters to success in the FA Youth Cup in 1988 and 1994. He was briefly caretaker manager in September 1996 and when Arsène was appointed he became the Frenchman's number two, a role he undertook until May 2012.

The FA Youth Cup game was a very close encounter. I soon noted that Andros was playing on the left wing. He started well and was easily the best player on the pitch in the first 20 minutes. I heard Arsène say to Pat, 'I like the Tottenham lad playing on the left wing, do you know him?' I was keeping my fingers and legs crossed in the hope that Pat did not turn to ask me if I knew about this left-winger who was tearing the Arsenal defence to pieces. Fortunately he did not and as we went on to win 1-0 the importance of Andros's performance was somewhat diminished.

When academies were introduced to cover all young players in the London area, we set up development centres at Potters Bar, Brentwood, Hale End, Middlesex and Croydon with a coach in charge of each one. Ken Fisher, our south London scout for many years, was placed in charge of developing the Croydon centre. He has been a loyal servant for Arsenal for many years and he was still scouting for the club at the time of writing.

One of the boys who impressed Ken was **Luke Ayling**, who was born in August 1991 and so was having to compete for a place in the academy with boys nine or ten months older. I felt Luke wasn't quite ready to play in his own age group and I put it to him and his parents that he should stay with the development centre and that I would sign him for the under-nines team the following year. They agreed and Luke played for the academy team during the following season and for the next four years.

At the beginning of the under-13 season, he was doing well enough to move into his own age group. His future, though, was by no means secure. One of his first games at this age saw Luke play at right-back against Bristol City away. Steve Leonard was managing the side and Luke was having a bad time when facing a speedy winger, so he was substituted at half-time to save him from further embarrassment. Luke's parents were very angry as they had driven all the way from London to watch their son play only half a game. I am sure that many years later they can now appreciate that Steve's decision was the correct one as it helped Luke to retain his confidence and go on to big success.

When it came to deciding whether to offer Luke a scholarship at 16 there were some doubts about his lack of pace. But it was decided to give him the platform not only because of his ability and football intelligence but also his attitude, desire and dedication.

He made good contributions to the youth team and played in the 2008/09 side that won the FA Youth Cup, signing a one-year professional deal that summer before joining Yeovil Town on loan in March 2010 and making his first-team debut.

Luke was released by Arsenal at the end of the season and returned to Yeovil, signing a permanent contract. He had to adjust to the type of football played lower down the Football League and he would quickly become aware of the trimmings he had enjoyed at the Arsenal. These would be missing at Yeovil.

This clearly did not deter Luke as he just wanted to play football as a professional in a stadium with a crowd watching. He soon became a regular first-team player and his performances were noted by a Bristol City scout, leading to his transfer to the Ashton Gate club in the summer of 2014. He was now playing regularly in the Championship and after two seasons of steady progress, Leeds United bought him. He has since played hundreds of games for Leeds. It gave me great pleasure to see him playing a League Cup match at the Emirates Stadium during the 2019/20 season, which Arsenal won 1-0. Statistics for 2020/21 showed that Luke was one of the most successful tacklers in the Premier League.

Christian Burgess was a very quiet, intelligent and disciplined footballer. I remember myself and my scout, Gary Nott, watching Christian play and he stood out as a defender.

He was very competitive, he read the game well for his age and he was the outstanding boy on the pitch. It was what we were looking for – somebody who was maybe head and shoulders above everyone else.

We offered Christian a six-week trial and he impressed so we offered him academy forms and he stayed with us for five years. He was a terrific lad to have in the academy – he was a quality person as well as an intelligent, very competitive and disciplined footballer. Unfortunately, he didn't develop too many physical qualities by the time he was 12 and that's why it was decided to release him.

It's always a difficult decision to let a young player leave but, looking back, I realise that I made several mistakes through not allowing boys to develop through puberty. Sometimes you think they're on the small side, they're a bit delicate and they're not going to be strong enough or physical enough or quick enough to become professionals. That was poor judgement on my behalf and it might have been other people's point of view as well. I didn't wholly make the decisions – they were collective. It would have been myself and the coaches.

Christian moved on to the Tottenham academy, where he wasn't offered a scholarship at 16, so he remained at school to do his A levels.

Four years after Christian left Spurs, his dad Tony came to see me. He was excited to tell me his son had signed a two-year contract with Middlesbrough. After successfully completing his A levels, the lad had started a degree course at Loughborough University where he impressed for the university team in a friendly against Middlesbrough reserves. He was invited for a trial with the Teessiders and offered a professional deal. Middlesbrough allowed him to complete his degree course at the local university. Good for Tony Mowbray, their manager at the time, for doing that.

Unable to force his way into the Middlesbrough first team, Christian moved away from the north-east and, after a spell at

Peterborough, he became captain at Portsmouth. In 2021/22, Christian was one of the stars at the Belgium club Union SG who only just missed out on the title when, after finishing top of the table, they finished second in the championship play-off, securing Champions League qualification for the first time.

What a career Christian has had. It's fantastic what he's achieved, and what a great advert he is for any lad who's turned down twice and perhaps thinks his footballer career is finished. I'd be delighted to see him playing in the Champions League.

Naturally, a player released by a club of the stature of Arsenal, at whatever age, has a chance of a trial at a smaller club. Whenever I released someone I sought to get them fixed up elsewhere. However, it is far more difficult to arrange a further opportunity for a released player if you are working for a lower-league club. For such a player, a young man with great dreams, it is a very big blow.

All clubs have a responsibility to encourage young players to think about an alternative career to football and should encourage their active participation in their educational studies so that if they hear those horrible words 'I am sorry but I am not renewing your contract for next season', they can, at the very least, think they have an opportunity to do well in another career.

My own experiences helped me explain why it was important to study hard while at a club. I knew that without my teaching qualifications I would have found it hard to obtain a decent job at the age of 28 when my career as a professional footballer ended after several seasons where I often found myself sitting out matches due to injury. With a wife and three children to support, the future would have looked very bleak. You can't pass on your experiences to young people but you can at least advise them and hope they will listen.

The Premier League held various inter-academy tournaments and we were invited to play in one such event at Bisham Abbey with our under-tens squad. During our first game a young boy was kicking a ball to his dad on the side of the pitch. Impressed by the lad's technique, Steve Leonard asked the father if the boy played for a team. It transpired that the 11-year-old played for Coventry City and they had come down from Birmingham to see the lads from the Arsenal academy play. 'My lad is a very keen Arsenal supporter,' said the dad.

The youngster was **Daniel Sturridge**. At the end of the season, Daniel was invited down to London to play for the Arsenal under-11s against Manchester City in a Sunday-morning game at Brentwood School. A room was booked for Saturday night in a nearby hotel for Daniel and Mike, his father. It was small but convenient for the venue.

After a training session with the Arsenal academy youngsters on the Saturday morning, I was driving home feeling very relaxed after what had been a good week's work. I was looking forward to the game against Manchester City when my phone rang. Mr Sturridge was at the end of the phone complaining about the state and size of the hotel.

He had brought his family down with him and he said they were going home if I could not find him another hotel big enough. I drove down the A127 towards Southend to find another hotel and found suitable accommodation just off the road, so I booked three rooms for the Sturridge family. Mr Sturridge was happy with the new arrangements. Our under-11 squad beat Manchester City and Daniel scored three in a 4-1 success.

Another young player making his Arsenal academy debut that day was Kieran Agard, who scored the other goal. Later, Kieran's goals put Rotherham United in the Championship at the end of the 2013/14 season. He subsequently moved on to Bristol City for £1m. Not bad for a young player who, when he was 16, was thought not good enough to get a scholarship at the Arsenal.

Meanwhile, we kept in touch with Mike Sturridge and, when Daniel was 14, I heard that he had left Coventry City. I invited him and his dad to have a day with us at the Arsenal academy.

Steve Bould was the under-14 coach. I asked Steve to meet Daniel and take him for a one-to-one coaching session; he gave up his time gladly and put on a very good session. Over a buffet lunch it became clear that we would have to bring Daniel and his family down to London and buy or rent a house for them and also give Mike a scouting job. In today's academy world this would not be a problem but at this particular time it seemed a big gamble. Who is to say what a 14-year-old footballer will turn out to be when he is 20? We decided against the move. Three months later Manchester City signed Daniel. They sold him five years later to Chelsea for £8m.

Ian Poveda was a tiny little boy when he attended trials, aged eight. He showed exceptional skills. One of our coaches described him as a circus act when he saw him juggling the ball from his feet to thigh and head. He was sharp and energetic, producing good performances for his academy team.

He was picked to play for the under-12s in an eight-a-side tournament in Spain that included four giants of Spanish football – Barcelona, Real Madrid, Atlético Madrid and Villarreal – plus Paris Saint-Germain and Arsenal. Despite Arsenal finishing only fifth, Ian was voted as the tournament's best player.

Two weeks later his father came to my office and told me he was moving abroad with his company for the next two years. As his wife, living in south London, would not be able to bring Ian to training or matches then Mr Poveda said he was taking his son with him to look after his education and football progress.

Although disappointed, I could not argue with this decision and wished all concerned all the best of luck in this new venture. When the new season got under way, I was in my office when Francis Cagigao, head of international scouting at Arsenal, rang me from a tournament he was attending in Holland.

'Guess who is playing for Barcelona?'

'I've no idea.'

'It's Carlo Poveda.'

At the start of 2023, Carlo was playing for Blackpool on loan from Leeds United.

One player fits into a slightly different category in that he was perhaps the only academy player who Arsenal did want to sign but he chose to leave – for Spurs.

I had only been in post for just over a month when Graham Nicholls asked me to come down to Kent and watch a youngster play for his district team. That lad was **Jamie O'Hara.** He had been training with Chelsea, and Graham believed that Arsenal should consider getting him to sign for the cub. The first thing I noticed was that Jamie was bigger than the rest of the other players and he was also head and shoulders the best player once the game kicked off.

I thought Arsenal should seek to sign him as quickly as possible. I told Steve Leonard that I intended on visiting Jamie's parents the following week.

Unbeknown to me, Steve sent a parcel to Jamie. It was the new Arsenal kit for Jamie's size. When I arrived some days later at his house, Jamie answered the door and was wearing the new kit that Steve had sent him. I knew then that we would sign him.

Jamie was a credit to the academy in terms of performances, attitude and behaviour. However, at 16 and with his dad being a keen Spurs fan, Jamie joined Tottenham Hotspur. He started his professional career very well but injuries prevented him from ever reaching his full potential, although he did play for Portsmouth at the 2010 FA Cup Final which Chelsea won 1-0.

In 2017 I watched Jamie appear on a different big stage when he was a contestant on *Celebrity Big Brother* and during which his larger-than-life personality shone through. He is now a well-regarded pundit on talkSPORT radio.

Nigel James has his own football coaching school in south London and during my time at Arsenal he would bring some of the young players up to the academy. On one occasion he came with his son, **Reece James,** then aged eight and playing as a centre-forward. He was a great dribbler with the ball and had an eye for scoring goals. We wanted Reece to join us at Arsenal but Nigel and the youngster felt it was too far to travel regularly and preferred to accept an offer from Chelsea to join their academy.

At some point somebody at Chelsea felt his talents would be better used elsewhere as a full-back rather than up front. Reece is doing very well as a player, but I would have preferred it if he had been doing so at Arsenal.

After watching him play for his local club, our south London scout Michael Verguizas brought **Ebere Eze** for a trial with the under-eights.

He was a very skilful and dedicated player who loved playing football and he had an eye for scoring goals. His coach Rob Dipple came back from an under-ten tournament in France singing Ebere's praises after he scored 20 goals in the competition. Nevertheless, he lacked awareness when in possession of the ball. But his major drawback was that he had not developed physically by the time he reached 14 and he was released. With hindsight it would have been better if Ebere hadn't joined Arsenal at such a young age and had played Sunday football with his local club where there was not the pressure to release the ball early and he could have enjoyed running and shooting at will.

Ebere later had trial spells at Watford and then Millwall before finding success at Queens Park Rangers. He then joined Crystal Palace for a fee of £17m in August 2020. He performed with distinction in the Eagles first team in the 2020/21 season, leading to a call-up to the England squad in May 2021, although a serious injury in training that same day slowed his progress. Thankfully he has recovered well and continues to impress for Palace.

In the second year of academy football, we managed to assemble a very good group of under-nine players. **Chris Solly** was one of them. Although small for his age, he was tenacious and, allied to his skill on the ball, he served the team for two years before he began to struggle a little.

We decided to release Chris at the age of 12. It was disappointing to have to do so as he was a delightful boy and his parents were a pleasure to be with. It was felt that his lack of physique and pace would let him down at the highest level of football as he got older. When he was released by Arsenal he had a successful trial with his local club, Charlton Athletic.

At 18, Chris made his first-team debut for the Addicks in the Championship and he kept his place for many years. He captained the club and as of the 2022/23 season he is playing and coaching for Ebbsfleet United in National League South.

There were many occasions when I really could have used a crystal ball to see into the future but one case stands out more than most. In 2004 we played in an under-12 tournament organised by Genk in Belgium. Our translator for the three-day visit was a lady from Croydon whose son was constantly with her. He was with the Genk academy but was too young to play in the tournament. And he was an Arsenal fan.

We reached the quarter-finals, the competition was worthwhile and we returned the following year. Sure enough, our translator was there to meet us. She was very enthusiastic about the progress her son had made over the previous 12 months and told us proudly that he had been selected to attend the Anderlecht academy. The youngster was thus playing his last games for Genk, a club well known for its outstanding academy, having brought through players such as Thibaut Courtois, Christian Benteke, Divock Origi and Leandro Trossard.

Arsenal faced Genk in the final. We won on penalties but the young boy played well. His name was **Kevin De Bruyne.**

His mother then asked me if her son could train with the Arsenal boys for a week in the following pre-season as she was going back to London to see her family. I was pleased to be able to accommodate her request as she had put so much effort into making us feel welcome and comfortable during our stay.

Kevin was a quiet young man and clearly did not feel quite at ease playing alongside some of the more confident Arsenal under-13 players. He did show some ability, possessing strong football intelligence and fine passing skills. But there was still no way we could bring a lad from Belgium to live in London so that he could be a member of the Arsenal academy. The decision may have been different if he was already living in London. Certainly, we would have wanted to see more of him. Both parties said goodbye and we wished him all the best for the future.

Many years later Steve Leonard rang me and asked if I could remember the young player with red hair from Belgium. I could but I had long forgotten his name. Now the link was revealed. Kevin's journey had taken him from Genk to Chelsea and Wolfsburg. He was now playing for Manchester City and had become one of the best midfield players in the world.

Yes, a crystal ball would be very useful, but then again life would not be as challenging and perhaps a little too predictable.

* * *

George Dobson signed for the Arsenal Academy as an eight-year-old and typified the qualities required to become a professional footballer. As he reached his teenage years it was clear though that his lack of pace might let him down. Having spoken with him his dad arranged for George to attend the local athletics club and over the following three years he sought to improve his running ability whilst also attending his coaching sessions at the Academy. His desire, determination and effort resulted in him gaining a scholarship.

George was a centre half as a schoolboy but after his first year as a scholar it was clear that he would not be tall enough to become a central defender and we asked the coaching staff to play him in midfield. We had a lot of good midfielders and so George himself terminated his Arsenal contract. Following a brief period at West Ham United he went on loan to Walsall, eventually signing full-time for the Saddlers following a spell at Sparta Rotterdam. George became the youngest ever player to captain the Walsall first team and went on to play for Sunderland and AFC Wimbledon and he is currently playing for Charlton.

Steve Rowley gave magnificent service to the Arsenal recruitment department. I first came across Steve when he was a part-time scout for the youth development programme in the 1980s. He was often watching schoolboy matches in the Essex area and I was viewing the same games for Colchester United.

We always had friendly conversations on the touchline, but our friendship dimmed somewhat when he tempted three Colchester players, including Steve Ball, to sign apprenticeship forms for his beloved Arsenal. Our relationship improved when I started work for the Gunners' academy in 1998. By this time Steve was working alongside Arsène Wenger as he was in charge of scouting for the first team.

It was a very sad day when I learned that cancer had got the better of Steve and that he had died at age 63 in the spring of 2022. Steve had signed Tony Adams and Ray Parlour as 15-year-olds from the Essex area.

At his funeral, many colleagues, coaches and former Arsenal players were present to pay their respects. Tony gave a wonderful talk on his relationship with Steve over the years. Cesc Fàbregas and Robin van Persie sent messages of condolence in which they recognised how much influence Steve, who was associated with Arsenal from 1980 to 2017, had on their careers.

Chapter 8

South Yorkshire roots

I WAS born at the home of my grandparents Jimmy and Fanny in Park Road, Mexborough, on 10 September 1943.

My mum Rachel had a difficult time delivering me. The midwife had warned that I might be stillborn due to difficulty over the umbilical cord, but as soon as I arrived I gave out a cry which was a great relief to everybody waiting in anticipation for the new arrival to the Massey family.

My dad Gordon was part of a large family of six brothers and three sisters. One of his brothers, Roy, was only ten years old when he died, and I proudly inherited his name.

When I was four, my mum's dad, Tom Parkes, died and so my parents and I moved to live with my grandmother, Elisa Parkes, in Derwent Terrace. This was a semi-detached council house with three bedrooms, a living room, kitchen and a small bathroom. The living room was cluttered with a piano, sofa, dining table and chairs.

Mexborough is believed to have grown from its strategic defensive position on the River Don, possibly in the face of Roman or Anglo-Saxon invaders. The settlement was first referred to in the *Domesday Book* of 1086.

Mexborough was a good town during the 1950s, providing a wide range of amenities for its 10,000 inhabitants. Everyone did their shopping in the high street and in the market situated just behind it. There was a continual buzz about the place.

As a teenager I was a regular visitor to Harrison's sports shop where my mates and I peered enviously at the new football boots on display. We also frequented the music shop to stand inside the listening booth to hear the newly released rock 'n' roll records. My favourite singers were Elvis Presley, Buddy Holly and Roy Orbison.

But I was just window-shopping. I could not afford to buy the boots. Buying a vinyl record was also out of the question as I had no record player.

Like many people I was a keen cinema-goer. UK attendances peaked at 1,430 million people of all ages in 1949, with 1951 not far behind at 1,360 million. Apparently the 2019 total was 176 million. I queued with my mum to see the film *Snow White and the Seven Dwarfs*. We waited 45 minutes. On edging close to the entrance, a 'cinema full' notice shot up. I never did see that film.

As a young boy, the two most exciting days in Mexborough were the annual fair and the day trip to Cleethorpes.

The fair was held at the town sports grounds, the Mexborough Athletic Club in Hampden Road, which had a 5,000 capacity. The sports ground consisted of a cricket square where the town's team played and to the side of the long boundary was a football pitch.

The whole field was cordoned off with a 3ft fence. To one side of the football pitch was the grassed area that ran down near the touchline. This was where fans stood when supporting their team. The changing rooms and clubhouse were nearby.

The fair consisted of side stalls, refreshments and an athletics event open to the public. I was ten and after my running escapades my mum entered me for the 100 yards. These events were staggered depending on your age. When my event was announced I went to the marshal and he put me at the start of the track. I was up against seven other runners, much bigger and two or three years older.

I had no chance of beating any of the other runners. Nevertheless, on the gun I ran my heart out. My mum was crying at the unfairness of it all but I just kept running as fast as I could even though I was going to be last. This was a big lesson to me and all the youngsters who I have coached that when playing sport, particularly at a high level, there is no room for the player who throws in the towel even if his team is losing 6-0.

The Cleethorpes trip was organised by the Hope Working Men's Club where my dad was a member. A hired train took us to the seaside. Whole families, grandparents included, piled aboard. On arrival at Cleethorpes, we kids raced out into the sea, then later enjoyed the fairground attractions, ate too much and just had a great day out.

The Massey family were very close-knit and the central characters were James and Fanny. They gathered at their house on Saturday nights to make a ten-minute walk to the Hope club – even the wives were welcome on Saturdays.

They would sit in one big group at a regular spot adjacent to the bar and stage on which many acts came to perform in the 'big room'. The family entertained themselves and liked to chat and drink on Saturday nights at the end of a hard-working week. All the men worked at the pit, the steelworks or at the Mexborough Loco, the large railway locomotive maintenance depot, which would close in 1964.

At closing time on Saturday – last orders then were at 10.30pm – the family would walk or totter back to Park Road where fish suppers would be waiting. Cousin Olaf would play the piano and a good singsong would complete the evening.

My dad often said he needed no friends because all his brothers and sisters were his friends. His brother Stanley was the only one who chose not to work in the South Yorkshire industries and as a youngster he left for London. He became a fireman and then brought his girlfriend, my auntie Louise, down to London. They settled in Rainham, 13 miles east of Charing Cross, and had a little girl, Pat. Little did I realise when we were growing up and seeing each other twice a year during the school holidays that Pat would change the course of my life when I was 50 years old.

Other than academic terms, namely the three years from 1962 to 1965 when I went to Saint Paul's College in Cheltenham, I lived in Mexborough for my first 24 years.

Mexborough is in the middle of a triangle consisting of Rotherham, Doncaster and Barnsley. For decades, many coal mines surrounded the town. From one of them William Hackett quit to join the British Army in October 1915 and, like many pitmen, he was enlisted to serve in one of the many frontline sapper battalions digging tunnels and laying mines in France.

On the night of 22 June 1916 and into the following day, a tunnel Hackett was working in near Givenchy-lès-la-Bassée collapsed when a German mine exploded, trapping him and his comrades. After 20 hours knocking through an escape tunnel, Hackett helped three men to safety before, ignoring the probability of further collapse, he stayed to care for a seriously injured soldier who couldn't be moved. Tragically, despite further rescue attempts, the roof did cave in, burying them both. Hackett's bravery earned him a posthumous Victoria Cross and he is also honoured with an imposing memorial in his hometown.

Most people lived in a council house, the men grafted at work and the wives looked after the children and the household duties. When I was growing up in the late 1940s and 50s I cannot think of a woman or girl who went out to work. Thank goodness for the move to equal opportunities of today.

When I was eight I was playing on the swing at the local park. A neighbour's boy came running into the park shouting, 'Masseys have got a telly.' In great excitement I sprinted home and there it was on the sideboard, a 12in black and white television. We sat watching the test card before *Children's Hour* started at 5pm.

Previously, the only other times I had a link with for television was when my mate Barry Hodgkinson's dad bought a TV. They lived on the opposite side of the estate. Mr Hodgkinson opened his house to all the local youngsters to watch *Children's Hour* pm. Sometimes there were up to 40 children there and we all paid one old penny to watch for an hour.

* * *

Of course, the rapid advance of television technology would help bring football into millions of living rooms. In doing so it further popularised the game and eventually turned it into a multibillion-dollar industry with players at the highest levels earning astronomical sums.

The first television match was a specially arranged Highbury friendly between Arsenal's first team and reserves on 16 September 1937. The following year two Wembley matches were broadcast – the FA Cup Final, featuring Preston North End and Huddersfield Town, and the annual England v Scotland clash.

After the war, TV coverage remained static with only the FA Cup finals and the occasional England-Scotland game being shown live.

In December 1954, I was very excited when I watched the BBC broadcast of the second half of the friendly at Molineux between English champions Wolverhampton Wanderers and the Hungarian champions Honvéd, whose team contained many of the famous 'Magical Magyars' who had finished as World Cup runners-up earlier that year and who had thrashed England 6-3 at Wembley in 1953 and 7-1 in Budapest in 1954. Wolves came from 2-0 down at the interval to win 3-2. Afterwards, their manager Stan Cullis pointed to his team in the dressing room and told reporters, 'There they are, the champions of the world.'

Having noted that the home side had heavily watered the pitch before the game, there were many who disagreed. In the aftermath, previous suggestions that a European club championship be organised were at last taken seriously and acted upon. It helped that by now technology had also advanced, such that games could be played in midweek under floodlights.

Adverts for new televisions, often in matchday programmes, encouraged many new purchases. By 1956, around one third of people in Britain owned a television. In comparison only one in 20 households had the benefits of central heating. You could freeze to death watching the TV in those days.

There then began a battle between the TV stations and the various football authorities who were keen to protect the game and felt that live coverage would impact on attendances at other matches. Burnley chairman Bob Lord led the successful campaign to prevent televised games on Saturday afternoons. This is still the case today as the FA, Premier League and Football League do not allow live coverage between 2.45pm and 5.15pm on Saturdays.

The BBC showed brief highlights of games on its Saturday night *Sports Special* from 1955 to 1963. ITV agreed a deal worth £150,000 with the Football League to screen 26 live matches in 1960/61 but this was abandoned when Arsenal and Spurs refused them permission to show their games against Newcastle United and Aston Villa respectively.

In 1962, ITV tried again and were this time more successful. Anglia launched *Match of the Week*, first showing Ipswich Town v Wolves on 22 September 1962 and ITV started local coverage under the title *Shoot*. In 1964, the BBC started *Match of the Day* on BBC 2, the first programme featuring a thrilling 3-2 Liverpool win at Anfield against Arsenal. The programme was moved to BBC1 after England's 1966 World Cup success and the number of viewers rose considerably. ITV's regional coverage was also extended in the late 60s with London Weekend Television's *The Big Match* kicking off in 1968.

The demand for football on television grew through the early 1970s and 80s and has continued to grow ever since.

* * *

As a child I attended St John's Primary School. Organised football started in my life when I was nine when I was selected to play for the school team. My junior school classroom was in the church hall, around a mile away from the main school which did not have sufficient classrooms for all its pupils. On Friday afternoons we had to make the one-mile trip from the church hall to take part in the final assembly of the week. We had to walk in pairs and a strict 'no speaking' policy was implemented. Imagine today a group of ten-year-olds asked to walk for a mile without speaking.

I was walking with my friend Peter Holmes and he started chatting to me. I said he should not be speaking. Mrs Pilkington, an old lady, came up to me and scolded me for talking. When we reached the assembly hall, Mr Popple, the headmaster, approached me and said that I was talking on the way to school. I said, 'No, sir.' With that he hit me as hard as he could across the face. He ranted, 'Did you speak?' and he made to hit me again very hard. His actions forced me to say, 'Yes, sir.'

When I returned home my mam asked what was wrong with my face as Popple's fingermarks could be clearly seen on my cheek. I told her what had happened. The next day our class had an activity at the school. The headteacher came up to me and apologised. Unbeknown to me, my dad's eldest sister Elsie had visited the school and confronted Mr Popple. He admitted he was out of order and she had made him apologise.

Smacking on the face was commonplace in the 1950s. I also remember being rapped on the knuckles with the edge of a ruler for getting my sums wrong. When I attended secondary school, it was a clip around the head or the cane, while up until the 1970s the PE teacher used a slipper on the backside for any boy that might be disruptive. I regret to say that after I became a teacher in the 70s, I used the slipper on five occasions during my subsequent 25 years of teaching. There were no confrontations, as I put it to the boys, who were in the final years of schooling, that the option they faced was to go to see the headmaster and he would inform their parents or they could have the slipper and no one else would know. All chose the slipper.

Of course, physical punishment in today's society is out of order but it is very difficult for a teacher to control and relate to a pupil who is hell-bent on causing havoc. Teachers have a very difficult role; they must be able to teach their subject by establishing classroom control and this requires real skills as it means being able to establish a special relationship with every pupil in their class.

I found this to be the same when coaching a group of young footballers. Getting the very best from each boy requires a coach to develop a care and understanding of them. I used to be very disappointed if a parent came up to me to say he felt the coach did not like his boy and that he instead had favourites in his team.

There are 15 or more boys in a squad of players and up to 30 pupils in a school class. All are from varied backgrounds and with different temperaments. I have always maintained that it is the responsibility of the coach or teacher to build a relationship with each child in their charge. Doing so means they have a greater chance of helping youngsters reach their full potential.

I remember Benik Afobe playing for the Arsenal under-16 side in a match at West Ham United. He had been going through a barren spell in front of goal, so Steve Leonard, his coach, took him to one side before kick-off to tell him not to worry about his drought and to remind him that he could be a good player as a professional one day. After ten minutes of the match Benik scored and he ran over to Steve with his thumbs up. Situations such as these enhance the relationship between teacher and student.

On Saturday mornings at the age of ten I would walk two miles to the bus station with some of my friends. I then caught a bus for a five-mile journey to Wath upon Dearne where a new public swimming pool had opened. As this was then the only one in the area it was very popular and there would be a long queue waiting for the 10am session.

When we did finally get into the baths, the water at the bottom end would be up to our waist. As there was no tuition, we had to teach ourselves to swim before we would dare explore the deep end.

The swimming was just one part of the excitement because after we exited the pool there was the pleasure of standing under the warm shower which was fixed to the ceiling in a small cubicle, into which four of us could squeeze and enjoy the luxury of hot water raining down on us. The idea back then of being able to have a daily hot shower at home was out of the question.

At the bottom of the terrace where I lived was a wider road where, during the evenings, we would have a game of football with two coats on the ground for goals. We played floodlit football when it got dark and the streetlights came on. The only time the game was stopped was when the odd car came along the road and we all moved to the side for it to pass by. Unfortunately, one game was abandoned because we forgot to pick up the ball and the car ran it over. However, only a limited number of cars came by as few local people owned one in the early 1950s. Skipping, hopscotch, and whip and top were other activities that we took part in. They all helped to keep our minds and bodies healthy.

It is very understandable that today's parents do not allow their children to play outside on their own as we did. Unfortunately, the result is that many of them become armchair children with television and computer games taking up much of their free time. Children may be better fed than in our day but they are perhaps less healthy for being inside much more than we were. In her mid-60s,

Grandma Parkes became housebound, sitting all day in a particular chair. She loved to have a bet on the horses and in those days horse racing was often on terrestrial television.

I had, like everyone else where I lived, failed the 11-plus. That meant that rather than attend a grammar school I would be a pupil at a secondary modern, where pupils were destined to leave at aged 15 with no qualifications. The jobs available for everyone were at the pit, steelworks and in other manual occupations. In comparison, grammar school pupils would largely be able to opt to stay on until they were 18 in order to take O levels and A levels at 16 and 18 respectively. They could then perhaps go on to university or college followed by a rewarding career. I attended Adwick Road Secondary Modern School along with other pupils from working-class backgrounds.

At 13, a lifeline arose when I was able to take the 13-plus exam. Much to my surprise and the great joy of my parents, I passed. This enabled me to transfer to the Mexborough Technical School where the curriculum was divided into three compartments – engineering, building and secretarial. I was placed in engineering but without having a practical brain I was more at home in PE and on the sports fields. This proved detrimental to my GCSE exam results and I later failed all but two, English and History. I was, though, persuaded by my parents and Clary Mason to resit my exams and with thorough revision I passed seven subjects, allowing me to attend sixth form, which in turn widened out my opportunities in life.

Mexborough Technical School was just ten minutes away and so I could return home for lunch. When I set out back for the afternoon classes my grandma would give me a betting slip and 6d (2.5p). I would call into a general store that also served as a bookmaker and put her bet on. I was always delighted to pick up the winnings each time her horse came in. Her favourite jockeys were Lester Piggott, one of the greatest Flat racing jockeys of all time, and Australian Scobie Breasley, a great rival to Sir Gordon Richards and then, later, Piggott.

I subsequently found out that my second wife Julia had on occasions as a child gone on an outing to the races to cheer on Piggott as he was riding her uncle Tom and aunty Peggy's horse. This was named Pebsham after their farm in Bexhill-on-Sea. Julia met Piggott on several occasions and he was always friendly towards her.

My football upbringing was very different to the talented of today who train and play with an academy, enjoying three coaching sessions each week with a game on a Sunday versus another academy. All with nets, a referee and wonderful pitches to play on.

There are some disadvantages, however, as some coaches shout and bark at the boys from the touchline, instructing them how to play. Parents, also on the touchline, become disgruntled and frustrated if their boy is having a poor game or if their team lose. No wonder some boys are put off playing as they get older.

When I was assistant academy manager at Arsenal, a young lad, who was 14, told me he was packing in football as he preferred to go scrambling on his motorbike on Sundays. The season beforehand he had scored 30 goals for the under-13 academy team.

On another occasion a parent told me that his son, who was 11 and had just started at senior school, had begun playing rugby for the school and as he enjoyed it so much then he had decided to stop playing football and concentrate on rugby instead. While I was disappointed, I have to say that the boy in question was clearly a very talented young man. He was Adam Ball, who became a professional cricketer with Kent and captained the England under-19 team.

A boy who makes a mistake playing for his academy team is often criticised by his coach who wants to win the game rather than examining the personal development of each player in his charge. When I was playing for my school team we didn't play in front of critical parents, and our coach was our teacher who was refereeing, so he couldn't show any bias and give us instructions on how to play and win the match.

The 1966 England World Cup winners all played in the same environment where I developed my own football skills. All were world-class players and I am sure that they did not have coaches telling them how to play in the early teenage years. They would have a passion to play the game and be allowed to improvise and develop their own football intelligence. Despite all the wonderful facilities and coaching provided by academies, there is a danger of producing stereotype players who lack the ability to improvise and make the right decisions when in possession of the ball.

* * *

When I started at the technical school at aged 13, the one subject I was really looking forward to was PE, which gave us a double lesson of football in the winter months plus one lesson in the gymnasium, which was fully equipped with wall bars, beams, ropes and other apparatus.

It was still a multipurpose building as it was used for morning assemblies and monthly dance evenings for year five, six and seven pupils – now years 11, 12 and 13 – that were organised by our PE teacher Clary Mason.

Nevertheless, the facilities were amazing when compared to the hall at my previous secondary modern school which was used as a dining room at lunchtime and was surrounded by classrooms, such that when we had a double lesson of PE, it was interrupted when the bell went at the end of the first session and pupils crossed the hall to attend their next lesson.

After school ended, I attended my first gym club and as I looked around at my class-mates I felt confident that I would be ahead of them in gymnastic ability. I raced into the gymnasium and started climbing one of the ropes. As I looked down from the top of the rope, the smallest boy in the class came running into the gym and followed up his run with an Arab Spring, consisting of a cartwheel with a twist, before he moved straight into a backward somersault. Everyone marvelled at his ability.

His name was Stan Wild. We became friends and he eventually went to Carnegie College of Physical Education in Leeds. He continued working to develop his gymnastic ability and he represented the Great Britain gymnastic team at the 1968 and 1972 Olympic Games.

Chapter 9

A profession – or professional football?

WHEN I was 16, I was set to leave school. I had been offered apprenticeship forms – the predecessor to scholarships – by Barnsley, Sheffield United and Sheffield Wednesday. The Owls were my first choice because of my grandad James Massey's career there.

Instead of joining the Wednesday, who had won the Second Division in 1958/59, my PE teacher Clary Mason persuaded me and my dad that I should stay on at school for two years and then go to college for three years to undertake a certificate course in PE. He suggested that I could play professional football when I had completed the course. He stressed how, by gaining a teaching qualification in a subject I loved, I would be guaranteed work in later life doing something I enjoyed. I agonised over what to do for a considerable time.

I thought being a PE teacher was a great, rewarding job. I had a passion for sport, physical activity and healthy living and felt it would be rewarding to try to motivate and educate young people about all the benefits of these practices. I liked the idea of increasing participation levels by planning, organising and delivering enjoyable lessons for students at different ages and abilities. I was aware, even then, that staying fit and healthy was also good for a person's mental health and that a good PE teacher could play an important role in young people's subsequent lifestyles.

I understood that team games encouraged working together and helped build lifelong friendships.

I felt that Mr Mason's advice was worth following and I also felt fairly confident that I could become a professional footballer once I had completed my studies.

Although disappointed not to be joining a professional club, I decided not to take up the Sheffield Wednesday offer and decided to remain at school for the next two years.

I was a member of the Mexborough Methodist Church and one of the most enjoyable activities they organised was the Saturday youth club for 14- to 18-year-olds. I would watch the likes of Billy Fury, Cliff Richard and the Vernons Girls on the 12in black and white television. They'd sing their latest rock 'n' roll hits on the show *Oh Boy*, which ended at 6.30pm.

The boys would then play indoor football in the hall where, perhaps surprisingly, no windows were ever smashed. There was a table tennis table and a snooker table, easy chairs in a side room where you could chat with your friends and a record player playing the latest hits non-stop. The club was run by two young women volunteers who were regular worshippers at the church.

One Saturday evening the whole atmosphere changed when a gang of Teddy Boys arrived unexpectedly. They were all wearing their long, coloured coats, drainpipe trousers and shoes with thick crepe soles. With their hair greased back they looked intimidating and they had gone to stir things up.

I was 16 and of the dozen or so Teddy Boys, some were around my age and others older. They stayed until closing time and as I made to go home, a distance of around three miles away, one accused me of stealing his watch which he demanded I give back. I did not have his watch and told him so. It was 10pm and I was keen to catch the bus at the nearby stop.

I was rushing down the long flight of stairs to the street when my friend from school, George Pendlebury, who was on the fringe of the Teddy Boy set, came running towards me to let me know not to go any further as the gang was waiting for me at the bottom. We both sprinted in the opposite direction. My nearest shelter was my grandparents' house where my dad and all his brothers and their wives had their supper on Saturday evenings. When I entered the front room, I was pale. After I said what had happened, all my uncles went to find the boys. Thank goodness they did not locate them as I suspect quite a bit of blood, mostly the Teddy Boys', would have flowed. As for George and myself, we laid low for a while before venturing out again.

In my schoolboy years, if you didn't get selected for the school team, then you had no other opportunities to play for a football team as there were no matches on a Sunday because the day was set aside for church Sunday school. Even those boys who did play competitive football only did so during the autumn and spring terms as very often games were cancelled during the winter months when pitches might be waterlogged, frozen or snow-covered.

In the summer term at the senior school, we were able to choose cricket or athletics. I opted for the latter and enjoyed participating in the field events such as the shot put, discus and javelin. I became quite good at throwing the javelin and won the South Yorkshire Schools under-14 championship. This gave me an incentive to practise regularly and as I gradually worked on my techniques then my personal best continued to improve.

When I was 17 and in the sixth form at Mexborough Technical School, I was chosen for the South Yorkshire Schools team in the Yorkshire Schools Athletics Championships. To my surprise, I won the javelin competition with a personal best of 180ft.

I then went on to win the Northern Schools Championship. This meant I was selected to represent Yorkshire in the English Schools Athletics Championship at Chesterfield. I travelled down on the team bus and we were met by the parents who would be looking after us for the weekend. I was made to feel very welcome and after dinner I sat in their lounge watching television while also scanning the official programme for the following day's English Schools event. Coincidentally, the TV was screening the Great Britain versus USA athletics event being held at the White City Stadium. Looking through the lists in the programme, I was keen to see the names of the boys taking part in my competition. I was disappointed when I read the name of John McSorley and this feeling changed to gloom when I heard his name on the television, just as he was about to throw the javelin for Great Britain.

But I still calculated that if he was on international duty in London on the Friday evening then he was unlikely to turn up less than 24 hours later for the schools championship. I was eagerly looking forward to the next day's competition, hoping to throw a personal best and come away with a top-three place.

The following day was sunny and the stadium was buzzing with excitement with young athletes from all over the country warming up for their event.

The time came when I heard that all javelin throwers should report to the organising marshal. As I approached, I saw an Adonis in an England tracksuit registering for the competition. McSorley, who was 18 months older than me, had turned up.

He threw before me and his javelin flew through the air, landing at well over 200ft. I had a disastrous time and my best was only 135ft. This was well below my personal best and I finished third from last. Where was the never-say-die spirit of that ten-year-old who had run with so much determination against older boys at the Mexborough summer fair?

Now aged 18, I had allowed myself to become deflated before the competition began. Even with the presence of a rival who I knew was far better than me, I had let myself down. The mental and psychological approach to performing is so important. I wonder if my own performance would have been better if I had not known beforehand that a full England international was in the competition. McSorley went on to represent England in the hammer, javelin and discus at the 1962 Commonwealth Games in Perth, Australia, and eight years later he took silver at the games in Edinburgh.

While I was in the sixth form, I played football for Yorkshire Grammar Schools against Birmingham and District Grammar Schools at Barnsley's Oakwell ground. I crashed home the third from 15 yards out in a 5-3 victory on a muddy pitch.

After playing well for Yorkshire as an under-17 player, I was selected to have trials for England Grammar Schools. Forty boys from all over the country attended the week-long trials at Cambridge University, where in 1848 a group of students had written a set of 11 rules which they hoped everyone could agree upon. At the end of the trials, I was delighted to learn that I had been selected to play against Scotland at Celtic Park.

The England team included two players, Howard Wilkinson and Graham Taylor, destined to lead their country out at Wembley as managers.

England had played Scotland at football for the first time at the Kennington Oval on 5 March 1870. The organiser was FA secretary Charles Alcock who, inspired by the inter-house 'sudden death' knockout competition he experienced at Harrow School, then created the FA Cup, the longest-running cup competition in the world, the following year.

Although the 1870 game is not considered a full international – only two of the Scotland players, Arthur Kinnaird and Robert Smith of Queen's Park, were Scottish-born – the event, and four further matches, acted as the precursor to modern international football with the first full fixture taking place between Scotland and England in Glasgow on 30 November 1872. Interestingly, match reports contain no reference to any English player passing the ball. The game was played under Scottish rules and follow-up encounters in England were under English rules. When the two FAs met with their Welsh and Irish counterparts in 1882 to regularise the rules – or laws, as they were known – it led to the standard two-handed throw-in from behind the head and the clear marking of the touchlines.

Terry Oldfield, one of my best friends from Mexborough Technical School, was also selected to play at Celtic Park. He was an astounding centre-half and team captain and many professional clubs were chasing his signature.

Travelling to Sheffield to join the rest of the England squad, my train passed the Parkgate steelworks where my dad worked as a crane driver. There he was, standing on the side of his crane giving me the thumbs up! And on the evening of the game, I got off the coach at Celtic Park to be greeted by my mum and dad and the always supportive Clary Mason who had driven my parents to Glasgow.

The game itself was disappointing; we lost 1-0 and I had a poor match. But much worse was to follow. It was distressing to see Terry collapse in the dressing room at half-time. During the first half, Terry had to head many high balls away from the Scottish goalkeeper's kicks. He recovered the next day and was able to go home with the rest of the team. However, several weeks later, after having tests at the local hospital, the specialist had devastating news for Terry – he was advised not to play football again. He had a weak or thin skull and heading the ball would be extremely dangerous in the long term. Terry was the first of several young players I knew who lost fine careers in the game due to injury or ill health.

After my dismal performance at Celtic Park, I was determined to attend the following year's trials at Cambridge University and make sure I was selected for England Grammar Schools again. I then intended to justify my selection with an outstanding performance. Maybe score a hat-trick!

I was delighted to make the trials again. On the previous Friday I had played in a very competitive school inter-house match. As

I was playing in the Doncaster League for the school old boys' team on Saturday afternoon, I was left out of the school team match on the Saturday morning. But Clary Mason arrived the following morning saying that the school team had only ten players and asking if I could play. I did so before going on to play in the Doncaster League fixture in the afternoon. Fifteen minutes into my third match in 24 hours I was sprinting for the ball when I suddenly felt a severe pain in my right thigh. I had torn my quadriceps and couldn't continue.

Over the weekend, I rested up and rubbed oils into the torn muscle and hoped that the injury would miraculously clear up.

I travelled down to Cambridge intending to play in the first trial game using a leg strapping. I was hoping the injury would have healed but this was wishful thinking. As soon as I began running, the muscle gave me so much pain that I had to withdraw immediately. It then proved a long week as I sat out the trials and watched the games. I was not going to be picked for the England Grammar Schools squad, but even so, I thought the injury was a temporary one, something that I would shake off in time. I didn't realise then that injuries would subsequently play a big part in my footballing career. Injuries would restrict both the level and the number of times I would be able to play at a professional standard.

It took two months for the injury to recover. It was a lesson for any young player not to play in too many games in a week. The best schoolboy players can often be selected for their school year group and play for the school year above them. If they live in an area that has a school district team, they are selected to play in these teams on Saturday mornings, and Sundays they are playing in the academy team. It is the responsibility of the academy staff to monitor the number of games played by their younger players.

As I was coming towards the end of my school years, I was persuaded by Aston Villa to go for a trial in the summer of 1962. I was accompanied by my uncle John. The Villa manager was Joe

Mercer, who had a brilliant playing career with Everton, Arsenal and England and who was to go on to become a great manager, especially at Manchester City where he won the First and Second Division titles, the FA Cup and League Cup and the European Cup Winners' Cup. I played with a group of trialists against the Villa youth team and I had a good game, scoring twice. Afterwards, John walked up to Mercer, who later acted as the England caretaker manager in 1974, and asked him if he liked any of the trialists.

Mercer, whose side had finished seventh in the First Division in 1961/62, looked at him as if to say, 'Who do you think you are, poking your nose into our affairs?' John followed up by stating that he was with the number nine. Mercer's face lit up and his tone altered immediately, saying he would like to see us after I had changed. He took us to a restaurant and later dropped us off at the station. He was keen for me to sign. In a trial for Barnsley, I scored seven goals and their manager John Steele was also desperate to give me a contract.

I was, however, reluctantly forced to turn down both offers. I had undertaken an interview at St Paul's College in Cheltenham, Gloucestershire, and had been accepted on to the PE certificate course there. My thoughts of being a professional footballer had to go on the back burner. This began in September 1962 and would end in May 1965.

Chapter 10

How a trainee PE teacher
becomes a Miller in the holidays

WHILE IT was always satisfying to know that St Paul's College would help me qualify as a PE teacher, the downside was that I had to prioritise playing for the college each Wednesday and, crucially, on Saturdays. It was expected that college sport, especially if you were on a PE programme, would always come before any other activity in which a student might consider taking part. There was prestige attached to winning sporting competitions against other colleges. But the rules, of course, meant I could not have signed for a professional club.

In the last weekend of my first term in 1962, the college side didn't have a fixture. Ronnie Massarella, chairman of Yorkshire League side Doncaster United, had already said that I was welcome to play for his club on any spare weekends and he would pay my travel expenses back to Yorkshire. Even better, he would collect me before games – the arrival of his car always caused great excitement as it was a pink Cadillac. We did not have many cars coming down our street, let alone snazzy American ones.

Ronnie was the Yorkshire-born son of an Italian immigrant family. At the age of ten he used to sell the family's homemade ice cream from a wooden wheelbarrow to coal miners at the pit head anxious to clear their throats. When he took over the running of the business, his vans would come round the streets on our estate, to the delight of local youngsters[1].

Doncaster United had gained promotion from Yorkshire League Division Two in their inaugural season of 1959/60 but were immediately relegated, only to bounce straight back up in 1961/62, finishing second out of 14 teams. In seventh place were Sheffield FC who, as the oldest club in the world, had celebrated their centenary only a few years earlier.

My debut would be against Stocksbridge Works FC who had become the dominant force in the Yorkshire League in the 1950s. They won the title in 1961/62 and would triumph again in 1962/63, scoring 83 goals in 30 matches and losing just four times. Doncaster had struggled to score at the start of the season and were to total just 35 league goals across the campaign, the lowest by far, as relegation was avoided by just three points. Ronnie wanted me to up the scoring rate.

The match was at Stocksbridge's hilltop Bracken Moor ground and was played in a gale. With the wind behind us in the first half we had all the play but could not score. High-flyers Stocksbridge were constantly on the attack in the second 45 minutes but also could not find the net. With just five minutes remaining I found myself with the ball on the edge of the opposing penalty area. Despite facing the wind, I struck my shot perfectly and it flew into the top corner to give Doncaster a shock 1-0 win. I was the hero that night and still beaming with pride when I met my friends, who were still going to the church youth club.

Back at Cheltenham. I was still smiling when I went for the evening meal in the main hall where staff and students would dine

---

1 Ronnie Massarella turned the family firm into one of Europe's biggest ice-cream producers. When he died in 2015 his UK-wide Massarella Catering Group was a £40m concern with more than 100 outlets and 2,000 employees. But he became best known in the UK and far beyond as the leader of Britain's showjumping teams during the glory years of such household names as Harvey Smith, David Broome, Nick Skelton and John Whitaker. For 32 years he was the British team's manager, taking them to seven Olympic Games.

together before notices were read. At that point my joy suddenly ended. I heard vice-principal Jack Priestley mention my name and telling me to report to his office later. What had I done wrong?

It had been discovered that I had left the college premises at the weekend without a permit to do so and that this was considered gross misconduct. I had a strip torn off me and was told never to leave the college again without being given an exit pass – I didn't!

No doubt the college rules were being protective as many students were away from home for the first time and as such a big responsibility was put on the teachers to care for their well-being. Yet I had never been told off at school or home and now here I was as a 19-year-old getting a scolding.

Fortunately, I faced no problems in playing over Christmas 1962 when I returned home. I had left to go to Cheltenham ten weeks previously. It seemed a long time ago. It was great to have the time to go to the youth club and visit my old friends.

Ronnie asked if I would play for his team at Mexborough Town's Athletic Club ground on Boxing Day. I jumped at the chance. The match was a friendly as Town were in Division Two of the Yorkshire League but, unlike Doncaster, they were scoring regularly and winning matches.

When my uncle John heard that I was playing, he challenged Mexborough Town chairman Mr Roebuck to a pint of beer that Doncaster would win. The bet was quickly accepted as in truth the away side had no right to think of victory.

More than 1,000 spectators crammed into the ground; there was always a good turnout on Boxing Day. The game kicked off at 11am, leaving time for supporters, nearly all men, to go to the club for a lunchtime pint before going home for dinner.

Doncaster won 2-1; I'd like to say that I was the star and scored two goals. I had an undistinguished game and other than two average efforts I failed to get involved. It was a lucky win as Mexborough had all of the play but they missed their chances and we took ours. How often does this happen in football? At the end, John was delighted to go to the club and enjoy his free pint.

One young Doncaster player who I played with and who went on to have a good career in professional football was forward Rod Belfitt. We formed a good partnership up front, were both 18, and we played with great enthusiasm and energy, scoring many goals between us. Like me, Rod was invited by an Arsenal scout for a trial in London but he declined the offer and was eventually signed by Leeds United. He went on to have a successful career with, among others, Leeds and Ipswich Town.

St Paul's College catered for everyone who wished to play football regardless of their standard and they ran four teams. My friend Dave Wilkins, a staunch Coventry City fan, was the secretary and organised all the games for the season.

Soon after I turned down Arsenal in the summer of 1964, the college team had an important last game of the season at home to Loughborough College, the top college team of the day. It was a competitive match but after 30 minutes the Loughborough centre-half put in a late challenge and caught me above the ankle. I went down feeling a great pain and had to be carried off the pitch and taken to hospital. The X-ray showed a fracture of my fibula just above the ankle. The season finished with my leg in plaster for six weeks. I wondered if I would recover from this injury, and if I did, at which club could I restart my football journey.

My broken fibula healed well over the coming weeks and I was ready to return to college to finish my final year. Although college football was a good standard it was not the same as playing for Arsenal. I was keen to earn a professional contract and the teaching certificate would come in handy if I failed to make the grade. Little did I know that the certificate would prove to be a godsend.

Another of my dad's brothers, Harry, lived in Rotherham and he was an avid fan of the local professional club, watching them for many years at every home game. He took great pride in telling me that he knew the manager Danny Williams as he would see him every week at the local betting shop.

After I had turned down a professional contract in London, Harry asked me who I was going to play for the following season. I had no idea. The next day he saw Danny and asked him if I could train with the Rotherham United players during the forthcoming 1964/65 pre-season build-up and I soon reported to the Millmoor ground on the first day of training.

The 1964 Rotherham side was a young one with the majority of players being in their early 20s. They had established themselves in the Second Division (today's Championship) the previous season.

The players were very friendly, particularly Brian Tiler who became the captain, aged 22, the following season. I knew Brian from our school days having played against him when he was a pupil at Dinnington Technical School, just outside Rotherham. Brian went on to play for Aston Villa and then joined Harry Redknapp at Bournemouth. He seemed destined for greater things in football but tragically lost his life in a car accident when he was travelling back to his hotel after watching a World Cup match in Spain in 1982.

Every day I travelled the ten miles from Mexborough to Rotherham by bus. On the way we would go through a small town called Rawmarsh, where the Parkgate steelworks was the centre of activity. Sitting on the bus watching people make their way to and from work, children going to school and with passengers getting on and off, I could feel a real buzz in the town. Shops had impressive frontages, plenty of goods were being sold and hundreds of steelworkers noisily chatted with one another.

Some two decades later I made the same journey in my car to watch Rotherham play the club I was then working for, Colchester United. The difference was immense. The steelworks had closed, shops were boarded up and few people were walking around the streets.

The steelworks had been axed at the same time as Margaret Thatcher closed the coal mines. Mexborough was in the middle of the River Don and Dearne area and several pits were important to the nearby villages – Kilnhurst, Denaby, Manvers and Barnborough to name just a few. When I was a boy growing up in Mexborough, most men earned a living either at the coal mine or the steelworks.

From being a teenager to the day he had a heart attack on his 50th birthday, my dad worked at Parkgate as a crane driver. Like everybody else, we lived in a council house. Dad's job was to earn enough money to pay the bills and put food on the table while Mum's role was to look after me, the house, and my grandma – her own mother – whose husband died when I was four.

Mum would do the shopping in a series of small shops. Shop assistants would serve individual customers directly; the idea of customers helping themselves was unheard of. Many ingredients such as butter and flour had to be weighed and bagged by the staff before being sold to the customer. On occasions, shopping was delivered to customers' homes via a delivery boy on a bike or in a van.

Mum would also cook, wash all the clothes, towels and bed clothes, iron and clean. I did help as I got older.

Although there were a few private houses, most people lived to the same standard. Money was certainly scarce but I, like my friends, had a very happy upbringing. From eight years of age I was able to go to the local park with my friends, and our parents would have no worries about us coming to any harm. We played football until it was nearly dark. In the summer we played cricket.

After the first training session at Rotherham United, a cross-country run was organised with trainer Albert Wilson accompanying the players by riding alongside us on his bike and shouting out encouragement. I was asked to participate in the whole of pre-season and play in the reserve friendly matches. I did well enough for Danny Williams to sign me on amateur forms before I went back to college.

On 22 August 1964 I made my competitive debut, playing for the reserves in a 5-2 home win over South Shields in the Northern Regional League. I scored my first goal on just two minutes and ended up with two, although I was outscored by my outside-left colleague David Chambers. The Rotherham side on the day was: Morritt, Wilcockson, Simpson, Brandon, Haselden, Lancaster, Himsworth, Rabjohn, Massey, Chappell and Chambers.

I managed five reserve-team appearances before going back to Cheltenham. The *Sheffield Star* reported how I had turned down Arsenal and was returning to finish my college course.

As I had a commitment to the college football team then I was only able to play again for the reserves during the holidays at half-term, Christmas and Easter. The reserves played their home games at Millmoor and would be watched by around 2,000 fans. Some supporters worked at Parkgate steelworks and they included workmates of my dad. When I did get the opportunity to play I did well and so my dad was bursting with pride when his colleagues were singing my praises.

I also scored another double in an 8-1 defeat of Darlington reserves and ended 1964/65 with ten goals in total in 14 games. I was on the winning side nine times and lost twice.

Chapter 11

Netting a professional
contract for the Millers

I HAVE heard many people say that a lack of English players in the modern game is due mainly to so many foreign players playing here. This may be partly true but I believe another key reason why youngsters do not get the opportunities they did previously is the play-offs, which began at the end of the 1986/87 season.

Before the system was introduced, three teams were automatically promoted from the Second and Third Divisions, and four from the Fourth Division. By the beginning of March each season most teams were not involved in the battle for promotion or the survival fight. Managers could give their best youngsters a run of five or six games in the first team instead of, as today, ten minutes here and there. This would allow them to see if the player might be good enough for their squad for the following season.

Danny Williams, a legendary player for over a decade with Rotherham United, was the manager at Millmoor. He made a club-record number of 461 league appearances and he turned down offers to sign for Arsenal and Leicester City, such was his love for Rotherham. At the age of 14 he suffered an injury that left him on crutches for five months. He worked down the pit during the Second World War, signing for the Millers in October 1943 and scoring for the first time in a 3-0 away victory over Doncaster

Rovers on 22 September 1945 in the Third Division East League consisting of nine local sides.

After competitive league football was resumed at the start of 1946/47, Williams played all 49 Third Division North and FA Cup fixtures and scored his first league goal in a 4-3 defeat of Barrow at home watched by a 9,974 crowd. Rotherham finished second but only the champions were promoted.

Rotherham had one of their finest sides over the following seasons and finished second again in 1947/48 and 1948/49. The title was won in 1950/51 and Williams, playing at inside-right, scored eight league goals. He also netted twice in the FA Cup but failed to score when Rotherham lost 2-0 away to Hull City where the Boothferry Park crowd was 50,040.

In 1954/55, Rotherham almost made it into the top flight of English football for the only time, ending the Second Division season in third place, equal with champions Birmingham City and the second promoted side, Luton Town, on 54 points. The Millers lost out due to an inferior goal average, having won eight and lost one of their final nine matches and ending the campaign by thrashing Liverpool 6-1.

Williams's last first-team game was in the 1959/60 season and he became reserve-team player-coach before taking over as first-team manager in 1962.

I played three reserve games in April 1965: a 1-1 draw at Bradford City, a 2-1 success at Crewe Alexandra and a 4-2 defeat at Doncaster Rovers. I scored at Crewe and Doncaster. I must have shown enough talent to enable Williams to give me my Football League debut at Cardiff City on Saturday, 24 April 1965. Rotherham were the longest-serving club in the Second Division by this stage.

I lined up against the great John Charles, who was finally ending his playing days. He had a wonderful career with Leeds United, where, with 38 league goals in 1956/57, he finished as the top scorer in the First Division. He then joined Juventus and was one of the two British players that successfully adapted to life in Italy; Eddie Firmani was the other. Doing well when playing in another country must have been difficult. John remains a legend in Turin, the home of Juventus. He was also world class as a centre-half.

There is no doubt that forwards have the hardest role in football. Not only are all their basic skills tested, such as kicking, controlling and passing of the ball, heading, and awareness of the players around them so they can bring them into play, but they are also expected to score goals.

Being able and willing to shoot quickly from different angles and from any distance using both feet must be developed by constant practice.

Forwards also act as target men for clearances and long balls. Making decoy runs to draw defenders away for other players to move in on goal is a skill that requires intelligence and speed.

Bravery to go in where it hurts in pursuit of a goal can be the vital difference between winning promotion or avoiding relegation. Forwards who score vital goals are loved and songs are sung about them that stretch back generations. John Charles is now long gone but every Leeds, Juventus, Cardiff City and Wales supporter, plus followers of many other clubs, know his name even though they never saw him play.

Also playing for Cardiff at inside-forward was Ivor Allchurch, known as the 'Golden Boy of Welsh football' and another Welsh great who, when he retired in 1968, had made a record 68 appearances for his country. He also held, with Trevor Ford, the record number of Wales goals, with 23. Ivor scored twice at the 1958 World Cup finals in Sweden when Wales, missing Charles who was injured, were unlucky to lose 1-0 in the quarter-final to Pelé's Brazil side that went on to win the tournament. Allchurch and Charles would not have looked out of place up front for the world champions.

Cardiff and Rotherham were just below halfway in the Second Division and so the respective managers experimented with their line-up. Cardiff's XI contained eight players under the age of 21. At left-half, Barrie Hole, who during his career made 30 Wales appearances, was from a football family – his father, Billy, had made almost 400 appearances as a winger for Swansea Town, while his brother Alan was also a centre-half for the Vetch Field club. Barrie was a great passer of the ball and could be relied upon to arrive late in the box for an effort on goal.

The Cardiff manager was Jimmy Scoular, a hardman on and off the pitch who captained Newcastle United when they won the FA Cup in 1955 and earlier helped Portsmouth win the First Division title two seasons running.

Cardiff, who joined the Football League in 1920, had done well in the 1964/65 European Cup Winners' Cup, a competition held between the respective national cup winners each season up until the late 1990s, losing out 3-2 on aggregate in the quarter-finals to Spanish side Real Zaragoza. The competition was won by West Ham United, who in a marvellous match beat TSV Munich 2-0 at Wembley in the final.

This was how the sides lined up at Ninian Park:

Cardiff City: Wilson, Rodriguez, Baker, Williams, Murray, Hole, Johnson, Allchurch, Charles, King, Lewis.

Rotherham: Williams, Wilcockson, Carver, Tiler, Haselden, Hardy, Lyons, Bennett, Massey, Hellawell, Pring.

There were no substitutes, set to be introduced for injuries at the start of the following season.

With only pride to play for, it was no surprise that the crowd was small, totalling 9,794 on a ground whose club-record attendance was 57,800, set by the visit of league leaders and eventual champions Arsenal on 22 April 1953. Ninian Park's record attendance was for a Wales international against England in 1961 when 61,566 packed out the ground.

Cardiff's main stand had been burnt down on 18 January 1937 and the old stand was replaced by a brick and steel construction some 60 yards long on the halfway line. Under this stand I got ready in the away dressing room for my Football League debut.

The match was a decent one which the home side won 3-2. Rotherham had signed John Galley from Wolves midway through the season and he had done well to score nine goals in 18 league and FA Cup matches before getting injured. In his absence, midfielder Brian Tiler had been pushed up front to partner Albert Bennett, who in the summer of 1965 was, after media speculation dating back a couple of years, transferred to Newcastle. Bennett left having notched 69 goals in the previous three seasons.

With Tiler at number four, I was handed the number nine shirt and I was able to score twice, with my first league goal putting us ahead on 21 minutes when I netted what was described in one of the papers as 'a smooth effort'. With my back to the goal, I received the ball from Welsh international Keith Pring, I swivelled and, with one touch from my right foot to my left, I hit a shot that squeezed beyond Bob Wilson in the home goal. My success, which came from good control of the ball with both feet, increased my confidence.

Allchurch equalised just before half-time, then Peter Rodriguez put his side ahead and Cardiff doubled their lead through Peter King.

I was faced with a tough opponent in Scottish under-23 international centre-half Don Murray, who before kick-off told me that if I went near him, he would 'break my bloody leg'. During half-time I told Danny Williams these comments but he shrugged and said, 'Welcome to professional football, son.'

I battled away against Murray and I scored with a 25-yard ground shot past Wilson. Unfortunately, we could not force a late equaliser. Dennis Busher's match report in the local paper was headed 'MILLMOOR DISCOVERY' and I was pleased to receive some warm praise from him and other reporters. Williams had been pleased with the team's performance as he had an amateur centre-forward and goalkeeper playing.

I stayed in the side at Belle Vue, Doncaster's ground at the time, for the semi-final of the Sheffield County Cup, a tournament that in 1965 was taken seriously by local professional clubs. Today, such a match would see line-ups composed of reserve players and youngsters, although back then both teams put out their first XI.

I scored in the seventh minute with a flick past the keeper, and again in the 55th, so we were heading for the final before the Doncaster manager chose to push his centre-half, Keith Ripley, forward. Ripley scored twice in the final five minutes to force extra time. Ripley scored again to take his side to an unlikely victory before a crowd of 5,704.

I then played in the penultimate game of the season. Gigg Lane, Bury, witnessed a single goal by the Millers' number ten John Galley in a team where I lined up at number eight alongside Frank Casper, who had come up through the ranks at Millmoor. He went on to play over 100 times before moving to Burnley and making 230 league starts for the Clarets. Frank played as an inside-forward, which today would be a mixture of a striker and a midfield player. He had good skills on the ball, pace and an eye for goal.

I had played for the Don and Dearne Schools team against Frank, who was representing Barnsley, in a Yorkshire Schoolboys under-15s final over two legs. He soon announced his presence in the first match at Oakwell. The large Barnsley crowd cheered when the home side won 3-0 and Frank had a good match.

In the return, played at Denaby United, there was a crowd of 700 to watch a schoolboy game. We put up a much better performance and I scored in the first half to reduce the arrears. Our hopes were ended when Barnsley equalised after the break and we lost 4-1 on aggregate.

The Bury side contained Colin Bell. He was to go on to become one of Manchester City's greatest-ever players and helped them to win the First Division, FA Cup, European Cup Winners' Cup and League Cup (twice) before injury forced him to retire early. He died in January 2021.

Victory meant Rotherham ended in 14th place in a division won by Newcastle United, who were joined in the top flight for 1965/66 by Northampton Town. Swindon Town and Swansea were relegated.

The Bury keeper Chris Harker, best known for being involved in the incident that led to Brian Clough suffering what proved to be a career-ending injury at Roker Park on Boxing Day 1962, was the man of the match. Rotherham should have won more handsomely with the goal coming after I fed Galley, who dashed clear to finish in style. Galley was signed from Wolverhampton Wanderers, who had picked him up from their nursery team, Wath Wanderers, in Wath upon Dearne.

Galley had scored a hat-trick on his Millers debut at Coventry City in December 1964. My college friend and Sky Blues fan Dave Wilkins had two tickets for that match and I had accepted his offer to accompany him to Highfield Road. When I opened the matchday programme, I became aware that Galley had moved from Molineux. I had high hopes of being the regular number nine for the Millers in 1965/66 and I was therefore somewhat dismayed that Galley had signed on at Millmoor. I was even more disgruntled when he scored three times as I could not envisage a situation where Rotherham would play with two target men in the first team. It would be up to me to prove my right to be picked before Galley as the regular target man, assuming, of course, I could first earn a professional contract. Galley went on to have a distinguished career scoring many goals for, among others, Rotherham, Bristol City and Nottingham Forest. He finished with 166 in total.

At the end of each college football season the teams held their annual dinner at a Cheltenham hotel. My final one was in 1965, and Dave arranged for Pat Saward to give a speech at the dinner. Pat had played, generally as wing-half, between 1955 and March 1961 for Aston Villa and he was a member of the 1957 FA Cup-winning and 1960 Second Division championship-winning sides. He also won 18 caps for the Republic of Ireland. Saward joined Coventry City in October 1963 in the role of player-coach and he became assistant manager at Highfield Road in 1967.

Saward had a good eye for a player and 'found' Willie Carr and Dennis Mortimer, who after leaving Coventry was a member of the Aston Villa side in the 1980s that captured the First Division title and European Cup. In his role of coach at Coventry, Saward led the youngsters to the FA Youth Cup Final.

At the end of the evening, Pat was looking at the programme statistics for the season and he saw that a Roy Massey was well ahead in the scoring charts so he asked Dave to introduce me to him. Sitting together in the hotel lounge, we spoke about football for two hours. Pat was a knowledgeable man and he asked me if I would go up to play a few games at Coventry the following season. I had to turn down this opportunity as I was committed to Rotherham. Little more than 18 months later, on Boxing Day 1966, I would score one of my best-ever goals against Coventry and create a controversy the next day when we entertained the Sky Blues at home.

I felt my early first-team games had gone well. I had scored three goals in three games including efforts with both feet and a header. Ever since the head at my junior school had picked me to play as a number nine, I had scored lots of goals for school and at college. I was confident I could take my ability to stick the ball into the net at amateur-level football into my professional career. I think, despite my subsequent injuries, I proved I could score goals with a record of one in every three matches.

I felt I had also combined well in the games with my team-mates and had continuously sought to find space including running behind both full-backs to try and collect the long ball. I always did this when playing at centre-forward. I was quite pacy and sought to tire out my opponent.

I prided myself on making my centre-half opponent earn his wages by constantly dragging him away from the middle of the park, which in turn allowed midfield players space into which to run. I possessed an awareness of how to put other players through on goal. I think I would have played at the highest level if I had not been badly injured in August 1965.

Now it was up to Danny Williams to decide my future. I was aware that in the past several top players had remained amateurs during part of their careers, such as Bill Slater, who played for Blackpool in the 1951 FA Cup Final while working as a teacher. Was Williams going to offer me a professional contract, which I had decided I wanted, or was I going to begin looking for a teaching job and combine this with playing at semi-professional level?

Chapter 12

Physically hurt and mentally abandoned

I HAD gained my teaching diploma. Whatever happened in the future I had something I could fall back on. Now I was determined to have a successful professional football career and I reported to Millmoor on 1 August 1965 with the enthusiasm of a ten-year-old. I had turned down, among others, Arsenal but I still had the ambition to play at the highest level of the game. I was only 21 and could see myself playing for 14 years. After that – who knows?

After the first week of pre-season training, club secretary Len Holmes gave me ten brown wage packets from the safe. I had signed as a professional at the end of the previous season. Professionals were paid their basic salary during the summer weeks and I had a considerable sum of money given to me.

I gave the cash to my dad, Gordon, to buy a decent car. He worked as an excavator driver with the Park Gate Iron and Steel Company and had an old A40. He went to work at 6am and in the winter I could hear him cranking up the engine to start the car. Sometimes it would take 15 minutes. Sweat poured off him and I believe that the strain contributed to his heart attack on his 50th birthday. Dad purchased a more reliable car that started by turning the ignition key. I was pleased for him.

Danny Williams had resigned during the summer in order to manage Third Division Swindon Town. He had great success in Wiltshire, leading Swindon to the 1969 League Cup Final at Wembley where they beat Arsenal 3-1 to produce one of the biggest cup shocks of all time. That same season Swindon also won promotion, following which Danny moved on to manage Sheffield Wednesday. Danny lived to the ripe old age of 94 before he died in February 2019.

The new manager was Jack Mansell. He had a reputation as a top coach and had been employed by clubs in the Netherlands, including Telstar. In his first team talk he spoke about a new 4-4-2 playing system of four defenders, four in the middle of the park and two up front. Jack intended abandoning the traditional WM formation that was introduced into football following the change in the offside law in 1925. Then called 'the one back system', it is best known today as the two-man offside rule. Alarmed by the shortage of goals, officials had changed the law so that a player could only be offside if there were fewer than two rather than three players between him and the goal.

The 'experiment' was deemed to have worked as more goals were scored. In response, the new Arsenal manager Herbert Chapman adopted the WM formation of two full-backs, a centre-half, two half-backs, two inside-forwards, two wingers and a centre-forward. This was known as the pyramid formation and as a consequence out went the old straight-line formation of five defenders and five forwards.

A new trainer, Alf Willey, had been appointed alongside Mansell. He was a small, sergeant major-type of person, well educated, and he changed the whole structure of the pre-season fitness programme.

Physical fitness is essential at every decent level of football and no team can carry players unable to last the pace. Stamina is also important as most players are on the move for almost the whole match. A player may not have the ball but they still need to support their team-mates, either acting as decoy or to be available to take possession. They might have to chase down an opponent to make a tackle or mark him closely. Quickness off the mark and the ability to sprint five to 20 yards are vital to a good footballer. Unlike stamina, which can be maintained by playing regularly, sprint sharpness requires constant practice throughout a season.

Before the 1960s, pre-season training was mainly aimed at giving players a solid foundation on which to build their speed and much of the work consisted of long-distance running. It was true that in an age when players were nowhere near as fit as they are today then quite a few would return after the summer needing to lose a few pounds but it was still quite a boring time.

In fact, most training sessions, whatever the time of year, were never too exciting. They generally involved lots of running on the cinder track that divided the pitch from the terraces and stands.

Under Danny Williams, every Monday morning the players would do what was called six-six-six. Players would be divided into two groups at diagonal corners of the ground. Under the watchful eye of trainer Albert Wilson, players would run, as fast as they could, a full circuit of the pitch back to their starting position. After a recovery walk to the next corner, the players would run another lap. This they did six times. The next six sprints covered half the pitch from the corner to the opposite corner. The final six sequences were to sprint down each side of the pitch with the recovery walk from corner to corner behind the goal. Players were absolutely shattered and went in for a bath which completed the day's work.

It was believed for many decades across English football that if you did not see much of the ball during the week then you'd want more of it during the match on Saturday. Balls were often locked away and out of bounds for players. At most clubs you'd have players who'd seek to find hidden balls and play games such as 'keepy up' by using every part of their bodies to get the ball over a net in no more than two touches. Coaches, who were really fitness trainers, would try to intervene and take the ball away.

How crazy it all was. Imagine not practising with the most important object of your trade. Little wonder that England had fallen behind internationally.

On the very first day of pre-season training in 1965 I arrived to pleasantly find Alf Willey just finishing putting some poles in the ground. These were on the corners of rectangles at 20 yards by ten yards.

Alf demonstrated with four players on each corner. On the whistle, players had to run as fast as they could around the rectangle and back to the original pole, then turn and run around the other direction and back to the pole. After 30 seconds of rest this was to be repeated; the players did this run ten times in total. We were on our knees at the end of this session. Alf's idea was to put stops and turns into the fitness training rather than running and sprinting in one straight line as in previous sessions. After four weeks the Rotherham players were fitter and stronger than they had ever been.

Rotherham had a young side, as nearly everyone was between 20 and 22 years of age. The players responded well in training and we were looking forward to implementing this new way of playing when the season started.

Jack Mansell had arranged a three-match pre-season tour to the Netherlands. The players were very excited at the prospect of playing abroad for the first time. Unbeknown to me it was to be a disaster. It changed my career path from being potentially a top player to eventually a role as a coach in youth development.

I was left out of the side for the opening game of the tour when we lost 2-1 against Mansell's former team, Telstar of the Dutch second division.

I was selected to play at number nine in the second match, against HFC EDO of Haarlem, and when I scored my second of the game on 38 minutes it meant Rotherham, who were backed by a handful of diehards, reached half-time 3-2 up. I was already off the field by then. As I was running towards the goal with the ball and hoping to score a third, the opposition centre-half, Krooder – all 14st of him – took off and launched into a tackle, a reckless one. With my weight on my right leg, his boot and full body weight crashed into my knee. I was in agony as the physiotherapist rushed over the pitch to examine my injury and assure me that I would be fine.

I knew immediately I could not continue playing in the game and I already feared I might have suffered long-term, perhaps even career-ending, damage. I was taken off on a stretcher and the physiotherapist bandaged up my knee in the dressing room as the pain began to ease slightly.

Krooder had made sure that I wouldn't score any more goals. Local correspondent Benny Hill reported, 'The first fear was Massey had broken his leg.'

I was quoted as saying, 'I heard a crack and thought I had broken my leg. The "crack" was similar to when I broke my ankle 18 months ago, when I was playing in college football. I was relieved when I was able to get up and hobble off. Just my luck that this should happen to me in my first competitive match as a professional.'

On seeing the swelling around my knee, the Dutch specialist told me the injury was ligament damage and that I would play again in around six weeks. I was somewhat reassured by this news but nevertheless I was left out of the Rotherham United 1965/66 squad photograph. I was told to stay away from training.

We did not have a telephone at home in Mexborough and so while I subsequently rested at home I didn't hear from the manager or the physiotherapist, who were, with the trainer, the only full-time club employees looking after the players. I was also not given any exercises to do. I spent a lot of my time worrying that my career was over and felt desperate at seeing the swelling only slowly going down. Finally, when I felt my knee was strong enough, I used the public phone box and arranged to see the physiotherapist who, when he carried out an examination, decided I could start training again.

On my return to training, I took part in a regular late-morning session with the rest of the squad. It was great to be back but I was, naturally, tentative as the knee did not feel 100 per cent.

With the club's permission I had agreed to teach youngsters PE at a local school in the afternoon. I was keen to put my teaching certificate into action. The boys were listening to me as I demonstrated some dribbling skills. As I did a little side step, my knee gave way and once again I was writhing in agony on the floor. As I did not want to be embarrassed in the middle of a coaching session, I got back on my feet and somehow finished the lesson although my knee was very painful. I managed to go home on the bus to Mexborough and I hobbled from the stop to our house.

Alf Willey took me to see a specialist, Mr Papworth. He diagnosed a cartilage problem and I was in hospital the next day having an operation. In those days you had to stay in bed for ten days before you could put any weight on the operated leg. Mr Papworth told me that the cartilage had been in pieces, forcing him to take it out bit by bit. To my relief, he said I should be fit in eight weeks.

There was no gym at Rotherham so I was unable to do body-strengthening exercises. I thus, once again, stayed isolated at home and fretted about my career.

Finally I got the go ahead to restart training. My knee was feeling fine and I was optimistic about the future.

On my first day back I trained in the morning and participated in a five-a-side game in the afternoon. As I received the ball, a side-step saw me fall to the ground and once again I felt severe pain. I revisited Mr Papworth, who assured me there was nothing wrong with my knee and that the problem was just adhesions breaking down in the joint. I didn't have much faith in his assessment as the knee was very swollen. I was told to rest.

Several weeks later I restarted training on my knee and finally my problems seemed to be settling down. I managed to play some reserve games, and Jack Mansell called me into his office and said I was to be substitute for the Second Division game at Millmoor on 11 December 1965 against Birmingham City, who had been relegated from the First Division at the end of the previous season. Substitutes had been introduced at the start of the 1965/66 season with only one per game allowed for an injured player. Keith Peacock of Charlton Athletic was the first substitute when the 21-year-old replaced injured Addicks goalkeeper Mick Rose on 11 minutes at The Valley against Bolton Wanderers in August 1965.

A Millmoor crowd of 10,684 watched the Birmingham game and at the interval the home side led 3-0 with two goals by Les Chappell and one from Sam Hardy. The manager told me to get ready as I was going to play the second half. He knew I had been going through a hard time and this was his way of returning me to first-team action. It was a marvellous feeling to replace Hardy and move on to the field with the crowd cheering knowing that their side were set to gain two points in my home league debut at Millmoor. I left the dugout from in front of the main stand, built when Rotherham Town and Rotherham County had combined forces in the 1920s to form Rotherham United. Directly opposite the main stand there was terracing along the Millmoor Lane side. Above it there was a small cover.

The Railway End terracing to the right of the main stand had been covered in 1957 and in November 1960 the floodlights – which we already on by half-time against Birmingham – were first used for a League Cup tie against Bristol Rovers. Rotherham made it into the final of the first League Cup that season, losing 3-2 on aggregate against Aston Villa over two legs.

To the left of the main stand, the Tivoli End terrace, named after the nearby Tivoli Cinema, remained open to the elements.

The name Millmoor failed to do justice to the ground's surroundings; they were bleak as it stood among a collection of scrapyards. Yet the small ground was, thanks to good maintenance and liberal doses of bright-red paint, a cheerful place that, especially when fully packed, had a great atmosphere, as Rotherham fans were passionate about their side.

In the first five minutes of the second half against Birmingham, I received the ball on the halfway line and I played it inside the full-back for winger Barry Lyons to run on to. I sprinted into the Birmingham penalty area in an attempt to meet the oncoming cross but as I stretched for the ball, I felt something go in my knee. It had given way again and I was forced to hobble on the wing for the rest of the game. Birmingham soon pulled a goal back and the final score was ultimately to be a 4-3 victory for the visitors. Geoff Vowden scored three for the Blues, who had been struggling in the first half of the 1965/66 season. As a result, their directors had replaced Joe Mallett with Stan Cullis, whose managerial record at Wolverhampton Wanderers from 1948 to 1964 was superb. Cullis, whose style of football was heavily based on an extraordinary level of fitness in which he employed speed and athleticism rather than skill on the ball, was a former England captain.

I limped off the pitch at the end of the game and there was no sympathy from some of the home fans who hurled abuse at me as they felt I was responsible for their team losing.

The following Monday I was in the manager's office saying I had to retire from football as my knee was failing me. Mansell said that he would seek a second opinion.

I certainly did not want Mr Papworth involved and I visited another knee specialist in Sheffield. He felt my knee as I settled down on the couch. After five seconds he told me that following my last operation a piece of cartilage had been left floating about in the knee joint. This was a ray of light that gave me something to cling on to. Perhaps my career could be resurrected?

The operation went successfully in that the piece of cartilage was removed but the specialist did tell me that my ligaments had now stretched so my knee was never going to be strong enough to carry on playing at a decent level. At the time I thought I would be able to prove him wrong by working hard in training and playing my best on the field. Sadly, he was ultimately correct.

I was able to return for Rotherham reserves at Roker Park in a 3-2 defeat to Sunderland reserves on 8 January 1966. The following weekend I hit two in a 5-2 victory away to Workington reserves. A 3-2 home win against Southend United in the third round of the FA Cup set up an away tie at First Division champions Manchester United. Everyone was very excited to be playing a United side containing George Best, Denis Law, Bobby Charlton and co. I was selected as substitute and, sitting in the dugout, I heard the great roar of the Old Trafford crowd as the home side emerged from the dressing room. Rotherham also enjoyed great backing with an estimated 12,000 of their own supporters in the 54,263 crowd.

Peter Madden, our centre-half and captain, a great Millers stalwart, was unable to play as he was injured. John Haselden, a 22-year-old reserve centre-half, had rarely played in the first team and took Madden's place. He was outstanding and a 0-0 draw, during which Keith Pring twice rapped Manchester United's woodwork, meant the sides met again the following Tuesday. I was again named as substitute, a disappointment that was tempered by the knowledge that I would be on the crowd bonus scheme at the end of the week.

The kick-off for the replay was 7.30pm, and at 7.15pm I visited the toilet, which was between the two dressing rooms. I saw George Best in his leather jacket speaking to somebody at the entrance to his team's changing room. He seemed so relaxed that I guessed he was injured and unfit to play. I excitedly returned to our changing rooms and told my colleagues that Best wasn't playing. This cheered everyone up as he was a match-winner.

We ran on to the pitch to a tremendous roar from our supporters. Manchester United came out a few minutes later with George, tucking his shirt into his shorts, emerging a few seconds after everyone else. I did hear that Matt Busby did not bother with George in the team talks, simply telling him to go out and play. The incident at Millmoor appears to back up this story.

The game itself, played before a packed 23,500 crowd, was another tight affair and was 0-0 at 90 minutes. Rotherham looked like earning a second replay but five minutes from the end of extra time, John Connelly scored the winner for United. Many decisions went against the home side. Firstly, there was what seemed a perfectly good Les Chappell goal when the ball was scrambled home following a John Galley cross. Wolverhampton referee Jack Taylor, one of the finest men to blow a whistle, signalled the goal. United goalkeeper Harry Gregg, a Munich hero in 1958, had even kicked the ball back to the centre spot but Rotherham's cheers were stifled when, after a lengthy consultation with a linesman, Taylor, who later refereed the 1974 World Cup Final between West Germany and the Netherlands, awarded a free kick for offside.

Just before the first half ended, Gregg's punch of the ball saw it hit Galley and appear to cross the line before England international Nobby Stiles kicked it clear. Galley still insists it was a goal. Despite the result, the two games were great occasions for Rotherham and their fans. Although I was only the substitute, I had the pleasure of collecting a £25 bonus in my pay packet at the end of the week.

This proved to be my last bonus of the season as I did not feature again for the first team.

I did play three more reserve games in 1965/66: a 4-1 victory against former Football League club Gateshead in which I scored once, a 1-0 victory away to Oldham reserves in which I did not score, and a 2-0 home defeat against Carlisle United reserves. Following that, my season was over due to injury.

My first season as a professional footballer had been disastrous. I had scored twice in the first two league games at the end of the previous season but had started only one match in 1965/66.

I had been badly let down by the specialists abroad and in England and by Rotherham. I wonder if, had Danny Williams remained manager, the Millers would have acted differently? Danny had seen me score goals in my three games at the end of the 1964/65 season. He knew what I could do. Not so Jack Mansell; maybe he thought I was just a college kid? I could not complain I was not getting picked as I was injured but, at the same time, I was sure that if I had been able to get fit, I would have done well.

Getting fit as quickly as possible was destroyed due to the wrong diagnosis by the specialists. Rather than resting up, I required an urgent operation. On my return to training, I then kept breaking down and was only then sent for an operation. This was done badly and I suffered another breakdown. I was wrongly told my knee was fine. By the time my problem was properly diagnosed and an operation performed I had lost vital strength in my knee which subsequently ended my professional career five years later.

I often wonder what might have been if I had not got injured in the Netherlands in 1965 or had been better looked after following the injury. I am confident that I would have played at the highest level, including internationally.

There are many discussions on mental health and depression in these modern times, but back then I had to cope largely by myself with my injury.

The thought of not being able to play football for a living was a nightmare. I'd become subdued and depressed when I was recovering from my operation and I stayed at home until I was able to walk to the bus stop so as to travel to Rotherham, where I then faced a lengthy walk to Millmoor. My parents were aware of my anguish. We were into March 1966 and the season was coming to an end and I felt I had no real sign of making a recovery.

Mexborough Methodist Church team with Roy in the middle of the front row

Jimmy Massey, Roy's grandfather, was a top-flight goalkeeper with Sheffield Wednesday and was an FA Cup winner in 1896

My parents Gordon and Rachel

Scotland Grammar Schools v England Grammar Schools at Celtic Park in 1961

SCOTTISH SCHOOLS FOOTBALL
ASSOCIATION

UNDER 18
INTERNATIONAL MATCH

SCOTLAND

v.

ENGLAND

CELTIC PARK, GLASGOW
(Kindly granted by Celtic F.C.)

WEDNESDAY, 19th APRIL, 1961
Kick-Off 7 p.m.

PROGRAMME - THREEPENCE

Team line-ups for Scotland Grammar Schools v England Grammar Schools at Celtic Park in 1961

SCOTLAND V. ENGLAND

THE game this evening for boys of under 18 years of age on 1st September, 1960, is the seventh of the series. Results to date are—

1955 — Scotland, 1 .... England, 2
1956 — England, 1 .... Scotland, 0
1957 — Scotland, 3 .... England, 0
1958 — England, 4 .... Scotland, 3
1959 — Scotland, 3 .... England, 3
1960 — England, 2 .... Scotland, 1

It will be noted that England have won four of the six played by the odd goal. We have been fortunate in having good friends in Celtic F.C. who have given us the use of their ground on each occasion the game has been played in Scotland.

The duration of the game will be 40 minutes each way.

The Scottish team was chosen from over 40 nominations. Trials were held in Glasgow and Perth and following the Glasgow v. Rest of Scotland match at Airdrie on March 18th, 15 boys were selected to take part in matches with youth teams sponsored by Motherwell F.C. and Celtic F.C.

All the Scots have played in Schools representative football. Craig, Roxburgh and McBeth played against England last year at Burnley while all the others have figured in Glasgow or Lanarkshire teams. Both our goalkeeper and Roxburgh have played for Scotland in Youth International matches this season.

Our referee this evening is Mr A. McKenzie of Coatbridge, linesman in this match in 1959 and one of the recent promotions to Class 1 on the S.F.A. list. Both he and his linesmen, who are also on the official list are very active referees in schools football.

The visitors, drawn from the Public and Grammar schools of England are the cream of the annual schools week conducted by the Football Association at Cambridge University. Schools football in England is run by the English Schools F.A. for boys of up to 15 years only, so there is no organisation similar to our own for boys up to 18 years. The F.A. therefore, invite some 80 boys for a week's course, at Cambridge and Oxford on alternate years, where coaching, trials and .... matches take place.

[continuation repeated:]
teams. Both our goalkeeper and Roxburgh have played for Scotland in Youth International matches this season.

Our referee this evening is Mr A. McKenzie of Coatbridge, linesman in this match in 1959 and one of the recent promotions to Class 1 on the S.F.A. list. Both he and his linesmen, who are also on the official list are very active referees in schools football.

TONIGHT'S TEAMS
SCOTLAND
(NAVY BLUE)

G. — K. McFARLANE, (Whitehill Sec. Glasgow).
R.B. — J. CRAIG, (St. Gerard's Sec. Glasgow). Capt.
L.B. — J. R. GOODWIN, (Dalziel H.S. Motherwell).
R.H. — G. HEANEY, (Our Lady's H.S. Motherwell).
C.H. — J. YOUNG, (Camphill Sec. Paisley).
L.H. — N. TONER, (St. Augustine's Sec. Glasgow).
O.R. — J. SAMSON, (Whitehill Sec. Glasgow).
I.R. — M. McGOLDRICK, (St. Mungo's Academy, Glasgow).
C.F. — J. McGUIRE, (St. Mungo's Academy, Glasgow).
I.L. — A. ROXBURGH, (Bellahouston Academy, Glasgow).
O.L. — A. McBETH, (St. Mungo's Academy, Glasgow).
Reserves—J. WATSON (Coatbridge H.S.) Goal.
G. CALDWELL, (Cumnock Academy) L.B.
T. KING (Airdrie Academy) O.L.

ENGLAND
(WHITE)

G. — J. JACKSON, (St. Clement Dane G.S.)
R.B. — K. J. GILKS, (Whitley Abbey Sec. Coventry).
L.B. — P. JACKSON, (Charlton G.S.)
R.H. — G. TAYLOR, (Scunthorpe G.S.)
C.H. — T. OLDFIELD, (Mexborough G.S.) Capt.
L.H. — K. R. HALL, (Almondbury G.S.)
O.R. — H. WILKINSON, (Abbeydale G.S.)
I.R. — A. BRADER, (Queen Elizabeth's G.S. Horncastle)
C.F. — R. MASSEY, (Mexborough Technical School)
I.L. — H. J. P. SWAIN, (Clee Humberstone Foundation School)
O.L. — G. SLEIGHT, (Normanton G.S.)
Reserves — A. D. THOMPSON, (Barrow G.S.)
R. P. FITCH, (Panniters School).

Referee—Mr A McKENZIE, (Coatbridge).
Linesmen—Mr W. McALLISTER, (Glasgow).
Mr W. S. BLACK, (Glasgow).

Another big night for football fans should be Thursday, 27th April at Hampden Park when St. Mungo's Academy and Coatbridge .... the final of the Scottish Secondary Championship Shield.
C.F. — R. MASSEY, (Mexborough Technical School).
I.L. — H. J. P. SWAIN, (Clee Humberstone Foundation School)
O.L. — G. SLEIGHT, (Normanton G.S.)
Reserves — A. D. THOMPSON, (Barrow G.S.)
R. P. FITCH, (Panniters School).

ASTON VILLA FOOTBALL CLUB
LIMITED

Registered Office :- ASTON VILLA GROUNDS,
TRINITY ROAD, ASTON,
BIRMINGHAM, 6.

F. J. ARCHER
Secretary

J. MERCER
Manager

30th, October, 1962.

Mr. R. Massey,
House "A" Room 6,
Rosehill Hostel,
Evesham Road,
Cheltenham, Glos.

Dear Ray,

We have just had your address sent
to us by Mr. Downes, and we are writing to
you to find out what the position is in regard
to your playing football for us on Saturdays,
we know there are certain rules regarding
College , and we would like to know if you
would be available, and if so, what procedure
we should pursue if you are agreeable.

It is not far from Birmingham and
would not entail a lot of travelling, so would
you be as kind to drop us a line stating your
views on this matter.

We hope this finds you well, and we
send our Best Wishes.

Yours Sincerely,

Manager.

Aston Villa manager Joe Mercer writes to Roy regarding his availability to play for
the club in the 1962/63 season

ARSENAL FOOTBALL CLUB LTD.

TELEGRAMS:
INLAND — GUNNERETIC LONDON N.5.
OVERSEAS — GUNNERETIC LONDON
TELEPHONE: CANONBURY 3312.

W. R. WALL.
SECRETARY.
W. A. WRIGHT, C.B.E.
MANAGER.

GROUND ADJACENT TO ARSENAL STATION,
(PICCADILLY TUBE)

ARSENAL STADIUM,
LONDON, N.5.

WAW/MR

15th January, 1963.

R.Massie, Esq.,
Saint Paul's College,
Cheltenham,
Gloucestershire.

Dear Ron,

　　　　　May I refer to a recent meeting you had early
this month in Doncaster with our Mr.J.McDonagh who informs
me that you are keen to have a game at Arsenal during your
mid-Term holiday or in April when your College games are
finished.

　　　　　I am pleased to confirm this arrangement, also
that your Club, Doncaster United, have approved this earlier
on, and wonder if you would inform me of the approximate date
of your mid-term holiday so that in due course I can let you
know when we can arrange for you to visit us here at Highbury.

　　　　　I shall look forward to hearing from you.

Yours sincerely,

Billy Wright

Manager.

Arsenal manager Billy Wright writes to Roy Massey regarding his availability in the second half of the 1962/63 season

The Arsenal squad 1963/64 with Roy Massey fourth from left in the back row

Brian Tiler of Rotherham United

Harold Wilcockson (left) and Colin Clish in a fierce arm wrestling battle at Rotherham are being cheered on by (left to right) myself, John Haseldene, John Galley, unknown and Michael Hegarty

My manager at Orient and Colchester United was Dick Graham

I played against Howard Wilkinson when he was at Brighton and Hove Albion

I annoyed Coventry City manager Jimmy Hill when I scored with my hand for Rotherham United at Millmoor

I was happily married to Christine Sutterby for many years and we had three beautiful children

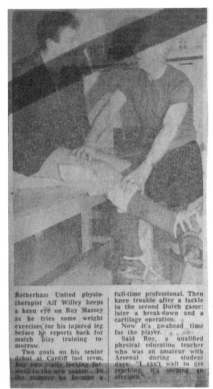

MILLMOOR CASUALTIES ARE RECOVERING

Tiler, Haselden shine

Injuries were to end Roy Massey's professional playing career before he reached 28 years of age

After months out injured at Rotherham United, Roy Massey finally gets the all-clear to return to action

THIS TREMENDOUS LEAPING HEADER BY ROY MASSEY EARNED ORIENT THEIR TRIP TO ST. ANDREWS IN THREE WEEKS. (PICTURE: JOHN CHINNERY).

Great, but how much further?

ORIENT 1, BURY 0
(F.A. Cup, third round)
Ian Kessler

Heading home the goal that secured victory in the FA Cup tie against Bury

NOW FOR TOWN

ghth

the rejuvenated Ocelot,
t Britain in the Little
e Bay this weekend.

lk and Sack, which will
rightlingsea firm of Sail-
take place Saturday and

will be taking part for
since then he has only
ellcat 35, Emma Hamil-

ational Catamaran Week
n Kitson and has com-

the European Tornado
im second place after a

rs which did not entirely
ins, a fifth and a sixth,
d a fourth.

LES

RY

BT

win at Reading on Wednesday
les and Brian Gibbs. Bickles
ad intensive treatment yester-
r Saturday's match at Notts
nful kick on the knee but is

on Saturday in the South East
Counties League while on
Wednesday the reserves travel
to Millwall in the London
Mid—Week League.

Tickets
on sale

UNITED'S second round
Football League cup tie at
Ipswich on Wednesday, September 3 will NOT be an all
ticket match. But the U's
allocation of stand seats go
on sale at the club offices
today between 10.30 am and
12.30 and 2.30 and 4.30. If
any remain they will be sold
on Saturday morning (10.00-
12.00) and on Monday from
10.00.

Season ticket holders have
until midday Tuesday to
claim their seats and any not
picked up will be sold after
this time.

If the match ends in a
draw, the replay will be at
Layer Road on Wednesday,
September 10 at 7.30.

YOUNGSTERS RALLY

Colchester Youth 2
Ipswich Youth 2

THIS was another strong
South East Counties League
finish by United's youngsters
at the Garrison ground on
Saturday morning. Goals in
the last five minutes by
Twidell, with a 25-yard
rocket, and Webster, earned
a point after Addo and
Sharpe had set up a 2-0
advantage for Town.

Ipswich played under the

considerable disadvantage of
being without their regular
goalkeeper who didn't turn
up until half time and was
not allowed on after the
break since the visitors had
not named a substitute. It
was here that United rather
missed the boat since they
seldom put enough pressure
on a shaky deputy.

Colchester: Smith; Partner,
Twidell, Bloss, Davies, Dines,
Smart, Webster, Weavers, Kil-
bourne, Ford. Sub: Taylor.

United's hat-
trick hero, Roy
Massey. Roy's
threesome was
the first hat-
trick scored
away from
home in league
or cup by a
United player
for nearly ten
years.

Yorkshire for Colchester

COLCHESTER'S 1970 cric-
ket week promises to be the
most attractive yet.
Yorkshire and Surrey pro-
vide the opposition and in
addition Essex have also
plumped to have the Sun-
day League match against
the Tykes at the Garrison
ground.

The Yorkshire match starts
off the week on July 25 and
the Surrey game begins on
July 29.

Yorkshire were last at
Colchester in 1960, when
they struggled to draw, and
Surrey provided the opposition in 1954—another match
which was drawn despite a
fantastic innings from
Doug Insole who scored an
unbeaten 172 out of 254
while at the wicket.

BRENTWOOD SHOCK

A shock for Brentwood
fans, their ground is not
among the venues in the
provisional list of fixtures. It
is believed that the accommodation is considered by the
county committee to be
inadequate to hold a big
crowd for the Sunday match
which a week there would
involve.

Headquarters Chelmsford
gets a more prominent place,

however, with four champion-
ship matches, one against the
South African tourists on
September 2, and three
Sunday League fixtures as
well.

Harlow Sports Centre and
Thames Board Mills ground at
Purfleet, each of which housed
good gates for Sunday League
matches, are given another
chance. Harlow is to stage a
three-day match with the
Pakistan B XI in June and
also a Sunday League clash
with Gloucester in August;
Purfleet stages another
Sunday League fixture with
Middlesex in mid-July.

All players have been
retained by Essex reported
the secretary of the club,
Major C. A. Brown, this week.

Roy Massey
hat-trick
settles it

Reading...0 Colchester...3

IPSWICH TOWN scout Reg Tyrell watched Wednesday
night's replayed first round Football League cup tie at
Elm Park. And his report to Town manager Bobby Robson
will certainly have underlined the fact that United must
not be taken lightly.

This most comprehensive
win over a side which
previously hadn't lost a match
this season, was a just reward
for an all round team
performance of the highest
calibre which had the home
side reeling for most of the
game, such was the speed,
skill, cover and finishing
power shown by the U's.

Reading had their moments,
notably in lively opening
spells to both periods of the
game. But apart from these
brief shows of their un-
doubted talents it was United
all the way.

INTO TROUBLE

At the back, apart from a
tendency early on to play
themselves into trouble instead of clearing first time,
the striking power of Les
Chappell and Peter Silvester
was reduced to the most
minimal of threats and
flankmen George Harris and,
to a slightly lesser degree,
Tom Jenkins, were shut out
of the game.

But efficient as United were
in defence it was in midfield
and up front that they really
showed their worth and
Mickey Brown, often such an
under-rated player, emerged
as the pick of the bunch.

He tackled like a terrier,
ripped the Reading defence to
shreds with lightning, probing
runs from the middle of the

park, and sprayed about the
sort of passes which just had
to bring the results.

Danny Light and Ray
Whittaker, too, making up as
diminutive a midfield trio as
any side will boast but, on
the right, certainly as potent
as any, also played their most
important roles to near per-
fection. And all their efforts
were helped by the hard and
clever running of the front
three, Jim Oliver, Roy Massey
and Brian Gibbs.

CREATED HAVOC

And to top the lot manager
Dick Graham seems to have
brought off a really shrewd
stroke of business by signing
Massey for a bargain £5,500 a
few weeks ago. The striker
landed the first hat-trick
scored away from home by a
United player for nearly ten
years, his incisive opportun-
ism creating havoc around the
Reading goal.

The first goal came after 43
minutes and the only surprise
was that it took so long for
United to go in front. Gibbs
crossed hard and low from
the left, Roy Brown failed to
gather an awkward ball
cleanly, and in a flash Massey
stabbed it home.

Silvester missed a good
early second half chance
when United were under some
pressure and then was
magnificently tackled from
behind by Bickles as he raced
clear. Referee Challis quite
rightly ignored penalty
appeals and in the 72nd
minute, as the U's once more
began to dictate the whole
course of the game, Massey
struck again. Light swung a
superbly judged centre into
the goalmouth, Fred Sharpe
outnumbered two to one had
no chance, and Massey
headed a magnificent goal.

GREAT SAVE

Reading's reply was almost
as decisive with Dixon running well on the blind side to
go clear. But Graham Smith
made the save of the match
to keep the number two's shot
out and seven minutes from
the end Massey wrapped it
up.

Brown swerved through the
square Reading defence and
was desperately unlucky to
see Roy Brown get his hands
to a stinging 25 yarder. But
Massey, in the right spot at
the right time once again,
stroked the ball home to
clinch for United a long
awaited tilt at their old rivals
Ipswich next Wednesday
week.

The teams

Reading: Brown; Dixon,
Thornhill, B. Wagstaff, Sharpe,
Meldrum, Jenkins, T. Wagstaff,
Silvester, Chappell, Harris. Sub:
Sainty.

Colchester: Smith; Joslyn,
Hall, Gibbs, Bickles, Wood,
Light, Massey, Oliver, Brown,
Whittaker. Sub: Howlett.

Attendance: 11,065.

Peter Hills

CUP TIE SCORES
BOOST THE RESERVES

Colchester Res. .... 2 Southend 2

MAYBE IT was the news that the first team were knocking
Reading out of the League Cup, but as the scorelines came
through from Elm Park to Layer Road on Wednesday
night so did the performance of the Reserves improve.

Fielding their youth team
plus new 'keeper Peter Goy,
Terry Dyson and Mickey
Cook, they were two down in
27 minutes. Both goals were
laid on by Eddie Clayton who
grabbed by leader O'Connor
who, after heading home from
three yards took advantage of
a miskick in the box by
Partner.

It looked so easy for
Southend's more experienced

side at this stage, but with
Goy settling down in goal
Colchester was a different
outfit altogether in the second
period.

Their first goal, however,
was out of the curio department. Dyson in midfield was
blatantly grabbed round the
waist by Vickery but man-
aged to shake off the Southend man and as referee
Byford let play proceed rifled
out a pass to the left.

Here a huge miskick by
Robinson let in Kilbourne
who smartly took advantage.
And when, six minutes later,
Dennis headed home a Dyson
free-kick, a Colchester win
appeared to be on the cards.
But Southend shrugged off a
casual approach and re-
maining exchanges were even.

Colchester: Goy; Partner,
Twidell, Bloss, Davis, Dennis,
Pitt, Webster, Cook, Dyson, Kil-
bourne. Sub: Sutton.

Southend: Steel; Robinson,
Heeck, Plunger, J. Chambers,
Clayton, Hunt, Vickery, O'Con-
nor, D. Chambers, McKinven.
Sub: Cotter.

A hat-trick in the League Cup for Colchester at Reading

My wages were being paid weekly but I did not spend any money as I did not want to go out. It was a difficult time. One day my mum read in the local paper that a red Triumph Spitfire was for sale and the seller lived nearby. I had passed my driving test and I went along to see the car with my dad. I liked it and after paying the agreed price I drove it home. Knowing that I had the cash to pay for it made me feel good.

I could now drive to Rotherham for treatment each day and the following season I had the luxury of driving to training each day in my car, although I did have one scary moment. Driving home at 50mph, I drove down a steep hill just outside Rawmarsh, a stone hit my windscreen and shattered it. I could not see anything other than broken glass. I slammed my foot on the brakes and smashed out the remaining glass with my fist so that I could see properly, managing to stop at the roadside. I was badly shaken and I drove the car slowly to my local garage where I had a new windscreen fitted.

The season ended with Rotherham finishing in a highly creditable seventh place in the Second Division, which was won by Manchester City who gained promotion at Millmoor with a 1-0 victory courtesy of a Colin Bell goal. Under Joe Mercer and Malcolm Allison, City went on to great things over the following six seasons.

Les Chappell, a product of Rotherham's successful apprentice-ship programme, scored 16 in the league. Les had an eye for a goal and was a typical fox in the box player with an instinct to be in the right place at the right time. I would have enjoyed playing more games than I did with Les as I believe our styles were well suited. He was small and sharp and formed a very good partnership with target man John Galley.

Galley finished with 18 league goals in 1965/66. He was a typical target man for the era. He had a good physique, showed strength and had the ability to receive and control the ball in tight situations. He was a very good header of the ball. All these skills meant he was a regular scorer. When John later joined Bristol City he enjoyed great success. John's scoring record at Ashton Gate means he is assured of a great welcome any time he returns to watch a game.

Chapter 13

A return to on-field action
and teaching off it

I TRAINED every day on my own throughout the summer of 1966. England won the World Cup under Alf Ramsey, later to be knighted, and like every football fan I eagerly anticipated the start of the new season.

I was approached by Ken Knowles, the deputy headteacher at Kimberworth School. He was a keen Rotherham United fan who had heard that I was a qualified PE teacher and wanted me to teach PE at the school, which was just five minutes from Millmoor, on three afternoons a week.

This sounded like a good idea and Jack Mansell gave me permission to do so. It was good public relations for Rotherham with one of their players putting something back into the community. This aspect of clubs at the time was not considered a priority. Today, it is remarkable the input that clubs put into their own catchment areas.

Arsenal have had a fantastic relationship with the community under the direction of Alan Sefton who has been at the helm of numerous community projects for many years. Arsenal in the Community was established in 1984 and on its 30th anniversary, Alan received an MBE from the Queen for Services to Education and to Young People in the UK and abroad.

Before the term started, I met with the PE head Bob Earnshaw. He was the same age as me, 23, and was already running a school department.

Bob had trained as a PE teacher at the Carnegie College of Physical Education in Leeds. This opened in 1907. Among its successful students was Walter Winterbottom, who had played briefly for Manchester United before the Second World War. Winterbottom was England's first, youngest and longest-serving team manager, from 1946 to 1962, and took the national squad to four World Cup finals.

It was as the FA's director of coaching that Sir Walter – he was knighted in 1978 – made significant contributions to the development of English football as well as ultimately to my own opportunities. In 1946, many players, managers and club directors were dismissive of the need for coaching. Winterbottom was unperturbed and began by creating a national coaching scheme with residential courses at Lilleshall in Shropshire. Internationals were persuaded to take courses that led to coaching badges. The players developed their teaching skills by coaching in schools and some worked part-time for junior clubs.

Winterbottom assembled a cadre of young FA coaches that changed attitudes to coaching and, by doing so, became famous, successful managers – men such as Don Howe, Vic Buckingham and England bosses Joe Mercer, Ron Greenwood and Bobby Robson. Winterbottom later became director at the newly formed Sports Council, where he battled for more investment in sport from national and local government. Hundreds of new sports centres and swimming pools were built during his time with the organisation. Winterbottom's passion to make sport more important in society is to be admired and one I have believed in all my life.

In recognition of his contribution to English football there is a bust of Winterbottom on display at St George's Park, the FA's training centre in Burton-on-Trent.

Bob Earnshaw combined his school work with being a part-time professional footballer with Barnsley, for whom he made 252 appearances at outside-right and scored 37 goals. Players like Bob, even then, who combined full-time work with playing professional football, were few and far between. I learned a great deal from working at Kimberworth, particularly from Bob's coaching style and enthusiasm. The school produced many professional sportsmen including future Arsenal and England goalkeeper David Seaman.

I vividly remember coaching John Breckin at the school. He gained legendary status as a Rotherham player, making over 400 appearances and captaining the side when they won the Third Division in 1980/81, and he later became assistant and caretaker manager of the Millers.

Bob and I got on very well together, and although I moved south and he stayed in South Yorkshire, we are still good friends. After retiring from playing the game, Bob organised Barnsley's youth system for many years.

Having again not appeared in the first-team squad photograph, I was pleased to get through pre-season training without further complications to my knee, although it did not feel as strong as it was before I had suffered my injury in the Netherlands. I was able to play in late August against Carlisle United reserves but did not score in a 2-1 defeat. Until the end of December 1966, I played 11 times for the reserves and scored four goals. Frank Casper scored both goals in the 2-2 home draw on Bonfire Night against Doncaster Rovers reserves. I played four more reserve matches in the second half of the season.

These games were held at 3pm on a Saturday and when they ended, the result of the first-team match would be announced over the loudspeaker system. This might seem wrong but if we had won and the first team had lost, there was an additional excitement as each player believed this raised the possibility of being picked to play for the first XI in the next game. Team spirit means nothing unless you are in the first team, especially as an appearance meant you earned an added appearance bonus of around a third of your wages.

My next first-team opportunity in 1966/67 came on Boxing Day when Rotherham travelled to play league leaders Coventry City who were managed by Jimmy Hill. He had taken charge at Coventry in 1961 and had immediately set about modernising the club's image. Hill promised a 'Sky Blue Revolution' and he was to take Coventry into the top flight for the first time in their history. He later had a successful career in football broadcasting, and between 1973 and 1988 he hosted the BBC's *Match of the Day*.

I was at number seven. John Galley was at number nine and when he flicked on a long ball from keeper Alan Hill with his head, I ran on to it and, after letting it bounce, I volleyed past Bill Glazier, the Coventry goalkeeper, from the edge of the penalty area.

This goal made me realise how practice in training is vital. At the end of each training session, Jack Mansell would put on the same shooting session. Players lined up outside the penalty area holding a ball which they would throw into the air for their team-mates to try to get to quickly in order to volley the ball towards goal. The idea was to strike the ball at the right height, putting backspin on it as it headed towards goal in the hope that it would suddenly dip, preferably just under the crossbar.

This worked for me at Coventry that day and the goal came about because of hours and hours of practice. It was a real beauty, so good that some of the home fans in the 31,348 crowd inside Highfield Road applauded.

We lost the game 4-2, the key moment coming when Hill, a brave keeper who hated losing, was forced to leave the field when he fractured his finger trying to foil the Coventry centre-forward Bobby Gould.

In an era of one substitute, Galley went in goal. As Hill's gloves were too big for him and the club did not carry any spares, trainer Albert Wilson taped the gloves up to make them smaller. A Coventry supporter jumped over the advertising boards and leapt on Galley's back and sought to assault Wilson. Acting in self-defence, Galley had a go back at his assailant who was then arrested. When the case reached court, Galley told us, 'The guy's solicitor said I should have been in the dock as well, which was nice of him.'

Just 24 hours later, the sides met again at Millmoor before a crowd of 13,301. The away side contained at full-back Dietmar Bruck at full-back, who was born in Danzig (now Gdańsk) Poland and as a child escaped with his family from the war-torn borders of Poland and ended up moving to Coventry.

I put us into the lead after 71 minutes with a goal that has played on my mind since. The ball came across the six-yard box from our left-winger Keith Pring. In the middle of a group of players I dived to head the ball, which went past my head and was deflected into the net off my hand.

When the referee gave the goal – it was described in one paper as 'a magnificent header' – I naturally celebrated. The Coventry players were furious and they all remonstrated with the referee Colin Cook, while Jimmy Hill went to the touchline and on to the pitch to complain. However, neither the linesman nor referee had seen the ball strike my hand and the goal was thus allowed. The games were not all televised in those days but I know that it was my hand that scored! Should I have done the decent thing and admitted I had scored with my hand? Would Hill have done the decent thing? Perhaps not.

In May 1977, Hill, then Coventry's chairman, showed on the Highfield Road giant scoreboard the result from Goodison Park as Everton hosted Sunderland. The Wearsiders had lost 2-0. With their scoreline tied at 2-2, Coventry and Bristol City knew that, if they played out the remaining eight minutes of their match, which had, for unspecified reasons, kicked off late, a draw would be sufficient for both of them to stay in the First Division. Coventry had led 2-0 but were under pressure after the Robins had equalised and a Bristol victory would have put the Sky Blues down. The sides played out an uneventful final eight minutes and Hill's men stayed up.

At Rotherham in December 1966, Coventry pushed forward big Dave Clements and when his shot was fumbled by Rod Jones in goal their number six equalised in the last minute. In truth, the away side had been second best and hardly deserved a point. The Sky Blues won promotion as Second Division champions in 1966/67.

Years later, when I was working at the Arsenal academy, I was reminded of my own 'Hand of God' moment when we took the Arsenal under-13s squad to play in a tournament in Qatar. Pelé and Diego Maradona were there as guests. Both legends were very friendly to the boys and it was wonderful to meet them.

After our first game, our young players and staff were sitting behind the goal waiting for the next match. Maradona ran on to the pitch in his tracksuit and came over to the goal behind which the boys were sitting. Two local lads started crossing balls into the area for him to shoot and head into the empty goal. Our boys were cheering him. After ten minutes, no doubt getting bored with this activity, a cross came over to him at head height. Maradona thumped the ball into the goal with his hand. As he ran behind the goal and past our boys, he put his finger to his mouth and muttered, 'Shhh, shhh.' The boys knew about his goal in the quarter-final of the World Cup against England in 1986 and they laughed hysterically.

I retained my place in the Rotherham first team over the following weeks but the results were disappointing. We lost 2-1 at home to struggling Northampton Town on New Year's Eve 1966 when we failed to deal with the heavy, muddy conditions, but two days later came one of my playing career highlights. The 1965/66 final of the Sheffield County Cup at Millmoor had been held over from the previous season and we faced First Division Sheffield United, who naturally started as favourites. The teams were:

Rotherham: Hill, Wilcockson, Clish, Rabjohn, Haselden, Tiler, Massey, Williams, Galley, Chambers, Pring.

Sheffield United: Hodgkinson, Badger, Bernard Shaw, Barlow, Finnigan, Barry Wagstaff, Woodward, Fenoughty, Jones, Tony Wagstaff, Punton.

The match was watched by 9,710 fans, and on 29 minutes I put Rotherham ahead after I took the ball from one side of the pitch to the other before beating England international Alan Hodgkinson with a shot that gave me great pleasure. I was also pleased with my overall performance, especially as the match was played in icy conditions that made it difficult to retain your footing. Incidentally, Hodgkinson later became English football's first specialist goalkeeping coach.

The match was crammed with incidents galore. Towards the end, Blades winger Alan Woodward's tremendous shot crashed back off the bar with Alan Hill well beaten. Woodward scored almost 200 league goals for the Bramall Lane side over a 14-year period and he was a very good player.

On balance, we just about deserved our 1-0 victory and for older Rotherham fans it brought back memories of an earlier Millers side that in 1925 beat Sheffield United 4-1 in the same competition only days after the Blades had captured the FA Cup. That Rotherham team lost in the final to Barnsley but we had gone one better. Also overjoyed were the fans, some of whom rushed on to the pitch to celebrate when the referee Keith Styles of Barnsley sounded the final whistle. Skipper Brian Tiler proudly held aloft the trophy and we were all presented with winning medals. The goal was my third in four first-team matches so far that season.

We then lost 1-0 away to Plymouth Argyle where, after escaping on several occasions from my marker, Andy Nelson, I missed some decent chances.

In the FA Cup we faced non-league Nuneaton Town, who had earned the title of giantkillers after disposing of Swansea Town in the previous round. We drew 1-1 and were grateful to John Galley who went in goal again and produced a series of fine saves after Alan Hill left the pitch due to concussion.

The replay packed out Millmoor with 22,930 inside. Our biggest Second Division home gate during the season was 17,237 against Hull City – 5,000 fewer than for an FA Cup tie against a non-league side, such was the draw of the famous old competition in the 1960s.

We somewhat fortunately beat Nuneaton 1-0 thanks to a disputed effort from right-back Harold Wilcockson.

Our hopes of a good cup run were dashed when we lost after a replay to Birmingham City in the following round. The match at St Andrew's drew a crowd of 35,482. I had dropped out of the first team after the replay against Nuneaton but I was able to play four reserve fixtures in February and March, although I only scored the once from my position at centre-forward and our best result was a 1-1 draw away to Bradford Park Avenue reserves.

I returned to first-team action at Preston North End on Easter Tuesday. There were eight matches of the season remaining and Rotherham, with just eight points from the previous 14 games, were facing relegation.

I played at number seven in a hard battle. At 1-1 with two minutes left, I had a great breakaway opportunity to win the game before the home left-back Jim Smith, who during a long career with Preston played over 300 games including the 1964 FA Cup Final against West Ham United, came across quickly and denied me with a fine tackle.

Five days later, though, when playing at centre-forward, I was able to score in the 4-1 defeat of Cardiff City at home. I had slung the ball over to allow Frank Casper to put us ahead early on and at 2-1 up I calmed the nerves by scoring late on. Then midfielder

Colin Clish, signed from Newcastle United in December 1963, scored to make it a comprehensive victory against another of our relegation rivals. It was the season's biggest win.

I played before a 32,338 crowd at Molineux where Wolves, inspired by their new hero, Northern Irishman Derek Dougan, were two up on just ten minutes. The match was played on a Saturday evening as with the Grand National on TV in the afternoon there was a fear that some fans might stay away to watch the racing. Wolves' 2-0 victory helped the Black Country side to gain promotion behind Coventry.

After defeat to Ipswich Town, we beat Bristol City 2-1 at Ashton Gate. Wing-half Chris Rabjohn, another product of Rotherham's youth policy, opened the scoring with a great shot. With the match tied at 1-1, Galley hit our precious winner with 12 minutes remaining.

I scored my fourth first-team goal of the season against Carlisle United on the last Saturday in April but the Cumbrians left after a fine second-half performance with both points thanks to a 3-2 win. Every Rotherham player had been promised a £50 win bonus for each of the final five games of the season, the directors no doubt hoping this incentive would inspire the side to make sure we avoided relegation. We had collected after our victory against Bristol City and this was our chance to make it another highly profitable Saturday. I was playing alongside a young lad called John Shepherd, who was making his second appearance. In addition to scoring from close range, I made our second goal for Rabjohn to give us a 2-0 half-time lead.

Shepherd was going on at the interval about how he was going to spend his bonus on his summer holiday, but Carlisle were pushing for promotion – they finished in third place– and had other thoughts. They reduced the arrears just after the restart through Peter McConnell, a fine player, before then equalising through John Rudge and scoring the winner through centre-forward

Tommy Murray. I was next to Shepherd as the winning goal went past Alan Hill and heard him mutter, 'Fifty quid down the drain.' In truth, as the local papers noted, we had paid the penalty for 'a tendency to take things too easily' in the second period.

Three points came from the next two games. One was earned from a 1-1 draw at Blackburn Rovers, where I played against Bryan Douglas, capped 36 times for England, who scored the home goal, and against 35-times-capped England wing-half and captain Ronnie Clayton. These pair can rightly be described as great, and Douglas was equally at home out wide or as an inside-forward. Two points were earned from the last league game in a 3-0 victory at Bury. I had started 13 Second Division matches throughout the season, along with one substitute appearance, and scored four times. I had also made two FA Cup appearances and did not score.

These late-season results helped ensure that Rotherham finished six points above Northampton Town and seven clear of Bury, who were both relegated. Les Chappell was our top scorer with 17 goals, all in the league. Brian Tiler was an ever-present. The former Millers junior player had scored 22 league and FA Cup goals in 1963/64, but the following season he returned to his natural position in defence. He later moved to Aston Villa when Tommy Docherty became the Birmingham club's manager in 1968.

Rotherham had thus retained the distinction of being the longest-serving club in the Second Division.

With Galley not fully fit at the start of the 1967/68 season I had hoped to play in the opening fixture at home to Crystal Palace but instead Tiler was chosen at centre-forward. Palace won 3-0; it was a poor start. Rotherham then faced Notts County away in the first round of the League Cup and I played at number nine in a 1-0 success, the goal coming from debutant Les Bradd, who made three more appearances for the Millers before accepting the chance to sign for County in October 1967. He went on to have a great career and played more than 400 games for the Magpies.

I was delighted to have played my part in beating County so I was disappointed to be left out for the match at Villa Park three days later, a 3-1 win for the home team. I was also not selected on the August Bank Holiday Monday for the 3-1 defeat at home to Derby County.

Two days later I played in the reserve match at Mansfield Town and I was determined to show I was ready to return to first-team action. It ended 1-1 with Galley scoring; it was to prove my final match for my hometown club. I was soon to be moving south.

Chapter 14

Moving to Orient to enjoy hitting the net

ENGLAND'S 4-2 victory over West Germany in the 1966 World Cup Final attracted a television audience of 400 million worldwide, including Americans captivated by the skills and excitement of a sport previously scorned from Miami to Boston.

The USA's two main sports demanded rigid physical proportions: weight for American football and height for basketball. Association football – soccer as they call it – is for all sizes and shapes. Previous attempts to establish football in the USA had proved unsuccessful although in 1950 the national team shocked the world by beating England 1-0 at the World Cup in Brazil.

Bill Cox sought to put US soccer on a sound footing and in 1967 he successfully established the North American Soccer League (NASL) consisting of 20 teams over two divisions, with matches played in the summer. Cox attracted European coaches, including Freddie Goodwin of Scunthorpe United to New York Generals and former Welsh international Phil Woosnam to Atlanta Chiefs.

At the beginning of the English 1967/68 season, Jack Mansell quit Rotherham United to manage Boston Beacons. He was joined in the NASL by Gordon Jago, the Fulham manager linking up with Baltimore Bays. Despite significant sponsorship, the Beacons lasted for only one season.

Jack had recruited his friend Fred Green as his Millmoor assistant and to my great shock he was promoted to the vacant manager's post at Rotherham. Green was a decent man but had never played football, about which he knew very little. My concerns worsened when, following the reserve game at Mansfield, he informed me that Rotherham had agreed to transfer me to Orient (the word Leyton was dropped from the club's title from 1966 to 1987) and that a train ticket had been booked for me to travel to London to discuss transfer arrangements the following day.

This was not an ideal situation. On Sunday, 16 October 1966 I had visited Tony Fallon to see what he was doing that evening. He had gone to the Empress Dance Hall in Doncaster so I went home, changed and drove to Doncaster to join up with Tony and my other friends. Christine Sutterby, a secretary at British Ropes in Warmsworth, was present and I asked her for a dance which she accepted. We continued dancing until her untimely death, due to cancer, in 1990.

We had arranged to get married at the end of the 1967/68 season and had put down a deposit on a house in Sprotbrough, a nearby village. Going to London for talks was a bombshell, especially as neither Christine nor myself had home telephones. The following day my mum and dad drove to Christine's to tell her I was on my way south accompanied by my Rotherham colleague Owen Simpson, who, in addition to being wanted by Orient as well, was also soon to be married.

We met Dick Graham, who had become Orient's manager after the club, which was in dire financial straits, was relegated to the Third Division in 1966.

Orient had finished 14th in the Third Division in 1966/67. Average attendances were just 5,981 and the star had been 37-year-old Cliff Holton, a key figure in the Arsenal First Division title-winning side in 1952/53. Holton notched 17 league goals in 1966/67 including a hat-trick in a 4-1 win over Mansfield Town in the penultimate home game. A leg injury at the start of the following season ended Holton's career, in which he notched 294 goals from 570 league matches for seven clubs. Holton and I played one game together, a 5-0 thrashing away to Walsall.

Orient had a small squad and Graham was keen to sign Owen and myself. I knew I had no future at Rotherham, who wanted just £1,000 for me. Dick was aware of my knee injury and although I felt it was weak, I said it was fine. I signed for Orient in the afternoon and received a £250 signing-on fee.

I had been unable to discuss things with my future wife. In the event, Christine and I agreed that living in London was quite exciting although she insisted that we urgently bring our wedding plans forward. A year to the day after we had first met, Christine and I were married on Monday, 16 October 1967 at Bank Street Methodist Church, Mexborough.

We quickly settled into an Orient club house in Gants Hill and I was graciously given two days off by Graham to sort things out. The weekend before I first attended training, Orient beat Southport 3-0 and so everyone was in a good mood on my first day with my new employers. On my return home, it was 4pm and there were no signs of Christine. The house was locked and I was left standing at the gate. After 20 minutes I saw her getting off a bus from Ilford. 'Where on earth have you been?' I asked. 'I have been for a job interview,' she replied, 'and they have offered me the job.'

Christine had rung Plessey PLC at Tottenham Road in Ilford to enquire about any secretarial vacancies. The company needed staff and she was asked to immediately attend an interview, following which she was offered a post that she accepted. Christine stayed at the company until we moved to Colchester.

As I was a qualified teacher, I had come to an agreement with Orient that I could teach three afternoons a week at a local school. Lake House was a junior comprehensive and pupils ranged from year seven to nine. Year ten students would continue their education at the nearby Tom Hood School. Lake House lacked PE facilities and equipment, with indoor PE taken in a hall that was surrounded by classrooms. At double PE lessons, then when the bell rang halfway through the session, it was necessary to halt all activities to allow other children to cross the hall as they swapped classrooms.

Most PE lessons were in the playground. For games we used playing fields at Wanstead flats where I took the football lessons. For the first time I was teaching youngsters who had come to London with their parents from the Caribbean. They were lively and friendly. The boys loved football and cricket so I hired a cricket pitch in the summer for inter-school cricket matches. After my teaching ended at the school when I was transferred on to Colchester, I was sorry to leave the pupils as I had developed a good relationship with many of them.

Early in the 1969/70 season, a former teaching colleague of mine hired a minibus and brought 15 youngsters from Lake House School down to Colchester. Christine prepared lunch for everyone and they hoped to see me play league football in the afternoon, but unfortunately my injury jinx had restarted and I missed the game. However, we all had an enjoyable time. Lake House School is now a housing estate.

Black footballers were starting to make progress in the English game. Leeds United's outside-right Albert Johanneson played at Wembley in the 1965 FA Cup Final when his side lost 2-1 to Liverpool. He appeared 200 times for Leeds between 1961 and 1969 and was the first high-profile black player of the modern age.

Johanneson joined Leeds in April 1961 from Germiston Colliers in South Africa, where under the Apartheid system there was strict racial segregation. He was a shy man and this made him uncertain about his place within white British society. He was a courageous player as he was forced to endure racial abuse on many occasions including at the 1965 final. George Best later remarked, 'Albert was quite a brave man to actually go on the pitch in the first place, wasn't he? And he went out and did it. He had a lot of skill. A nice man as well ... which is, I suppose, the more important thing, isn't it? More important than anything.'

After finishing playing football, Albert became a recluse, suffering from alcohol addiction. He died alone of meningitis and heart failure in 1995, aged 55. His body lay undiscovered in his flat for weeks. What a tragic end to his life.

I was therefore pleased that in January 2019, Leeds United and the Leeds Civic Trust unveiled a blue plaque to commemorate one of the pioneers of today's black players whom football as a whole should remember fondly.

For the 1967/68 season, Orient had chosen to swap back to their traditional red shirts, last worn in the 1902/03 season.

I made my Orient debut at number nine in the third league match, a 4-2 defeat away to Reading at Elm Park, a stadium which is now long gone. Our goals were scored by midfielder Peter Allen, who holds Orient's all-time league appearance record with 424 starts and eight substitute appearances.

Making his second Orient appearance against Reading was goalkeeper Ray Goddard, aged 18. Ray was successful at Brisbane Road with 311 appearances before signing for Millwall and then Wimbledon where he was a member of the Fourth Division title-winning team in 1982/83. This is how we lined up for my Orient debut: Goddard, Howe, Simpson, Whitehouse, Wood, Halom, Werge, Allen, Massey, Thomas, Eadie. Sub: Price.

Prior to kick-off, there was an incident that would never be allowed these days when Bob Ndobah, who had attended Cheltenham College during the period I was there studying PE, jumped the barrier behind the goal and came on to the pitch to have a chat with me. He stayed for a few minutes and then went back on to the terraces and watched the action.

I opened my Orient scoring account on my home debut, a 2-1 home defeat to Brighton & Hove Albion. I collected a Mick Jones corner and turned to put a Seagulls defenders on the wrong foot before hammering home off the underside of the bar. It was a spectacular goal and gave us an early lead, but Brighton equalised from a Brian Tawse penalty. This was awarded after the ball seemed to leap up and hit the hand of well-travelled Tommy Anderson. A disgruntled home fan objected and ran on to try to assault the referee for awarding a spot kick, but fortunately the man in charge ducked to avoid being struck.

Orient's first victory of the season was in the eighth league match, 2-0 at home against leaders Walsall. Following my pull-back, Mick Jones netted one of the goals. Jones was an Orient regular in the 1960s and early 70s, mainly at full-back, making over 250 appearances. His never-say-die attitude and his attacking flair endeared him to the Brisbane Road faithful, and he later played with distinction for Charlton Athletic. Our victory was helped when Jim McMorran, Walsall's Scottish forward, formerly of Aston Villa, was dismissed by referee John Osborne after just five minutes following a touchline tussle with Bert Howe, previously of Crystal Palace.

Against Northampton Town, Eddie Thomas, signed from Derby County on the same day as myself and Owen Simpson, scored his first Orient goal. Thomas had a distinguished career with the Rams and had come south for his final season. He was clearly unhappy and his displays frustrated the manager. In one home game on a very muddy pitch, Eddie fell over in front of the dugout where Dick Graham was sitting. Eddie was substituted. Sitting in the dressing room next to Eddie I witnessed Dick come over and say, 'Eddie, I thought you was a good player when you scored goals for Scunthorpe and Newcastle.'

'Boss, I didn't play for Scunthorpe or Newcastle; I have been with Derby County throughout my career.'

'Bloody hell, I've signed the wrong Eddie Thomas,' said Dick. Eddie was soon back in Derby.

Graham was a hard taskmaster. In November 1967 at Oxford United, after a severe frost, one penalty area was frozen. When I jumped there after ten minutes I fell over and hit my head on the bone-hard pitch. I ran around for the next ten minutes with double vision.

It was embarrassing seeing two balls and I went over to the bench and shouted, 'Dick, I can't see.'

His reply was, 'I can see you, get back on that bloody field.' I came off at half-time and we lost 2-0. When we arrived back by coach at Brisbane Road, Dick, who had sulked throughout the return journey, turned to everyone and sternly said that he would see us all on Monday morning.

At 10am on Monday, every player was sitting quietly in the dressing room. The usual banter had disappeared and it was like being in a doctor's waiting room as Dick kept us waiting for 45 minutes. Looking back, I can't believe that grown men could be so fearful of a manager's wrath.

We heard his footsteps coming down the corridor. The dressing-room door was flung open and Dick walked in grim-faced. He shouted and screamed at every player for putting in such a poor performance.

I was at the end of the line hoping that his rantings would fade by the time he came to me. He was out of control, 'Massey, I don't want any wimps in my team. Don't get settled in at Gants Hill because you can go back to where you came from. You are not allowed to teach at the school because you are going to train every afternoon.'

Up to that point I thought I was playing well, so his outburst shook me to the core. After a subdued training session, I had to go to see the Lake House headteacher to tell him that I could no longer work there due to the extra training I had to do.

The headteacher, out of the blue, had, in fact, suddenly offered me a full-time PE job for the following September. Without thinking of the consequences, I had accepted the offer. I was unsure exactly how I might tell Dick Graham. Now he was telling me I couldn't even do the part-time teaching.

The next day I went to see the manager. 'What are you doing here?' he asked. I told Dick that he had gone against our agreement that I could teach in the afternoons as I now had to do extra training sessions. 'I can't remember saying that,' Dick said. 'Of course, you can carry on teaching.'

I left his office feeling confused. I was pleased to be allowed to continue my current school work but I still faced the tricky problem of telling Dick that I wanted to play for him on a part-time basis the following season. I decided to say nothing for now.

Against Southport I took advantage of hesitancy by opposition keeper Brian Reeves to head home Malcolm Slater's corner from just a yard out to score the first of Orient's first-half goals. The 3-0 interval lead was the final result. The local paper, the *Guardian and Gazette*, reported that I 'chased anything and everything' during the game.

Against Barrow I scored twice in a 4-2 home win. Opposition keeper Brian Else, who during his career with Preston, Blackburn and Barrow made over 600 appearances, had no chance when Peter Bebbington's back pass dropped at my feet for my first but he was at fault for my second when he fumbled a shot to present me with a gift that put us 3-2 ahead. Our final goal was scored by trialist centre-half Terry Mancini who had written via Holton to Dick from South Africa where his business venture had collapsed. After a successful training spell, his inclusion in the first team led him to make 105 consecutive league appearances. He skippered the O's when they won the Division title in 1970.

Victory against the Cumbrians kickstarted a good run as Orient won five, drew once and lost just twice of their next eight league matches. I had started playing well but my knee did not feel particularly strong, so I strapped it when playing.

In early December, Beatle-haired teenager Vic Halom, the London-born son of Hungarian refugees, was moved up front – he had played at centre-half on my home debut – to partner me in an FA Cup tie at non-league Weymouth. When he notched both goals in a 2-0 victory, he was pushed permanently into the number ten slot. Halom's opportunity arose after Graham dropped Eddie Thomas.

Halom also scored in the second round as we squeezed past another non-league side, Boston United, 2-1 after drawing the first game 1-1 away. Vic had taken some abuse from Boston fans at the away match for wearing gloves on a cold day. It is a common thing to do today.

Vic later played in the 1973 FA Cup Final for Second Division Sunderland, who were managed by former Newcastle United captain Bob Stokoe. The boss went down in folklore after he ran on to the pitch wearing his overcoat and trilby to hug his goalkeeper Jim Montgomery who made two brilliant saves in quick succession to help keep Sunderland 1-0 up against big favourites Leeds United.

In my first three months at Orient, I was temporarily coached by Stokoe as Dick Graham had given him a temporary job after he had been sacked as Charlton Athletic manager. Dick was a hard man but he had empathy with people who were in difficulty. He aided Bob at a time when it was needed and Bob later went on to manage Rochdale, Carlisle, Blackpool, and Bury again.

On Boxing Day 1967 I scored my fifth league goal of the season in a 3-2 loss away to Peterborough United, and four days later I scored my sixth as the sides met again as Orient took revenge in a 3-0 success. Orient had turned down Notts County's offer for Halom and after he made the first for Simpson, he drove forward to deliver a cross that I powered beyond Welsh international keeper Tony Millington into the Posh net. Mancini headed the third from a corner. It was our best performance of the season so far.

My good form continued when I netted my seventh goal with a glancing header from a Jones centre in the following league match, a 1-1 draw at home to Shrewsbury Town. I was always a good header of the ball. Heading is one of football's fundamental skills and as such it has always been considered essential to introduce the technique as early as possible into the game for players of all ages. The problem is that a ball, especially during my own playing era and earlier, might be heavy with mud. Heading it might hurt the head and today there is real concern that youngsters in particular may need to be protected from heading regularly. It could be that the five-a-side matches where the rules see a free kick awarded against a side that hits the ball above head height may need to be adopted in all small-sided games up to eight v eight for the under-nine, under-10 and under-11 age groups.

Coaches stressed to me that the ball should be struck with the forehead, which, while strong and bony, is relatively flat. As a result the ball should be directed more accurately. Strong neck muscles should give added power to a header. A twist of the neck can send the ball off at an angle.

As a forward, my headers were concentrated on accuracy to send them towards and, hopefully, into the goal or to glance the ball delicately to a better-placed colleague to score. The best type of header for a forward was always to climb above the ball and power it downwards towards goal. In comparison, defenders concentrated on leaping high to send powerful headers to a team-mate or in any direction as far away from danger as possible.

The 1967/68 season saw Ron Davies of Southampton tying with George Best as top scorer in the First Division with 28 goals. Davies was a great header of the ball. Other forwards from that time with fantastic heading ability were Wyn Davies (no relation to Ron), Derek Dougan and Jeff Astle, who scored the winning goal for West Bromwich Albion at the 1968 FA Cup Final.

Astle had a great career but is now perhaps best known for the issues that have been raised since his early death in 2002, following which his family have successfully sought to prove that it was, at least in part, caused by his continuous heading of the ball, especially in training. This has led to a review in some parts of the game as to whether heading is suitable for youngsters.

Meanwhile, some former players such as Chris Sutton contend that the Professional Footballers' Association have not done enough to protect players, a charge which the union denies.

I am in no way qualified medically to have an opinion on the dangers and impact of heading a ball but if the game was played solely on the floor, then my friend Terry Oldfield would have gone on to have a good career.

Unlike in the past, the game today is played mainly on the ground, as players, including defenders and goalkeepers, have more confidence and ability on the ball than their counterparts of yesteryear. Goalkeepers playing the ball with their feet, passing to their defenders wasn't in the coaching manual during my playing career and for many years afterwards.

Thanks to excellent drainage, the pitches are also much better. When I was a player, in midwinter the pitches, even at First Division grounds, were very muddy. The ball would get very heavy. Heading a lighter ball on fewer occasions is clearly much better for the safety of players. I do not, however, feel heading can be entirely taken out of any part of the game, although to quote the legendary Brian Clough, 'If God wanted the ball to be played in the air, he would have made the sky green.'

I scored the only goal as Bury were eliminated from the FA Cup before Orient's largest home crowd of the season, 11,641. It was a tough encounter that was decided, reported *The Independent*, by a 'tremendous leaping header by Roy Massey'. It came from a perfect Slater cross. Orient had earlier that week turned down a £10,000 bid for my services from Walsall, with chairman Arthur Page saying, 'We don't want to break up a successful side.'

Birmingham City put us out in the fourth round of the FA Cup when they won 3-0 at St Andrew's before a 29,230 crowd.

Although he did not score, Fred Pickering, who played three times for England and scored five, including a hat-trick on his debut against the USA, was brilliant for Birmingham. My dad and three of his brothers drove down in my uncle Arthur's car from South Yorkshire for the game. I met them beforehand to give them their tickets and could see that my dad was ashen-faced. I asked him how he was feeling and was not totally reassured when he said he was fine. Only later did I find out that Arthur's car had broken down at the bottom of the hill outside the ground and the brothers pushed it to get it restarted. They managed to get home but were no doubt disappointed after our poor display. The next day was Dad's 50th birthday and when he was out celebrating with his brothers at the working men's club he collapsed after a heart attack and was rushed to hospital. He was put on a life-support machine and gradually recovered, but was unable to work again.

I was joined on the scoresheet in a 2-2 draw at home to Stockport County by outside-right Malcolm Slater, signed from Southend United in 1967. Malcolm's best season at Orient was 1968/69 when he missed just one match. As a youngster he was on the verge of signing for Celtic when two of his brothers were tragically killed in a drowning accident. He quit playing before Montrose persuaded him to get back into football.

The first Stockport goal was scored by Jim Fryatt, a much-travelled striker who is in the record books for having scored the quickest goal in league football when he netted after four seconds for Bradford Park Avenue at home to Tranmere Rovers in April 1964. His final league tally was just one short of 200 goals in 499 appearances, and he also won the NASL championship with Philadelphia Atoms in the early 1970s. At more than 6ft tall, Fryatt was a great, powerful header of the ball.

We then played Watford at home. Dick Graham gave a third start to 17-year-old Graham Archell who generally played on the left wing but this time featured on the opposite flank. The Watford player-manager Ken Furphy was playing at left-back and although he'd had a successful playing career, he was now in his mid-30s and his legs were not as quick as they had been. Ken would have noted in the programme that he was playing against a young and inexperienced player. Before kick-off, I noticed Ken sidling up to a young Graham and having a conversation with him.

We were losing 1-0 and Archell was having an undistinguished match. With the manager seeking to shake up the side, the youngster was taken off with Tommy Taylor coming on as a substitute. Afterwards, I asked Graham what Furphy had said to him. It was, 'Listen, son, I am going to let you play but if you start to run past me, I shall kick you over that bloody stand.' Needless to say, an intimidated Graham did not stay long in the game. Mental toughness is a necessary quality for a professional footballer.

I scored in early March in a 3-2 victory at promotion-chasing Gillingham, our first away win of the season. We took the lead thanks to two early goals by John Arnott, who just happened to be playing for Gillingham. Despite this victory, we had just 25 points from 29 matches and faced being relegated to the Fourth Division just seven seasons after Orient had been promoted for the first time to the First Division, where they stayed for just a year.

Frustrated by a lack of money to sign new players, Dick Graham then departed as manager, coincidentally in the week that I had informed him that I wanted to teach full-time and play on a part-time basis.

Before leaving, Graham suggested that Orient appoint a player-manager, an idea which was taken up by the board. Jimmy Bloomfield, who in the 1950s had scored 54 league goals for Arsenal, subsequently became player-manager, appearing 14 times at outside-right during the season. Graham soon found work as manager at Walsall and then in May 1968 he took charge at Colchester United.

There was real relief when Halom scored both our goals in a 2-1 home victory against Scunthorpe United before Owen Simpson and I netted in a 2-2 draw at Oldham Athletic. However, with only two draws from the following four games, Orient remained in deep trouble.

Continuing to blossom up front, Halom again provided some relief when he scored the only goal at home to Oxford United on Easter Saturday before two goalless draws on Easter Monday and Tuesday with relegation rivals Mansfield Town maintained our survival chances. Defeat at Bury on a Friday evening, though, left us with just 35 points from 40 matches.

Halom then netted in a 1-1 draw with Colchester at home before I headed a precious 86th-minute winner in a 1-0 home victory against Bournemouth, which meant we would avoid relegation and we eventually finished 19th with 41 points. This was four points ahead of Grimsby Town in 21st with Colchester, Scunthorpe and Peterborough finishing below the Mariners and also going down. The Posh had actually earned 50 points but had 19 deducted for making irregular payments to players.

At the top of the table, Oxford United, playing only their sixth season in the Football League, were promoted as champions. Joining them in going up were Bury, whose side contained one of the best midfielders of his generation in Scottish international Bobby Collins, as well as future Liverpool full-back Alec Lindsay.

With 12 league goals from 41 starts and one substitute appearance, then I was the top scorer for Orient, and my goal against Bury in the FA Cup gave me 13 in all competitions. Following the end of the season, team captain Brian Wood, who was a very confident centre-half who led by example, moved to Colchester. It was Wood who, because of Orient's cash crisis, had persuaded his team colleagues, including myself, to give up our 1967 Christmas bonus.

Chapter 15

Injury woes again

IN HIS first season at Orient, Jimmy Bloomfield worked alongside his coach Peter Angell, who had enjoyed a good career with Queens Park Rangers. Both were conscientious, decent and caring men. But they did not take too kindly when I announced that I wanted to play on a part-time basis as I intended teaching full-time because I needed to do a full year of teaching within five years of leaving college in order to become a qualified PE teacher.

The school gave me Wednesdays off to train with the senior players, plus I also trained on Tuesday and Thursday evenings with the youth team. Alas, the decision marked the beginning of the end of my O's career. Although I made the first team when the season started, it proved difficult to combine a teaching career while playing professional football.

The teaching gave me an insight into organising and communicating, and planning and preparing lessons. Studying the behaviour and needs of pupils was a great experience.

Orient's start to the 1967/68 season had been poor a year earlier, so there was relief as, following two draws, including an opening-day 3-3 with Rotherham United, who had been relegated under Tommy Docherty after the Scot had replaced Fred Green as manager during the previous campaign, Orient won their third league match of 1968/69. Vic Halom scored the only goal against

Mansfield Town and the line-up was: Goddard, Jones, Howe, Harper, Mancini, Taylor, Allen, Slater, Massey, Halom, Brabrook.

Youngster Tommy Taylor, who had made his debut as a substitute in the FA Cup tie against Birmingham City at just 15 years and 11 months, started the new campaign alongside Terry Mancini at centre-back. This defensive partnership flourished until Taylor moved to neighbours West Ham United for the 1970/71 season. Taylor was part of the Hammers' FA Cup-winning side in 1975, and returned to his first club in 1979.

I scored three in a pre-season 4-1 success against Romford Town but I failed to score in the first six league games of the season. I was relieved when I netted in a 1-0 success against Second Division Fulham, managed by their former England midfielder Bobby Robson, in the second round of the League Cup before a home crowd of 12,901. I hit the ball beautifully to give us a 15th-minute lead that we deservedly defended from then on.

Against Oldham I saw Halom notch his ninth goal in just 11 matches, although soon after that, cash-strapped Orient had to accept a transfer offer for him from Fulham. We had formed a creditable partnership up front, and I later discovered my former manager Dick Graham had suggested to Bobby Robson to also sign me in order to maintain my partnership with Vic. This may have been a fact, or it could have been Dick, the psychologist, attempting to motivate me to raise my game.

Less successful up front was Bloomfield, who later in the season moved himself to left-half. He quit playing at the end of the season to be a full-time manager.

After six defeats in seven league matches, everyone was relieved when I notched what was my only league goal of the campaign in the 1-0 away victory at Reading. The home rearguard made a hash of an offside trap and were caught sleeping as Taylor slipped the ball out wide to Malcolm Slater, whose accurate cross I steered beyond Roy Brown to give Orient a shock early lead. Reading thereafter kept up a non-stop attack but with Mancini in great form we held firm to capture two valuable points.

Having been booked – ironically for what was an innocuous challenge – for what was the only time in my professional career, I was forced to leave the field with a knee injury in a 1-1 draw at home to Watford. This was Orient's 17th league match and I was only able to make four starts and four substitute appearances in the next 29 Third Division fixtures.

As I was unable to train full-time because of my teaching, my form then dipped – and it was not helped by ongoing problems with my knee. Physiotherapist Charlie Simpson, a wonderful man, took me to see a specialist to enquire about how to strengthen the joint. I was told that the cruciate ligament was loose, so strengthening meant working on the quadriceps. I had already been doing quadriceps exercises for three years but nevertheless my knee never seemed to get any stronger.

Surgeons did not have the techniques to operate on weakened ligaments back then. Today, many players have cruciate ligament injuries and they make a full recovery after surgery.

During my absence, Dennis Rofe made the left-back position his own at Orient, and it was no surprise that when Bloomfield became Leicester City manager, he signed Rofe in August 1972 for a record fee for a full-back of £112,000. Rofe stayed at Filbert Street for many years before joining Chelsea and Southampton.

My lack of match fitness led to the O's dipping into the transfer market by signing Mickey Bullock for £8,000 from Oxford United to play at number nine. Barry Dyson arrived for £8,000 from Northampton Town at number ten and did well in 1968/69 with ten goals in 25 league appearances. Three of these came in the final four fixtures of the season, including the crucial only goal at Bournemouth in the penultimate match.

Bullock was a great Orient servant with over 300 first-team appearances, and he joined Dyson and Mancini on the scoresheet on the final day of the season. This was a game played on a Monday night under floodlights against Shrewsbury, another relegation-threatened side. Bullock scored with a glorious volley from 20 yards on five minutes with Dyson scoring a goal almost as good 13 minutes later. On the half-hour mark, Terry Parmenter was sent off after reacting to a poor tackle but despite playing the final hour with just ten men, Orient made it three when Bullock headed the ball into the middle for Mancini to score before the hard-working Dave Harper made it 4-0.

Victory raised Orient to 18th place and, by collecting seven points from their last five games, they made a great escape. I played no part. Defeat against Shrewsbury would have left Orient relegated below Northampton Town, who just four seasons after being promoted to First Division were now back in the Fourth Division. A remarkable drop.

Watford won the Third Division, while Swindon Town were promoted in second place and also won the League Cup by beating Arsenal 3-1 at Wembley in the final with Don Rogers scoring twice.

I had played no role in Orient's last-gasp escape and so I was grateful when Bloomfield offered me a contract to go back into full-time training. I was unsure what to do. I feared having another injury-ridden season. Having successfully completed my training to become a teacher, I considered becoming a full-time teacher and playing part-time football at non-league level.

Christine was pregnant and I wanted something to give us more security. Dick Graham again changed the direction of my life.

We had just installed a telephone at our flat and the first call was from my former manager, who asked me to consider joining him at Colchester United. Orient were prepared to sell me and the Colchester directors had offered £6,000 for a goalscoring centre-forward. Dick thought that I would be that man.

It was a drop down the Football League but I felt that this was my chance to resurrect my faltering professional football career.

The *Evening Standard* reported that my new boss felt I would provide the height hitherto missing up front in the Colchester attack. Graham also felt his side would be stronger at the back and on the wings in the 1969/70 campaign. The fee was the only one paid out that summer by Colchester with the other new faces all arriving on a free – goalkeeper Graham Smith from Notts County, Luton outside-left Ray Whittaker, Orient full-back Bert Howe, Southend wing-half Bobby Howlett and Tottenham Hotspur winger Steve Pitt.

MASSEY SHOWS POSH HOW

A STUNNING spectacle staged by Colchester's Ray Massey snatched victory from under Peterborough's bewildered noses and left them nursing their first home defeat of the season.

With three minutes to go, ex-Orient striker Massey blocked an attempted centre by Ollie Conmy deep in the Colchester half. Massey, who had a bad leg injury last season, ran 50 yards with the ball leaving Peterborough's surprised defence back-pedalling, and then planted a 20-yard shot past an immobile Mick Drewery in goal.

The result was hard on Peterborough who dominated the second half. But full marks to Massey for a supreme piece of goal-poaching.

The Colchester defenders deserved a medal apiece for the way they soaked up a continual pounding in the second half as the strong wind powered every Peterborough pass into their teeth.

Deflected

It never looked like Peterborough's lucky day. After only nine minutes Bob Turpie saw a shot deflected over goalkeeper Brian Sherratt's head, but the ball rebounded off the underside of the crossbar, on to the goal-line and then out.

Colchester got their first goal with a carefully prepared move in the 18th minute.

Massey, the man of the match, beat Wile on the left wing, crossed to crafty Ray Crawford, and the ex-England centre-forward, who is back from non-League football, nodded the

by DAVID THORPE

Peterborough - - 1
Colchester - - -- 2

cross down for Brian Gibbs to hammer the ball home.

Peterborough's equaliser came from a scrappy mêlée after a 40th-minute corner, but Tommy Robson, the pick of the "Posh," whipped the ball in with a firm right foot.

Peterborough flung extra men into the hunt for a winner and a weary Laurie Sheffield was pulled off midway through the second half so that swift little Bobby Moss could come on.

But Colchester were massively safe at the back, and though there were near miss thrills for the crowd a draw looked the likeliest result until Massey, playing only his third game since he returned to the first team after his injury, took that decisive hand.

A stunning goal for Colchester at Peterborough United

Roy Massey was grateful to Bobby Robson for bringing Ipswich Town to Layer Road for his testimonial match

ROY MASSEY'S
Testimonial Match

COLCHESTER UNITED
versus
IPSWICH TOWN

Monday, 8th November, 1971, Kick-off 7.30 p.m.

LAYER ROAD GROUND, COLCHESTER

Lucky Number for autographed match ball

Price: 5p

PERSONALITY PAGE

SO TOUGH FOR ROY

There are a score of hard luck stories in football but surely Roy Massey's takes some beating. The condolences of everyone—management, supporters and his colleagues go out to Roy who has recently learned that his playing career must be terminated so prematurely.

Poor Roy has borne his misfortune with great character and cheerfulness. Earlier this year he had his third cartilage operation. Last season, after a brilliant opening to the campaign, he was dogged by a nagging foot injury. That was really one of the cruellest blows of all. Roy, Yorkshire-born striker whose father won an F.A. Cup medal as goalkeeper for Sheffield Wednesday against Wolves in 1895-96, scored 11 goals in the first fifteen matches of last season.

It was the best start he had ever made to a League campaign and was highlighted by a wonder hat-trick in the Football League Cup tie against Reading at Elm Park.

Roy fought with persistence and courage, against all the injury luck that ironically followed. He emerged again to play at the end of last season and this term slowly fought his way back into the League side. He scored 4 goals in eight matches including a quite sensational last minute effort which was the winner at Peterborough—and who knows, that goal may yet turn out to be one of the most vital contributions of the season.

Then, just when it seemed Roy had turned the corner at last, came that final injury in a series of misfortune that has ultimately proved conclusive.

Roy, tall, gangling, superb in the air, had that knack of being in the right spot at the right time. It was a flair that first attracted the attention of Dick Graham when he was manager at Orient and Mr. Graham bought Roy, along with Owen Simpson, from Rotherham United.

Later, when at Brisbane Road, Roy switched to part-time and was persuaded to join his old boss again at Layer Road and as we all know

so well, until the injury hoodoo struck, Roy took on a completely new lease of life, his market value soaring after a terrific spell of scoring consistency.

So ten years of soccer, carrying such high promise, comes to an end. Roy began with Yorkshire and England Grammar Schools football. His College studies lost him a chance of turning professional with Arsenal who were keenly interested, but he went to Rotherham United, then in Division Two, and was an instant success. In his first game he scored twice in a 3-2 win over Cardiff City at Ninian Park, and that, plus his memorable Colchester hat-trick at Reading rank among Roy's biggest thrills. For the Reading feat he was presented with the match ball.

Roy's future probably now lies in the coaching side of the game. He is a fully qualified P.T. instructor and is going on another course at Lilleshall this summer.

From all at Layer Road one can only wish him and his family all the best of luck in his efforts to play some profitable and important non-playing role in the game he loves so much.

CAREER DETAILS
League only

Rotherham United:

	Appearances	Goals
1964-65	2	2
1966-67	13	4
Orient:		
1967-68	42	12
1968-69	17	1
Colchester United:		
1969-70	18	7
1970-71	13	4
Total	103	30

STATISTICS SPOT

TOTAL ATTENDANCE FIGURES

League
At Layer Road: 95,650.
Away: 81,092.
Best home gate: 7,777, v. Southend.
Lowest home gate: 4,286, v. Notts County.
Best away gate: 9,406, v. Southend.
Lowest away gate: 1,973, v. Newport Co.

F.A. Cup
At Layer Road: 30,692.
Away: 70,258.
Best home gate: 16,000, v. Leeds United.
Best away gate: 53,028, v. Everton.

Football League Cup
At Layer Road: 16,047.
Away: 17,606.
Best home gate: 8,095, v. B'ham City.
Best away gate: 17,606, v. B'ham City.

BEST WINS

League
4-0 v. Brentford.

F.A. Cup
5-0 v. Rochdale.

Football League Cup
5-0 v. Cambridge United.

HEAVIEST DEFEATS

League
1-4 v. Bournemouth.

F.A. Cup
0-5 v. Everton.

Football League Cup
1-2 v. Birmingham City (replay).

HAT-TRICKS

Ray Crawford (2), v. Crewe (League) and v. Ringmer (F.A. Cup).

RESERVE SCORERS

● Reserve scorers in London Mid-Week League and London Mid-Week League Cup (up to and including 10th March):
Leslie, 6; Lindsay Smith, 3; Whittaker, 2; Owen, 2; Jones, 2; Webster, R. Cook, Foley, Mahon, Massey, Hall, Brown, Dennis and Burgess one each.

APPEARANCES AND SCORERS

(LEAGUE, LEAGUE CUP & F.A. CUP)

Up to and including 22nd March

	Appearances	Goals
Cook	32	—
Cram	43	3
Crawford	44	26
Gibbs	43	8
Gilchrist	26	1
Garvey	41	1
Hall	39	2
Joslyn	8	—
Jones	29	—
Kurila	43	1
Lewis	17	5
Mahon	36	6
Massey	13	4
Owen	6	4
Painter	1	—
Sherratt	8	—
Simmons	15	5
Smith	36	—
Whittaker	5	—
Own goals	—	3

16

17

A nice tribute to Roy Massey from Colchester in the match programme for his testimonial

Contact Eddie Keegan at
Colchester United Football Club
Layer Road, Colchester, Essex
Telephone: Colchester 74042

A BIG THANK YOU

Now the dust has settled and the big game is over lets pay a tribute to the organisation and efficient work behind the scenes to ensure that everything went right when Manchester United came to town. True, the gate was not capacity but it was a man sized task for all to cope on the night of Tuesday Feb. 19. Chairman Mr. Jack Rippingale and club secretary, Betty Scott, want me to express their gratitude and thanks to the local Police, the Military Police and the many soldiers and other volunteers who acted as stewards. Well, they did a grand job and everything went off without a hitch.

No praise can be too high either, for the tremendous efforts of supporters over the previous week-end in clearing the pitch and terraces of snow to make sure the game went on. They were an example to all and Colchester United scored hands down when so many other clubs didn't make the big effort to beat the weather and get some action.

Finally, a word from myself over the general conduct of both sets of supporters at the Manchester United tie. They were great and it all proves that with proper organisation and good sense the game can go ahead as it should to everyones enjoyment.

B.W.

Roy Massey Talks About Youngsters

Many boys dream about becoming a professional footballer. Playing football and being paid for it, plus the glamour and excitement of the game, are great incentives for any youngster who has ability. If you are between the ages of fourteen and eighteen years, you might be wondering how to start a possible career in professional football.

A number of boys who play District football are seen by our scouts, and some players are brought to our attention by local team managers. However, if you have not been in this category, and you are like a trial with us, write to me at the club. Who knows, it might be the start of a successful career. Our own Steven Wright will be the first to admit that he was not a top schoolboy player at Alderman Blaxill School, and he played very few matches for the District team, but he has proved that with hard work and dedication, it is possible to improve and make the grade in professional football.

Each club has its own policy of developing its young players. Those boys who play well in our trials are invited back to play in a number of matches which are usually played on Sundays. After good displays in these games, the next step is an appearance in our reserve side. If a boy can hold his own in this standard, it is more than likely that he would be offered an apprenticeship. This is the first step to a career in professional football, but by no means is a successful career assured. Some apprentices fail to make the grade because their skills do not develop, or they have the wrong attitude towards training and practice. This is the less glamorous side of the game, and every boy who aims at becoming a footballer should also think of another profession in case he is unable to make the grade.

One thing is certain. If a young apprentice has the ability, then there is no doubt that he could command a regular place in our first team. Ian Allinson, and Steve Dowman, were both established first team players when they were eighteen years of age, and the club was pleased to offer professional contracts to Tony Evans, Russell Cotton and Geoff Harrop after serving their apprenticeships. Let's hope that they, and many more young players in the future will come through our youth policy and establish themselves as regular first team players.

The United Lottery
£1000 JACKPOT
THREE OF A KIND

13

A November 1983 Colchester programme report on young players by Roy Massey

FA CUP GAMES
Manager Massey sinks Lowestoft

Clacton Town 2   Lowestoft 1

TWO GOALS in the last quarter of an hour by Clacton player-manager Roy Massey gave the Town a thrilling victory in their FA Cup clash with Lowestoft at Old Road on Saturday.

It provided an exciting climax to what had been an entertaining, hard fought encounter that never wavered in interest.

stretched leg by goalkeeper Bob Catchpool prevented Barnard scoring, but Rudd was on hand to smartly hammer home. That goal came in the 59th minute.

Clacton immediately substituted Cooledge for Trovell and the move paid dividends. In the 75th minute Massey levelled from Robinson's headed flick.

Then, with a replay looking inevitable, Roy Massey struck again, via the prompting of Trovell's left wing cross and the assistance of Neil Partner.

Overall Clacton thoroughly merited this victory over tenacious opposition.

Roy Massey managed to score a number of goals when playing and managing in non-League football for Tiptree United and Clacton Town

Roy Massey was delighted when Liam Brady asked him in 1998 to work at the Arsenal academy. Arsenal 3-1 Manchester United, League Division One match at Highbury, Saturday, 1 April 1978; pictured: Liam Brady in action for Arsenal and Gordon McQueen of Man United.

Arsenal's Nigerian striker Alex Iwobi (C) runs with the ball chased by Crystal Palace's Senegalese midfielder Cheikhou Kouyate (L) and faced by Crystal Palace's English midfielder Andros Townsend (R) during the Premier League game at Selhurst Park on 28 October 2018.

In the Wings

*City's triumphant Under-14 Squad show off their winners medals! **Back row:** Sammy Morgan (Coach), Roy Massey (Asst. Coach), Ben Reakes, Michael Roberts, Matthew Joynson, Paul McKeaveney, Richard Kellett, Darrel Russell, Shaun Carr, Barrington Belgrave (who also won the 'golden boot' as the tournament's top scorer), Luke Williams, Albert Birbeck (physio). **Front row:** Michael Flynn, Paul Goreham, Ryan Green, Greg Oates, Clayden Cowell, Leon Jeane, Dean Scantlebury.*

MANCHESTER UNITED 0 NORWICH CITY 7 - No that's not a Canary fan's Fantasy League result! In fact, it's the scoreline from the Semi-Finals of a tournament for top professional clubs' under-14 schoolboy teams played in Sunderland last month.

And the potential City stars of tomorrow underlined their pedigree by beating Glasgow Celtic 4-0 in the Final the following day.

The prestigious five-day competition also involved Everton, Middlesbrough and Sunderland from England, and Scottish clubs Hearts and St. Johnstone.

City's talented teenagers actually swept to success with five straight wins. In their qualifying group games they beat St. Johnstone 2-1, Celtic 1-0 and Sunderland 5-2 before hitting the heights with their superb performances in the Semi-Final and Final.

Coach Sammy Morgan reflected: "The boys did very well. Their attitude, on and off the pitch, was just what we are looking for. It was nice to win, but that wasn't the main reason for going. The tournament is part and parcel of teaching the lads what is required if they want to become professionals.

"We had taken the group to Holland back in May for a week's training, including matches against Feyenoord, Den Bosch and Fortuna Sittard, and it was encouraging to see in Sunderland that lessons had been learned from the trip.

"It was also pleasing that we were able to give all 16 players who went to Sunderland a good run-out. They improved a lot during the week. At one stage in our game against Sunderland we were trailing 2-0, but the lads fought back well to win 5-2, and everything really gelled together from that stage onwards.

"There's enormous competition these days for the best schoolboys, so it must be reassuring to Norwich City to find their lads measure up so well against the boys at other leading clubs – and that's a feather in the cap of Roy Massey, who's been largely responsible for the scouting which has brought this group together," says Sammy.

TOURNAMENTS ABROAD

Youth Development Officer Gordon Bennett adds: "We think the boys benefit enormously from playing in tournaments like this against the best boys not only in

Britain but also from abroad."

During the recent summer holiday period, City's under-16's coached by Mike Sutton took part in the International Festival organised by the FA Premier League and Reebok at Keele University; while the under-15's with coach Colin Watts went to the Northern Ireland Milk Cup and played (a year out of their age-group) in the Sunderland under-16 professional club competition.

"All the boys will have gained invaluable experience and when, for instance, our under-16's can draw with Glasgow Rangers and Werder Bremen – recognised as standard-setters at schoolboy level across the continent – we know we must be working along the right lines," affirms Gordon.

MATCH NOTE: Under new FA regulations, professional clubs are this season allowed to run schoolboy teams on Sundays at all age-groups – and City have no less than SEVEN in action tomorrow: The under-15's and under-13's are at home to Cambridge United at the UEA Sports Ground (11am); the under-16's and under-14's visit Cambridge; and the under-12's, under-11's and under-10's all visit Nottingham Forest.

I worked for Norwich City from 1991 to 1998. It was an enjoyable time.

ACADEMY FOOTBALL ACADEMY

ACADEMY PROGRESS REPORT

NAME: BENIK AFOBE   AGE GROUP: U12   DATE: DEC '04.

Technical ability:

Benik possesses good individual skills. He receives the ball well and he is comfortable when in possession of the ball. His passing can sometimes be erratic, but he is working hard to develop skills on his left side.

Football Intelligence:

He is improving in this area of his game. He is a natural goalscorer, and some of his play is instinctive. However, he is starting to think about his game more, and realise the importance of his team mates.

Attitude:

I have always been impressed with his attitude. He has a most pleasant personality, and he loves training and playing, giving of his best at all times. He is always prepared to respond to a challenge.

Physical attributes:

Benik possesses very good physical attributes, displaying strength, pace and balance. He needs to continue working on his sharpness off the mark.

General comments:

Benik continues to make excellent progress and his contributions to the games programme have been first class. Always maintain your enthusiasm for the game Benik.
                                    well done!

Roy Massey   Assistant Academy Manager   Dec '04
signature   position   date

Roy Massey's assessment of Benik Afobe at U12 level

NAME: JACK WILSHERE AGE GROUP: U13 DATE: DEC '04

Technical ability:

Jack possesses excellent technical ability in the way he receives the ball particularly in tight situations. His dribbling and passing skills are good and he is comfortable when in possession of the ball

Football intelligence:

Although he occasionally tends to dribble when a pass might be a better option, Jack is a very intelligent young footballer. His awareness of his team mates and opponents is very good. I would now like to see him develop his long passing game

Attitude:

Jack is a very competitive young footballer, who never shirks a tackle or a challenge. As a result he occasionally gets in bother with the referee. However, I am pleased to see that of late, he is maturing his attitude; he doesn't retaliate, and gets on with his game

Physical attributes:

He is strong and tough with a great desire. These qualities will stand him in good stead for the future. He is not the biggest of players but neither is Jermain Defoe. He needs to work on his pace and running ability, and he needs to maintain his passion for the game.

General comments:

It was good to see Jack playing again after his operation just before Christmas. His contributions to the games programme have been very good, and I look forward to his continued development in the New Year.

Roy Massey   Assistant Academy Manager   Dec '04.

signature   position   date

Roy Massey's assessment of Jack Wilshere of the U13 squad

Jack Wilshere is now a youth team coach at Arsenal

St Albans, England: Bukayo Saka and Ainsley Maitland-Niles of Arsenal during a training session at London Colney on 29 January 2021

Roy Massey was delighted to receive a special present on his retirement from Arsenal in 2014.

Roy and Julia Massey

Chapter 16

A great start at Layer Road

COLCHESTER UNITED, nicknamed the U's, finished the 1968/69 season just outside the promotion places in the Fourth Division, which was won by Doncaster Rovers. Scoring goals was problematic with just 57 in 46 matches.

United were formed in 1937 after fans at the amateur Colchester Town decided to establish a professional outfit in order to enter the Southern League. In 1937/38, Colchester won the Southern League title in their first season, and followed a fine FA Cup run in 1947/48 – they reached the fifth round – by winning the title again in consecutive seasons, 1948/49 and 1949/50. They were then elected to the Football League, replacing New Brighton for the 1950/51 season.

The U's had spent 11 seasons in the Third Division South and Third Division, which was formed in 1958/59, before suffering relegation to the Fourth Division in 1960/1. Promotion was achieved the following season, only for the U's to be relegated in 1965, promoted again in 1966 and relegated again in 1968.

Christine and I quickly settled into a club house, recently vacated by John Martin who had moved to Workington Town, allocated to us in Layer Road, close to Colchester's stadium. This meant that, unlike at my two previous clubs where I did not live local to the grounds, I quickly got to know several Colchester fans and some of whom would come up, especially if we had won the previous Saturday, and chat about the matches. I enjoyed doing so.

I never got any stick from fans and, when Christine attended a match at Layer Road and heard two spectators criticising my performance and told them who she was, they were then good enough to not say anything more that she could hear.

At Millmoor, Brisbane Road and Layer Road, there were a smallish number of fans who turned up early and/or waited behind after the game to seek autographs from players. I was always delighted to be asked to sign an autograph book or a programme. All three clubs had fans who went to as many games as possible and could be heard at away grounds encouraging the players who were representing their club.

We liked Colchester, which is a historic Essex market town. It has a strong claim to be Britain's oldest recorded town as it was the capital of Roman Britain. Being relatively close to London, even in the mid-1960s people would commute to the capital for work. Colchester Castle is the main landmark. It was built in the 11th century on top of the vaults of the old Roman temple. Colchester was a centre of the woollen cloth industry for much of its early existence.

Colchester has been an important military base since the Roman era, and its garrison trained several battalions during the First World War. The garrison has been the base for the Parachute Regiment for many years. Colchester United would use its fields for training.

I debuted for Colchester in the 2-0 pre-season friendly victory against Israeli champions Hapoel Tel Aviv, who showed plenty of skill but no goal threat. A 2,000-plus crowd watched the action.

Layer Road, where Colchester Town first played in 1909, consisted of a main stand, built originally in 1933 and improved when Football League status was achieved. The stand was mainly wooden. There were seats in the centre with standing on the wings. To the right was the Layer Road wooden covered terrace, which it was said had been constructed by Second World War prisoners of war. The roof was very low while the gap between the front of the stand and the pitch was so low that the back of goal nets cut into the stand.

Opposite the main stand was the 'popular side', a terrace with a small rusty roof covering part of it. The left side of this terrace, much of which was uneven, was open to the elements. To the main stand's left was an open bank with a clock, giving this badly maintained terrace its obvious name, the Clock End. Layer Road was a small, ordinary arena. An average of 6,273 fans had attended each home game in the 1968/69 season.

I made my Colchester league debut at number eight on the opening day of the season, 9 August 1969, away to Lincoln City in a 3-3 draw. The line-up was:

Graham Smith, Bert Howe, Brian Hall, Roger Joslyn, Bobby Howlett, Micky Brown, Steve Pitt, Roy Massey, Danny Light, Brian Gibbs, Ray Whittaker. Sub: Jim Oliver.

The Lincoln side contained, at number three, Graham Taylor (more of him later) who went on to manage England. Their number five was Ray Harford, who rescued a point for the Sincil Bank side when he netted in the 80th minute after I had put Colchester ahead five minutes earlier with a powerful drive past the advancing Colin Withers, the former Birmingham City keeper.

We had suffered a shock when the Imps had scored twice, both through Rod Fletcher, around the 20th minute. Skipper Brian Gibbs put us level within ten minutes; his first of two headers was a great diving effort.

Gibbs had signed from Gillingham, where the previous season he had finished as top scorer for a fifth consecutive year. He made over 170 appearances for Colchester, netting 41 goals, including one in the pre-season Watney Cup, held between the top-two-scoring teams in each of the four divisions the previous season. Colchester famously won it at the start of 1971/72.

I later met up with Ray Harford when Bobby Roberts invited him to be his assistant at Colchester.

At that time, many Colchester first-team games took place on Friday evenings as floodlight matches had proved more attractive for the fans. On Saturday afternoons, Roy would watch the reserves, who played in the Eastern Counties League. For away games, this would mean travelling to places such as Soham, Chatteris, Wisbech and Stowmarket. Bobby Hunt managed the reserves and Ray enjoyed contributing to the team talks. I also enjoyed watching the reserves as several youngsters would be selected to play.

On one occasion at the start of a new season, I was on the reserve-team coach going to Soham and sitting next to Ray. He told me that while abroad on his summer holiday, he was staying at the same hotel as Ron Atkinson, the Manchester United manager, who asked him about his Colchester role. Ray said that the first-team games were on Friday evenings and so he went to watch the reserves on Saturdays.

Ray was told that if he wanted to progress in the game, he should go to First or Second Division games on Saturdays and get a ticket for the directors' box, thus making himself known. 'Who is going to know Ray Harford at Thetford or Newmarket FC?' said Ron.

Ray took this advice seriously and throughout the following season we rarely saw him at reserve games. By the end of the campaign, Ray had gone to Fulham as their first-team coach. As the Cottagers were short of money, he had a difficult time and lost his job following relegation to the third tier in 1985/86.

Ray was then appointed as manager at Luton Town in June 1987 and within a season he took the Hatters to their greatest success, coming from a goal down to beat Arsenal 3-2 at Wembley in the 1988 League Cup Final. Luton returned to Wembley for the following season's final but were beaten 3-1 by Nottingham Forest, the European Cup winners of 1979 and 1980.

Ray became manager at Wimbledon before Kenny Dalglish invited him to be his assistant at Blackburn Rovers, who went on to win the 1994/95 Premier League title. When Dalglish departed, Ray took his place. Ray later went on to manage West Bromwich Albion and Queens Park Rangers and was on the coaching staff at Millwall when he died suddenly in 2003.

Ray was a top-class coach and he had a wonderful career. He was great company and it was a sad day when I learned that he had passed away after a short illness.

I netted again in my second U's appearance as we drew 1-1 in the first round of the League Cup at home to Reading, managed by Jack Mansell, back home from the United States. We did well to earn a draw after our keeper Ron Willis had to leave the field in the 24th minute with a cut eye, Brian Gibbs going in goal until the 85th minute before Bobby Howlett took over for the final five minutes. Willis had been accidentally struck by the boot of my former Rotherham colleague Les Chappell and the damage to his eye duct meant he required an operation and would be missing for a while. The draw for the next round meant that a replay victory would give us a big tie against nearby First Division side Ipswich Town.

Our first victory of the season came when we beat Wrexham 2-0, with Ray Whittaker and Gibbs scoring. Despite this loss, the North Wales side went on to gain promotion with their outside-left Albert Kinsey ending up as the Football League's top scorer with 27 goals.

A first professional hat-trick

The fourth match of the 1969/70 season was the replay at Reading. It will live in my memory forever as my favourite game as a professional footballer because I scored all three goals – in the 43rd, 72nd and 83rd minutes. Reading goalkeeper Roy Brown did well to stop a Micky Brown effort at 2-0 but when the ball ran loose, I was delighted to knock home the rebound and record a hat-trick. The pick of the bunch was the second, a splendid diving header past Brown.

I did not see Mansell, who had actually congratulated me on my performance after the first game. But no way was he going to shake my hand as he would have been gutted that one of his old players had come back to put one over him. How often does that happen in football? My hat-trick was the first by a Colchester player for nearly a decade.

I then scored again as a point was earned in a hard-fought draw at Notts County whose side contained Don Masson, who had chosen to drop down two divisions from Middlesbrough to join a team struggling at the bottom end of the Fourth Division. He is arguably County's best player ever, his vision and skill in midfield helping take his side to promotion twice in six seasons before he cost top-flight QPR a £100,000 fee in December 1974. Rangers finished as First Division runners-up in 1975/76. A good goalscorer from midfield, Masson returned to Meadow Lane in August 1978 and as captain he took the Magpies into the top flight. He possessed a defence-splitting pass and he played 17 times for Scotland.

Playing away to Ipswich in the League Cup, we were watched by 19,012 including many U's fans who returned home disappointed as the home side were much too good for us and we lost 4-0. Consolation of a sort was that the three League Cup ties had attracted a combined total 35,200 fans, meaning the club would collect £2,500 in receipts.

I scored twice at Feethams, a ground now long gone, but as Darlington scored three we made the long journey home disappointed. I was able to beat debutant David Crampton with a 25-yard drive on 80 minutes to reduce the arrears to 3-2 but we could not force a leveller. The opening Darlington goal came from Terry Melling, whose penalty was fiercely disputed by many U's players.

I was also on the scoresheet in the following match as Colchester beat Crewe Alexandra 1-0 before a 5,084 crowd. I might have scored more as I missed a few chances. The 69th-minute goal came following a fine Jim Oliver run and I got on the blind side of Eric Barnes to flick the ball beyond Alex keeper Ernie Adams. It was my ninth goal of the season. Adams, who was returning to Layer Road after departing in the summer after two seasons with the U's, had a good game.

I continued my scoring run by netting the equaliser at Oldham before Brown scored the winner. The Oldham manager was Jack Rowley who, during a long career with Manchester United before and after the war, scored over 200 goals. He won the league title in 1951/52 and he scored twice in the 1948 FA Cup Final as Blackpool were beaten 4-2 in one of the finest matches ever at Wembley.

After failing to score away to Hartlepool at the dilapidated Victoria Ground in a goalless draw, I made it 11 from 13 matches in a 1-1 draw at home to Swansea City. The number seven for the Swans was Welsh international Len Allchurch. *Match of the Day* that evening showed that I was the top scorer in all four divisions. I had a brief taste of celebrity status and thought my career might finally be about to take off.

We had earned 13 points from the first ten league fixtures. It was a decent start but in the following two games, against Scunthorpe United and Newport County, we left the field without a point having lost 2-0 and 4-1 respectively. At Newport's Somerton Park, which no longer exists, we played horribly to be 4-0 down after 35 minutes and even a late effort by Ray Whittaker, a Fourth Division winner with Luton in 1967/68, failed to calm down our manager afterwards. We ended the match with ten men as I had to limp off on 70 minutes. As Steve Pitt had earlier replaced Brian Wood, then we had no replacement in an era of just one substitute. Brian later went into business with Dick Graham, when the pair worked at an Ipswich sports centre.

I missed playing at Wrexham where Micky Cook came on as a substitute to make his Colchester debut. Micky, just 18, was released by Orient in the spring of 1969 but after a successful Layer Road trial he was given a professional contract by his former boss. Micky established himself at right-back as the 1969/70 season progressed and he went on to become a U's legend with almost 700 appearances before becoming the club's youth-team manager

I returned to the side for the fixture at the weekend but, after 30 minutes, I was again forced to leave the field injured. I felt a pain at the top of my foot as I landed in a game that Colchester won 2-1 against a poor Bradford Park Avenue side who were voted out of the Football League at the end of the season. Taking my place on the field was Terry Dyson, one of the smallest players I played with. Terry was part of Spurs' Double-winning side of 1960/61 and he scored twice in the 5-1 European Cup Winners' Cup Final victory against Atlético Madrid in 1963 as an English side won a European trophy for the first time.

I couldn't play in the following four league matches, which brought a return of just a point. I did play at Somerton Park in the FA Cup first round but I had to again leave the field at the start of the second period. Jeff Thomas struck the winner for Newport, whose team included Ronnie Radford, who two seasons later struck home that marvellous goal against Newcastle United as non-league Hereford United knocked the First Division side out of the famous competition. The goal still features regularly on television.

I was forced to rest but after doing so until the new year I found myself still facing injury problems. Meanwhile, Christine had given birth to a little boy, Paul. While it meant I could see more of Paul and support Christine, it was a frustrating time.

I had my foot X-rayed. I thought it might be a fracture of my metatarsal but nothing showed up and I was told to rest.

I returned at Swansea City in January 1970 but it was clearly too soon and I was forced off on 25 minutes. Swansea won 1-0 in a game where the former West Bromwich Albion player Bobby Cram, the uncle of athlete Steve Cram, debuted at left-back for Colchester. Bobby, signed from Vancouver Royals, became team captain as he was the most experienced player at Colchester and had previously been an established top-flight player.

Like Harry Kane, he rarely missed a penalty. Bobby and I got on well together and he often asked how I was getting on during the times I was injured.

When I had another X-ray, it showed that I had a fractured metatarsal that had not previously shown up. I was forced to rest for another month.

Nearly two months later I came on as a late second-half substitute in a 2-1 defeat away to Exeter City before playing the next three games without scoring. My season then ended on Good Friday in a 3-1 victory at home to Aldershot when I left the field on 85 minutes. Ken Jones, signed from Millwall for £5,000 in November 1969, scored twice for the U's and he ended the season with 16 goals. This was two more than Brian Gibbs.

It was a season that had started so brightly for me with 11 goals by 27 September 1969 but thereafter I struggled with my fitness. I faced a tough battle to get fit as did Bobby Howlett, who suffered a broken leg against Brentford in April 1970. Bobby worked hard to return to match fitness and eventually turned out for Colchester reserves in September 1971. Unable to make a full recovery, he was released at the end of the 1971/72 season. Micky Brown had also suffered a bad injury at the end of 1969/70, so was unable to play again the following season and later left to play in non-league. Football can be a cruel business.

* * *

I was first aware of Graham Taylor when he played full-back for Lincolnshire Grammar Schools against Yorkshire Grammar Schools. Although I was attending a technical school, it came under the auspices of grammar schools and so I was eligible to play for Yorkshire and England Grammar Schools.

Before playing for Lincoln City, Graham played for Grimsby Town. This was ironic as he supported another local side, Scunthorpe United.

I waited to take my FA full badge coaching award until 1971, the year when I realised my playing career was at an end at just 28 years old. The course was held across two weeks at Lilleshall. Graham Smith, a friend and Colchester team-mate, attended with me. Graham Taylor was slightly younger than me and he was the course tutor.

Like Howard Wilkinson, Graham obtained his full badge certificate at 21. Both men had realised at a very early age that their playing careers could not go on forever. If they wanted to stay in football at a high level, then they would need to become excellent coaches by acquiring a vast knowledge of the game.

The pair had played professionally but not at the highest levels and it is not generally the case that players with outstanding ability go on to be successful managers. Examples include Sir Bobby Charlton who managed only briefly at Preston North End. This is probably the same in most sports. Players of natural talent, although having to work hard for their success, produce their skills without thinking too much about how they do it. The so-called 'bread and butter' player has to work hard in skill practice while also improving his football intelligence. This gives him an insight when it later comes to helping other players develop their game.

Later, while coaching at Colchester in a part-time capacity, I helped out with the first team at training. In 1989, Jock Wallace, who was a great manager for Leicester City, was appointed to help Colchester climb out of the Fourth Division relegation zone and avoid dropping out of the Football League. Jock appointed Alan Ball as his coach. An England World Cup 1966 winner, Alan was a wonderful footballer who also won the league title with Everton in 1970. Alan played with and against the best players in the world. He was a very friendly person and he invited me to help him with a coaching session. His topic was getting full-backs overlapping and putting in crosses that his two strikers at the near and far post could attack.

The full-backs concerned did not have the techniques to regularly deliver accurate crosses; most of the balls ended up short of the near post or way beyond the far post. Alan was clearly very frustrated as he was used to dealing with top-class players. He did not expect to go back to basics to coach players how to deliver good crosses. Alan was still fuming when he went into the dressing room afterwards, and, throwing his boots on the floor, he told us about the inadequacies of the players.

To be fair to the defenders, the training pitches were played on regularly and they were well worn with bumpy surfaces. They were entirely different from the prestige training pitches that the modern-day professional trains on and that includes the players at Colchester. Alan went on to manage several sides at various levels, experiencing the joy of promotion and headache of relegation with Portsmouth, relegation to the Third Division with Stoke City and finally, relegation from the Premier League with Manchester City.

After Graham Taylor, who had Alan as his coach for six months during his time as England manager in the early 1990s, had given me my pass for my coaching award, I saw him subsequently several years later when he was the Watford manager. In 1972 he started his managerial career at Lincoln City, where he had made over 150 first-team appearances. Four years later he took the Imps to the Fourth Division title. In 1997, he then joined Elton John at Watford – where the singer was the owner – from 1976 to 1987, and later returned for a second spell from 1997 to 2001. During the 1970s and 1980s, I was teaching and enjoying coaching the youngsters at Colchester, whose youth team played Watford away in the Southern Junior Floodlit Cup. Watford were in the top flight of English football as, thanks to Graham's guidance, they had moved up three divisions from the Fourth Division between 1977/78 and 1982/83.

Colchester were in the Fourth Division and clearly it was going to be a tough test for the youth players. We were all surprised and delighted that with ten minutes remaining at Vicarage Road we led 3-1. However, the Watford boys continued to press and scored two late goals, so a replay at Layer Road would decide the tie.

Graham came into our dressing room afterwards to congratulate our players. He invited me into his office for a cup of tea. He was disappointed at the result, but he told me that when he was looking at his youth matches, he sought to see which team had the best player on the pitch rather than which team had won the game. He knew in reality that few of the youth players would go on to play in the first team and so he recognised that it was likely to be the best players who would have the best chance of doing so. We lost the replay 3-0.

Under Graham's leadership, Watford were First Division runners-up in 1982/83 and FA Cup finalists in 1984. He took over at Aston Villa in 1987, leading the club to promotion in 1988 and finishing as runners-up in the First Division in 1989/90. He then took over the England team.

Many years later when I was working at the Arsenal, I was coaching our under-12 squad in the sports hall adjoining Highbury stadium. Above the hall was a banqueting suite and the FA had booked it for a meeting.

I was part of the way through my coaching when a friendly face appeared at the window looking into the sports hall. It was Graham, who by now was back managing Watford between 1997 and 2001. He opened the door and walked over to me shaking my hand and wishing me all the best in my job.

I quickly took the opportunity to ask him if he would say a few words to the boys, who were naturally thrilled to personally meet the ex-England boss. He had a joke with them and then said the only way to success was to be enthusiastic for the game, work hard and have a positive attitude. For a former England manager to come into the sports hall and have a joke and talk to the boys speaks volumes for the character of Graham, who sadly died in 2017.

Chapter 17

Forced to retire as Colchester beat Don Revie's Boys

OVER THE summer of 1970 I worked hard. When the new season began, I felt in good shape as I had experienced no foot problems. I had agreed, thanks to Reg Hayes, the local schools PE organiser, to teach, after training had finished, three afternoons of PE each week at a local school. I was really looking forward to the future. I knew I might not get straight back into the team as Dick Graham had signed the experienced Ipswich Town and England striker Ray Crawford, a 1961/62 First Division title winner under Alf Ramsey.

I was substitute for most pre-season games, but I played well enough in the reserves to earn a chance in the first team. I returned in the second match, a 5-0 League Cup first-round thrashing of new boys Cambridge United, who had been elected to the league to replace Bradford Park Avenue.

I then made two further substitute appearances before taking my place at number 11 in a 2-0 victory in the evening match at Barrow at Holker Street with Crawford netting the second before a crowd of just 2,442. It was a happy party that took the overnight train back to London after the game.

Late in September I was back in Cumbria and came on as a second-half substitute in a 1-1 draw at Workington before a crowd of 2,350. John Gilchrist, signed from Fulham in the summer, played at number nine.

On 3 October 1970, Colchester made the short trip to Peterborough United and, with the game at 1-1, I scored the winner on 88 minutes. Dick had swapped me to play number nine, with Gilchrist switching to outside-left. With the match drifting towards a draw, I hit a rocket beyond keeper Mick Drewery. I was swamped by my team-mates as we celebrated a dramatic winner; it was one of the best goals I ever scored. I had been out for so long, it was not surprising that my first goal in over a year left me delighted. I was always very happy when I scored but that goal was extra special.

The previous U's game had seen Crawford score all of Colchester's goals in a 3-0 success against Crewe Alexandra and he was to go on to score 31 times in all competitions that season.

Following the goal against the Posh, I played against Oldham at home but again left the field early. In four days at the start of November I was delighted to score in a 2-2 draw against Exeter City away and then net two at Newport County in a 3-1 win before a Tuesday evening crowd of only 1,973. I had laid on the first for Ken Jones on 28 minutes, and seven minutes later I put us back ahead after amateur Rod Jones had equalised, finishing from close in after winger Mick Mahon's effort was blocked. I doubled our lead with 55 minutes gone with a diving header. We were moving up the table with Dick saying afterwards, 'We love to play fluid, fast-moving football and I'm delighted with tonight's performance.'

What happened next

I played in the home game against Brentford on 28 November 1970. The game's highlights were televised on the following day for *East Anglia Sport* as the match of the week.

One incident has been shown on the TV quiz show *Question of Sport* under the 'What Happened Next?' round. A dog jumped over the wall and ran on to the pitch. The Brentford defender in possession of the ball played it back to his goalkeeper, Chic Brodie. The dog chased after the ball and, as the goalkeeper bent down on one knee to scoop it safely into his hands, the dog pounced and jumped straight into Chic, knocking him to the ground. The crowd cheered and hooted with laughter but it soon dawned on us that Chic was seriously injured. He had to be carried off on a stretcher with ligament damage. The injury affected his career and he had to retire early from the game. Chic later said, 'The dog may have been small, but it just happened to be solid.'

Modern technology is a wonder. Over 40 years later I was telling the story to a young Arsenal coach, Greg Lincoln. We were travelling home from a tournament in Spain. He typed into his mobile phone 'Colchester versus Brentford 1970' and we watched the dog incident. At least he could see that I wasn't pulling his leg.

I was playing well for Colchester and getting back to enjoying my games. We had played a village team called Ringmer, of the Sussex County League, in the first round of the FA Cup. Crawford again scored a hat-trick in a 3-0 win and in the second round we were drawn away to Cambridge, but before then we faced them away in the league. Although I managed to play the whole game, my knee again started troubling me. My appearance took my overall Colchester career statistics up to 41 matches, 35 starts, with 15 goals, four in the 1970/71 season.

I felt quite dejected and I once again found myself visiting a knee specialist at the Colchester hospital. The medial cartilage had been taken out in the previous two operations but now a bursa had developed on the lateral cartilage. This required another operation. In the first week of 1971 I was in a hospital bed, and my wife Christine was due to give birth to our second child. If it was a girl, we had decided to call her Justine.

Before I went down to the theatre, the nurse came up to my bed and said that my son had been born. Another boy, I thought, and then the needle was put in my vein and I was off to sleep. When I came round after my operation my dad was sitting at the bedside. 'Another boy then,' I said. 'What do you mean?' said Dad. 'You have a baby girl called Justine.' I can only assume that my mum who rang the hospital said that Justine was born and the nurse heard the name 'Justin'.

With Brian Owen also unlikely to play for a long time, Dick Graham signed midfielder Brian Lewis and forward Dave Simmons from Oxford United and Aston Villa respectively.

While I was in hospital, Colchester played non-league Barnet away in the third round of the FA Cup. I listened on the radio and we won 1-0 thanks to an effort by Mahon. Away to Rochdale, then in the Third Division, was the next step in the fourth round. The game was moved to the Wednesday, after it was postponed.

The tie ended in a 3-3 draw. The build-up to the replay was very exciting as the winners knew they would face Leeds United in the fifth round. I was pleased for all my team-mates when they beat Rochdale 5-0.

But there was also sadness in my heart. Not only was I not fit to play in this game but the specialist had informed me my right knee was in a terrible mess – the official diagnosis was an arthritic condition – and he advised me to stop playing as my knee would otherwise give me problems in later life. This was bittersweet advice.

I was 27 years old, with a wife and two children and a football career that was going nowhere. I was gutted not to play again, but in my heart of hearts I knew that my knee was never going to get any stronger to withstand the rigours of the professional game.

I was aware that unlike many footballers I had a good option to fall back on in teaching for a living. I was glad now that I had turned down the chance as a young man to sign for, among others, Aston Villa and Arsenal, in order to undertake my PE certificate. I could find alternative work that I enjoyed and I might still be able to enjoy playing football at a lower level.

When Dick read the specialist report, which stated that my problem was due to a degeneration of the knee due to my first injury years earlier in the Netherlands, he advised the Colchester United chairman not to send the report to the Football League because the degeneration of the knee would be a sticking point when it came to compensation. He had, however, already sent it and the club lost all rights to compensation. This was a blow to Colchester's coffers.

However, the FA Cup tie against Leeds, the First Division champions in 1968/69, was to provide much-needed financial security for the club. Leeds had lost in the previous season's final when, after drawing 2-2 at Wembley, they were beaten 2-1 by Chelsea in the replay at Old Trafford. Mick Jones, Leeds' number nine, scored in both games. He had a brilliant career with the club and played three times, twice when at Sheffield United, for England. I felt my own game resembled that of Mick's and without the fateful incident in the Netherlands in 1965 and the subsequent misdiagnoses, then who knows what I might have achieved as a player?

Leeds had never won the famous trophy and they would have to wait until 1972 to do so, when Jones created an opening for his forward colleague Allan Clarke to score the only goal in the final against Arsenal.

I had never seen such pre-match queues outside Layer Road. The ground was full to capacity. The *Match of the Day* cameras were present but no Colchester supporter could dare to dream that their tiny club could win this game.

At the end of 90 minutes, one of the greatest upsets in FA Cup history had happened; Colchester won 3-2. Crawford scored two goals and newly arrived Dave Simmons the third, giving Colchester at one time a 3-0 lead.

Leeds rallied and scored two late goals through Norman Hunter and John Giles; then in the last five minutes our goalkeeper

Graham Smith made a brilliant save from Giles. The final few minutes seemed a lifetime for the Colchester supporters. Then the whistle went for full time. What a wonderful achievement. Six of the 11 players who played on the day have sadly passed away at the time of writing, but they will always be remembered in the proud history of the U's, as all the players in the game will be. Victory took Colchester into the quarter-finals of the FA Cup for the first time in their history.

Smith had joined Colchester just before pre-season started in 1969. We had much in common in that he had studied to be a PE teacher at Loughborough, the top PE college in those days, and I had studied the same subject in Cheltenham. The other coincidence was that both our wives, Christine and Janet, lived in Doncaster before jet-setting over the country with their Fourth Division professional footballer husbands. Graham was at Notts County before he arrived at Colchester. As a qualified teacher like me, Graham taught at the local schools in the afternoons after training, and he was also on that Lilleshall coaching course tutored by Graham Taylor.

Smith left Layer Road to sign for West Bromwich Albion at the start of the 1972/73 season and at the end of it he moved on to play for Ron Atkinson at Cambridge between 1973 and 1976.

In 1975, Graham told me an unbelievable story, which changed his life from being a professional footballer into a major sales representative for Adidas. In the 1970s, Adidas was famous for its football boots with three stripes on each side of the boot. When Graham had arrived home the previous Sunday, he had a message from John Boulter, his neighbour during his time at Colchester. John was a former international athlete who competed at the highest level in the 800m. He had joined Adidas, an organisation with a fascinating history, where he later helped form the international relations team, which became very powerful across all levels of sport, especially at Olympic standard.

The message for Graham was that a flight to Brussels had been booked for him the following day. He caught this flight and was then collected at the airport and taken to meet representatives of Adidas who had a proposal for him. Boulter had recommended Graham to introduce Adidas's new football shirts with the three stripes down the sleeve to the top clubs in the First Division. Adidas, which first sprung to prominence when Jesse Owens won four Olympic gold medals wearing its spiked shoes in Berlin in 1936, wanted to be associated with winners.

At the end of the season, Graham stopped being a professional footballer and began working full-time for Adidas. He did this job for many years and was highly successful in persuading, among others, Liverpool, Manchester United and Nottingham Forest to wear the famous Adidas shirts. Thanks to Graham, Adidas was to be at the forefront of an increasingly competitive market.

The following Monday after the Leeds match, everybody was waiting for the quarter-final draw, which pitched Colchester away to play league champions Everton. By winning the title in 1970, Everton had won it seven times, level with Liverpool, Arsenal and Manchester United.

I could not feel the pleasure and excitement of the other players and Dick had some sympathy for me. He promised me a testimonial match. He also said that if I could get a job as a PE teacher locally, he would give me the opportunity (which he subsequently did and I accepted) on a part-time basis to rebuild the youth facilities at the club. He knew that I had watched the youth team play on Saturday mornings in the South East Counties League in the 1969/70 season, when the U's had closed down the team until restarting it in 1973.

So, unfortunately, when I did take over the running of the youth team later that year, Colchester had abandoned the youth development programme and I had to start from scratch. Initially I arranged for the few apprentices to play for Tiptree United in the

Essex Senior League and the under-16 side to play friendlies on Saturday mornings.

Dick asked me to go to Goodison Park and scout on the Everton team. I witnessed the derby with Liverpool one cold Saturday in February. As I collected my ticket, I felt very privileged as it was for the directors' box. The commissionaire took me up the lift to the guest room. There was a wonderful array of sandwiches and cakes and, as I sat down to watch the game, I could feel warm air coming up from under the seat in order to keep the guests warm during the winter matches. 'How the other half lives,' I thought.

I studied the match and the Everton team, who drew 0-0 with their rivals. Liverpool included two players whose moves into professional football were, like myself, delayed by completing their studies.

They were Brian Hall and Steve Heighway, who almost a year earlier had signed from non-league Skelmersdale United as an amateur for Bill Shankly's side. This enabled Heighway to finish the season at Skelmersdale and also complete his Economics and Politics degree before signing as a professional for Liverpool in May 1970. Heighway played at number nine against Everton and at number 11 was Hall, who had arrived in Liverpool from Scotland to study Mathematics and who, after graduating three years later, signed for the Anfield club. The pair thus had very different backgrounds from the vast majority of professional footballers. Both men, especially Heighway, enjoyed great success. In the 1970s, Steve Coppell also completed a degree in Economics at Liverpool University but did the course while playing for Manchester United.

I spent the following day writing a match report and drawing diagrams of the Everton team's free kicks and corners, plus indicating each player's strengths and weaknesses.

On the day of the game, the players gathered in their hotel for a team meeting before travelling to Goodison Park. Dick told the players that I had written what was the best and most detailed report he had ever received. He went through it with the players who then boarded the bus to take them to Goodison Park for a game that featured on *Match of the Day*.

Colchester lost 5-0 with two goals coming from Howard Kendall, who when he played for Preston North End at the 1964 FA Cup Final was the youngest-ever player in a Wembley final. The other scorers were Alan Ball, Jimmy Husband and a young Joe Royle, who had a great match. When I saw Dick in his office the following Monday, he grinned and told me my report was the last I would ever give him. The pain of defeat was lessened by the share of the gate receipts from a 53,028 crowd.

Hampered by a fixture backlog caused by the FA Cup run, Colchester ended the season in sixth, two points behind fourth-placed York City. Three consecutive defeats in mid-April proved just too much; sixth place would today be good enough to reach the play-offs but they did not exist in 1971. The average league gate was 5,603.

With Tony Hateley, a great header of the ball and a prolific scorer of goals at all levels, having joined Don Masson for a second spell at Notts County, the Magpies won the title. But Bournemouth had the player of the season in Ted MacDougall, who hit a remarkable 42 league goals. Ted later finished as the First Division's top scorer, with Norwich in 1975/76, scoring 23 goals. Ted netted nine against Margate for Bournemouth in the FA Cup in November 1971, the record by any player in the FA Cup proper.

My testimonial match was on Monday, 8 November 1971 against First Division neighbours Ipswich Town, who paid me the compliment of fielding their strongest team. With Brian Lewis in great form, his goals helped Colchester win 5-2. I watched that match from the directors' box saying afterwards that while I had been tempted to play, 'I felt it was such a good one that I think I might have spoiled it.' I was grateful to everyone who worked so hard to put on the game, to Ipswich for playing for free and to Bobby Robson, who when I rang him about sending a team had responded immediately by saying, 'We will be delighted to play in your testimonial', for bringing a strong side.

I was absolutely delighted with the crowd figure of 4,900 especially as I had only played a small number of matches for Colchester. U's fans were great to me.

The receipts generated from the event were over £1,000. Christine and I had been required to vacate our club house and the cash meant we could improve our new home in Great Horkesley.

Ken Runicles of the *Essex County Standard* said I was 'surely the unluckiest man ever on the club's books, whose injury-troubled career was brought to a sad end earlier this year'.

While I was grateful for those kind words, I didn't feel that I had nothing to be thankful for. I had a wife and two young children and I could look forward to my new role as PE master at Gilberd School, plus managing at Tiptree United, where I was training and running the team, and my job at Layer Road with the schoolboys. It meant I still had my finger in three footballing pies. I told Ken, 'I am pretty busy as you can see. But I am enjoying it.'

* * *

There were no uniform kits when football first started in the middle of the 19th century. But once the FA Cup kicked off in 1871/72, it was soon clear that a solution was required to the difficulty of telling two teams apart. As plain white shirts were cheap and freely available they proved popular, but teams also began to adopt their own colours for what were known as jerseys, a close-fitting knitted garment with no collar.

In 1879, Bukta became the first UK sportswear manufacturer. Around 1883, vertical stripes began to appear, becoming synonymous with football. Then came quarters, where the main body of strips, a term first used in the 1880s, was made from four separate panels. The halved shirts worn by Blackburn Rovers became famous. Some strips at county or international levels often had the appropriate badge sewn into the jerseys. There were a series of exotic shirt colours. Bukta's domination as a kit supplier was threatened in 1920 by a company that later became better known as Umbro in 1924.

There were several kit design innovations in the 1930s, with Everton adding a stripe to their shorts. The laced crew neck began to be replaced in favour of collared shirts with a short fly.

In 1953, Bolton Wanderers played in an artificial fabric material at the FA Cup Final. When England were heavily beaten twice by Hungary in 1953/54, it did not go unnoticed that the Mighty Magyars had worn a streamlined kit, and in November 1954 a newly designed 'continental-style' kit was worn by England for the first time. By 1957, virtually every English and Scottish team was wearing the new-look strips, the only difference being that teams north of the border often retained long-sleeved versions.

In the period in which I played there was a return to plain kits and this was because they looked better under floodlights. Leeds dropped their traditional colours for white shirts and shorts.

It was in the 1970s before clubs began to individually assert their identities again. In 1973, Don Revie led a revolution in kit design when he teamed up with Admiral so that the Leeds kit could be copyrighted, with replicas sold to the general public. The Elland Road side introduced a change kit of all yellow with a blue and white trim which they wore at all away games even if their white strip did not clash with their opponents'. The term 'change kit' became replaced with 'away kit' and is now universal.

Admiral targeted the top clubs and Manchester United switched to them in 1975, a year in which West Ham unveiled their new Admiral kit at the FA Cup Final against Fulham. Four years later, Liverpool became the first team in the Football League to carry a sponsor's name on their shirts but it took another four years before TV broadcasters relented to allow sponsored shirts to be shown. The design revolution was by then in full flow.

Chapter 18

A full-time PE teacher

IN THE summer school term of 1971, I found work as a part-time teacher working alongside Graham Smith at Colchester High School. I had unsuccessfully applied for PE jobs in South Yorkshire as Christine and I felt it was time to move back home to share life with family and friends.

No interviews came my way.

A knock on the door changed all thoughts of returning north. Reg Hayes knew me well through my school work and informed me that the headteacher Bill Glazier at Gilberd School needed a PE teacher in September. Four hours later I was sitting opposite Bill discussing my new appointment. I was taken to meet the PE head and could not believe it when it proved to be John McAleavy, who had been a student at St Paul's College at the same time as me in the early 1960s. Bristol-born John loved his rugby union. We got on very well together and he played a major part in my teaching career some years later.

The very next day I was speaking to Dick Graham and true to his word he gave me the post of running the Colchester United youth policy, which I accepted.

The following week I was approached and accepted the offer by Tiptree United secretary Ron Bearman to be the boss of the Essex Senior League side.

It was going to be a very busy time, especially as we had a young family, but I was looking forward to the challenges and over the next two years I learned a lot.

Nevertheless, the pull of going back north remained strong and I restarted looking at PE department head roles in the South Yorkshire area. Once again, though, my applications did not get me any interviews.

In September 1973 I received a telephone call from the secretary of Stanway School, a comprehensive on the outskirts of Colchester. Would I be interested in applying for the head of PE there? I was delighted to do so and was overjoyed when I was offered the job after an interview. I accepted and only later realised that there was no chance of returning to Yorkshire.

We bought a house in Stanway so that I could be near work, and I stayed in the role for over 13 years.

I enjoyed the teaching. Stanway had extensive playing fields where the pupils enjoyed football, rugby and hockey. It was the first school regionally to have an indoor sports hall. The gymnasium and PE staffroom was just down the corridor from the stage and main hall.

Two 15-year-olds had started a rock band and the headmaster had given them permission to practise on the stage after school. I often walked by while they worked together. My thoughts were that they were good lads and they enjoyed the music but I couldn't see them getting any further than playing in the school concert. The two boys, Damon Albarn and Graham Coxon, went on to form Blur, one of the greatest bands of their generation. This lack of ability to identify young talent was to come up on several occasions with me.

While I was working at Stanway School in 1977, Christine gave birth to our third child, Richard.

Later a post came up for head of PE at Thomas Lord Audley School, another comprehensive in Colchester. I applied and I was delighted to be appointed in September 1987.

The school was known as quite tough, and many pupils came from difficult backgrounds. This again was a great experience for me. I soon realised that the common element to helping youngsters reach their full potential was to build good relationships with them, and that comes from having a genuine interest in them as individuals.

In PE, teaching football and other sports within the curriculum means that interesting and challenging practices are essential in order for youngsters to be stimulated to achieve a high level.

On my first day at Thomas Lord Audley, I was teaching football to a class of year nine boys. I had a well-prepared lesson and was keen to make a good impression. The lesson was going well but as I stopped it to make a coaching point, I saw a young man on a motorbike riding towards us. I told the boys to stand still and as the motorbike came towards me, I put my hand up in a sign for it to stop. The bike slowed down and I thought this was a chance for me to show some strength and authority in front of the pupils. The motorcyclist came within a few metres and just as I was about to give him a piece of my mind, he put two fingers up to me, told me to 'f*** off' and sped past me. Before I could open my mouth, he rode off into the distance going through a gap in the fence. The boys fell about laughing and that was the end of my football lesson.

I was later taking a volleyball lesson with some year 11 students, among whom were two whose behaviour disrupted the lesson. At the end of the session, I told the pair to wait outside my office. I was fuming and had made up my mind to give them a right dressing-down. I confronted them and my voice reached a crescendo as I told them they must improve their attitude or else. My face was going bright red and the boys glanced at each other before starting to suppress their giggling. I was lost for words, their reaction stopped me in my tracks. Totally deflated, I sent them off to their next lesson.

It took me some time to gain credibility with these boys.

Although being head of PE at Thomas Lord Audley was time-consuming, I still remained very involved in the development of youth football in the Colchester area. I was chairman of the Colchester Schools Football Association, and along with my friend and colleague Mick Pirnie I organised four district teams. Since Mick and I retired from doing this work in the early 1980s, sadly no other teachers have been prepared to take on the district teams. It's a situation that is the case in many areas of school football today. Teaching demands are such that teachers do not have the time and energy to cope with extracurricular activities.

Academies have now taken over the development of youngsters' football, ensuring that something special has been lost, a special charm and pride for boys representing the district football team.

It was my experiences of coaching young players at Colchester United from 1971 to 1973 and 1977 to 1991, and at Norwich City from 1992 to 1998, that eventually helped me land a plum job as the assistant academy manager at Arsenal.

Chapter 19

Finding and coaching future Colchester stars

AFTER I was forced to stop playing professionally for Colchester United in 1971 I found permanent work as a PE teacher at Gilberd School in Colchester.

I was speaking to the U's manager Dick Graham who had previously told me that if I stayed living locally, he would offer me the part-time post of running the club's youth policy. True to his word he offered me – and I accepted – the post. This I was to do until 1973 when I became manager at Clacton Town, a post which ended in 1976.

I returned to Layer Road again in 1977 when Bobby Hunt, at the request of manager Bobby Roberts, accepted a self-employed role as reserve-team manager (and occasional player) which he combined by also working alongside former keeper Alan Buck for the U's development fund. Hunt would also be coaching United's apprentices for two afternoons a week. He asked if I would be interested in returning to my old role, with responsibility for youth development at the club. I accepted the challenge. Local papers reported that I had been 'appointed to mastermind the club's new youth policy'. We were set to organise pre-season trials.

When I first started work in 1971, I applied for Colchester United to be admitted to the South East Counties League (SECL).

When this was accepted, it meant we could play under-18 games on Saturdays against the bigger clubs while also starting to coach the 15- and 16-year-olds on two nights each week. My opening task meant putting out a new team in the SECL. Playing against the top London clubs' youth sides would help players develop a competitive spirit – and we would also be able to enter the Southern Junior Floodlight Cup and the FA Youth Cup.

The SECL was a wonderful league for developing young players in the 1970s and 80s, and all the young players who went on to play for the likes of Chelsea, Arsenal, Tottenham and West Ham gained their experience from playing in it.

I was grateful to Dick for giving me such an opportunity. As it transpired, I remained at Colchester long after he had departed.

After the euphoria of the 1970/71 FA Cup run, Colchester hoped to win promotion the following season. When that did not happen and the first team then began the 1972/73 campaign in poor form, Dick resigned. I will always remember him fondly. He gave me my chance in youth development and while I always thought of him as a hard man to please, I also felt he was honest and fair.

When Dick felt the team were playing below the standards he expected, then many a time crockery was thrown around the dressing room at half-time. Harsh words were said, so much so that some players were loath to enter the dressing room first at the interval as they knew Dick's frustration might get the better of him.

I returned to Colchester in August 2005 for Brian Owen's testimonial. After being forced to end his playing career early due to various injuries, Brian worked for the club as physiotherapist for many years. Many ex-players had been invited to the testimonial and I met up with four of my team-mates, Brian Gibbs, Brian Garvey, Mick Mahon and John Kurila, all of whom had played in the FA Cup victory against Leeds in 1971.

On spotting us, Dick, now in his 70s and requiring a walking stick as his legs were not good, hobbled towards us. As he approached, he grinned and said, 'I've just got one thing to say to you fellows.' 'What's that, Dick?' we asked. 'I am sorry that I was such a bastard to you,' he said, then turned and made his way back to his seat in the stand.

Jim Smith, an up-and-coming young manager with Boston United, replaced Dick in October 1972. Leading up to this appointment the press were suggesting some leading figures who might be interested in taking the post.

I had met Jim on the FA coaching badge course I attended in May 1971. He had offered me the chance to play at Boston but I had no other option except to refuse as I did not feel I would be fit enough to play in the Southern League.

Jim was unknown in Colchester. When he was given the new role of player-manager, the front cover of the *Evening Gazette* welcomed him but the paper's back page carried the emboldened headline 'JIMMY WHO?' He turned the tables on the doubters by gaining promotion to the Third Division the following season and after two further successful years he was appointed manager at Blackburn Rovers. He proceeded to have a successful management career with, among others, Newcastle United, Birmingham City, Derby County, Queens Park Rangers and Oxford United.

When Jim moved on to greater things, his coach Bobby Roberts, former Ipswich Town centre-half Allan Hunter and then former Ipswich player and coach Cyril Lea followed as Colchester manager.

Roberts took over in June 1975. He was unfortunate when his side were relegated in his first season but he took Colchester immediately back up in 1976/77. A second promotion to the Second Division was only just missed in 1979/80 but a year later, Colchester again dropped into the Fourth Division. When he failed to lead his side to immediate promotion, he was sacked in May 1982.

Allan Hunter, who when he played for Oldham Athletic between 1967 and 1969 was my toughest-ever opponent during my playing career, had taken charge of the final match of 1981/82. He had enjoyed a great defensive partnership at Ipswich with Kevin Beattie. His brief time in charge came during a period when John Lyons took his own life, following which Allan tendered his resignation in January 1983. Allan later came back to Colchester in a coaching capacity when Mike Walker took charge in April 1986.

Signed from Cambridge United, Lyons, who scored on his debut in front of the *Match of the Day* cameras as Colchester thrashed promotion rivals Sheffield United 5-2 in February 1982, was a talented centre-forward. He appeared to be enjoying his time at Layer Road, playing regularly and scoring his fair share of goals. Four days after he scored both goals in a 2-0 victory over Mansfield Town, I watched him play in a Friday evening floodlit match against Chester in November 1982 and he had a fine game. The following morning, I parked the car in Layer Road in order to take the youth team to Tottenham for an SECL match. I could sense that something was wrong when I approached the players and staff waiting for the coach to arrive. I was told the tragic news that John had taken his own life at his home in the hours following the previous night's match.

Between January 1983 and Walker's appointment, Cyril Lea was in the hot seat at Layer Road. Unable to gain promotion over the following three seasons and with promotion unlikely in 1985/86, he and his assistant Stewart Houston were sacked. Stewart, formerly of Manchester United, later became George Graham's assistant at Arsenal.

Walker made 451 appearances for Colchester and knew the club inside out. He steered his side to fifth in the Fourth Division in 1986/87 but lost out to Wolverhampton Wanderers in a two-legged play-off semi-final, and was surprisingly sacked in November 1987 even though Colchester were near the top of the table. After becoming reserve-team coach at Norwich he later became first-team manager in June 1992 when Dave Stringer was sacked as number one at Carrow Road. Roger Brown replaced Mike and was in charge from November 1987 to October 1988 when he was dismissed after Colchester suffered a club-record 8-0 defeat at Leyton Orient. Jock Wallace took over until December 1989.

I had a good relationship with all these managers. Although it was not easy to develop young players as professional footballers in the Colchester catchment area, we did have some success. Welsh international Cyril Lea was particularly keen to give youngsters a first-team opportunity especially as he had a limited transfer budget. There was a period when many of the players in the first XI had come up through the youth system.

Our policy was to try and recruit around half a dozen young players each season to become apprentices, who, back then, did much of the manual work around the ground. We did not have a significant scouting system and relied on boys writing to the club asking for trials. Many football-keen youngsters would write in. Once we had the numbers, we would organise trial games, from which we would select those we believed had a chance of becoming a professional. In some cases, a young player would stand out and he would certainly be invited to return and continue to show us his talents and take part in training sessions and in matches against local sides. With others it was more a case of instinct, seeing something in them or a feeling that a player possessed great enthusiasm which he could apply to his good skills.

Red-haired **Perry Groves** was among those who wrote asking for a trial at which, playing in midfield, he exhibited great confidence. He was invited back, continued to listen to our advice and was then signed as an apprentice and later as a professional.

Groves, who scored 30 times in 178 competitive games for the U's, went on to have a very successful career. He was transferred for £50,000 in 1986 to Arsenal where he twice collected a league winners' medal, making 53 appearances in two title-winning seasons, 24 as substitute.

Ian Allinson impressed with his strength, speed, directness and crossing ability. He was taken on as an apprentice in 1974 and debuted at aged 17 in April 1975. The Hitchin-born player made over 300 appearances in two spells (1974/75 to 1982/83 and 1988/89 to 1989/90) at Colchester. The second spell was under Wallace and coach Alan Ball and he helped them to claw their way away from demotion from the Football League in 1988/89 by scoring seven vital goals in 24 appearances. In his first spell, his winning goal against Bradford City at Layer Road in the final game of 1976/77 earned the U's promotion.

At the end of 1982/83, Allinson moved to Arsenal for nothing after a contract mix-up that deemed him to be a free agent. He was valued at over £100,000 and the loss of such a good player for no fee was a big blow. In the 1984/85 season, Allison scored ten top-flight goals for the Gunners to finish as their joint-top scorer with Tony Woodcock.

Tony Adcock came in for trials and it was clear that he was a striker who received the ball well, had good ball control and an eye for scoring goals. He was a very quiet lad who possessed great confidence in his own ability.

Tony was 18 when he debuted for Colchester. He had two spells at the club between 1980/81 and 1986/87, and then 1995/96 and 1998/99, in which he made over 300 appearances, scoring an impressive 137 times. In June 1987 he moved to Manchester City where along with David White and Paul Stewart he grabbed a hat-trick in a 10-1 demolition of Huddersfield Town. He also played for Northampton Town, Bradford City, Peterborough United and Luton Town and ended his career with 212 league goals.

Steve Foley, who was dogged by injuries throughout his career, and **Steve Leslie** came through the youth ranks and both played their whole careers with Colchester. Foley, who impressed as an elegant young midfield player when I first saw him, was aged 18 on his debut against Exeter in November 1971. He played over 300 times for the club and scored 56 goals before being forced to retire in the autumn of 1981 at the age of 27. Leslie was 17 on his debut at Grimsby in April 1970 and won promotion twice with the U's, in 1973/74 and 1976/77. He made over 450 appearances and later became an integral part of the Ipswich youth academy.

Lindsay Smith and **John McLaughlin** also had good careers and it was Cyril Lea who gave them an early chance in the first team when they were only teenagers. Both came to Colchester as a result of Dick Graham's long working relationship with John Rouhan, a PE headteacher at an Enfield school. Rouhan scouted for Graham when the latter was manager at Brisbane Road and this had led to Micky Cook signing for Orient. When Cook was subsequently released, Dick brought him to Layer Road.

Rouhan had informed me that Smith and McLaughlin were worth taking a look at and his views were right. Lindsay was a talented ball player, had an eye for goals and possessed good physique. He developed his ability over the following two or three years. McLaughlin was a full-back and he showed great enthusiasm, allied to dedication and a strong personality. It was agreed at the trial that he should be given further opportunities and he grasped it with both hands by working extremely hard to get into the first team.

McLaughlin was still an apprentice when Dick gave him his full debut at Hartlepool, aged 17. He moved to Swindon for £25,000 in December 1973 and later enjoyed a lengthy spell with Portsmouth before joining Bournemouth. Smith was only 16 years and 183 days old when he came on as a substitute at Grimsby in April 1971. He played in various defensive roles before settling down at centre-half and he made over 200 appearances before being signed by Cambridge United in October 1977. He later enjoyed spells with Plymouth Argyle and Millwall before returning to the Abbey Stadium.

I took my Stanway under-15s school team to play at Witham. I saw this tall lad running out and was thinking he was head and shoulders above anyone off the pitch but he was also the same on the pitch. **Rudi Hedman**'s skills were outstanding and he dominated the game and I just had to go and speak to him to come for a trial and he got his scholarship from there.

Hedman then came through the U's youth team and reserves before signing a pro contract under Lea in February 1984 soon after making his first-team debut against Bury. He played over 170 times for Colchester before Crystal Palace paid a £100,000 fee to take him to Selhurst Park.

Martin Grainger was another John Rouhan discovery from the London area. Aged 14, he had a quiet confidence in himself. He had a nice personality, never caused any problems on or off the pitch and got on with his job.

After making only 16 appearances in five seasons, Martin signed for Brentford for £60,000 soon after the 1993/94 season began. The Bees made a tidy profit on the no-nonsense defender when Birmingham City paid £400,000 for him in March 1996, and he was a member of the Blues team that made it to the Premier League when they beat Norwich City in the 2001/02 play-off final at the Millennium Stadium in Cardiff. He had previously played at the same ground in the 2001 League Cup Final against Liverpool, which the Merseysiders won on penalties following a 1-1 draw. Football also clearly runs in the family as Martin's son, Charlie, briefly played professionally with Leyton Orient and at the start of the 2022/23 season he was in goal for Dulwich Hamlet.

Andy Farrell was a quiet and studious local lad from St Charles Lucas school in Colchester. As few young players from Colchester came through to become professional players, he, and others in similar situations, were loved when they made their debuts. He was signed to apprentice forms and made his debut at aged 17 on the opening day of the 1983/84 season against Darlington. Soon afterwards he was a member of the U's team that played Manchester United at Layer Road in the League Cup. He played at either full-back or centre-half and it was a surprise to me when he was allowed to leave for just £5,000 in the summer of 1987 to sign for Fourth Division Burnley, for whom he later gained promotion. He made 237 starts and 20 substitute appearances for the Clarets and was thought highly enough of to be inducted into their Hall of Fame by Burnley fans.

John Taylor came from Suffolk for a trial. He was a tall centre-forward and had good skills which everyone has to have if they are going to impress. He was not overly pacy but had an eye for goal, and we took him on as a scholar. He played at schoolboy and youth level for Colchester and he also played many times in the reserve side only to be released after just a single first-team substitute appearance. After dropping down into non-league, Taylor became part of John Beck's teams at Cambridge who rose from the Fourth Division to the Second Division in 1989/90 and 1990/91 and almost made it to the Premier League at the end of the 1991/92 season. He enjoyed spells at, among others, Bristol Rovers and Bradford City, and later managed Cambridge.

Steven Ball was one of the best young players I have ever seen. In a match played at the Colchester training ground, he was representing St Helena School against Stanway under-14s in a cup final and his side won 6-1, with Steven scoring five.

I tried desperately to sign him as an apprentice for Colchester but for some reason he opted for Arsenal when he left school! I understand that he did very well as a youth player at Arsenal, where he went on to win the FA Youth Cup. He signed as a professional and I assumed that his career would take off. Steven was playing for Arsenal's reserves and his manager was Stewart Houston, who came over to watch an evening game at Layer Road. I spoke to him afterwards and asked how Steven was getting on.

I was disappointed when he shrugged his shoulders and said that he was struggling to make the grade at the top level. He praised Steven for his talent on the ball but he questioned his ability to win the ball back when the opposition had it. This requires anticipation, pace and agility, plus the ability to close opponents down and make well-timed tackles to win the ball and retain possession. Steven had not been helped when he had suffered ankle ligament damage and was out for nine months.

After failing to appear in the Arsenal first team, Steven returned to Colchester and played a handful of first-team games in 1989/90 before joining Norwich and Cambridge and then returning to Layer Road on a monthly contract. He later dropped down into non-league football where he also later got involved in management, with a spell at Maldon & Tiptree in 2015/16, combined with being a part of the Colchester coaching staff. After undertaking the role of assistant manager, Ball was the U's manager from July 2020 to February 2021.

Born October 1961, **Tommy English** went to Saint Helena school and played at centre-forward. He came to my attention when he scored five times against my Stanway School team.

I selected him for the Colchester District team at under-15 level and his goals helped us reach the last 16 of the national English Schools competition. We played Oxford Schools away at Oxford United's ground. This was a great occasion for all of us as in general the Colchester teams did not have too much success against the London District teams such as Newham, Barking and Waltham Forest. The boys from the London area always seemed to be more competitive and confident.

Colchester is on the Suffolk border and it is a wonderful place to live as life is easy-going but perhaps this environment means youngsters do not develop the competitive edge and the streetwise attitude of their London counterparts.

Against Oxford, Tommy, who also played at county level for Essex, was the player we relied on to win. Unfortunately he had a poor game and we lost 1-0.

Despite his performance, I was very keen to give Tommy a scholarship with Colchester but when top-flight side Coventry City approached him then he naturally chose to join a bigger club. He made his first-team debut aged just 17 against Arsenal at Highbury and later joined Leicester City before playing briefly for Rochdale and Plymouth.

After a spell at Canberra City, Australia, Tommy finally joined Colchester in the 1984/85 season where he linked up with his younger brother **Tony English,** who was capped at England youth level and who began his apprenticeship with Coventry before returning to Colchester. Tony gained legendary status with a fine career over many years at Layer Road that saw him make over 500 appearances.

Tommy was to have two spells with the club, between 1984/85 and 1986/87 and then in 1989/90. On 18 April 1986 he grabbed a hat-trick against Preston and four days later Tony scored three against Peterborough at Layer Road. The following week the pair were both dismissed after Tommy ran a long way to defend Tony who was involved in a melee with Crewe's Gary Blissett, who was also sent off.

Born November 1981, Tommy's son, Tom, also looked like he would become a professional player. He possessed amazing skills and even my wife Julia, who is not particularly a football fan, was impressed when she saw him playing. As he dribbled towards the defender, he put his right foot over the ball, then rolled it on to his heel with his left foot and with his right foot flicked it over his, and the defender's, head leaving the defender wondering where the ball had gone. Julia still talks of this incident.

I signed Tom English junior as a schoolboy for Norwich. When Tom, who had wonderful ball skills and great football intelligence, was 16, Liam Brady agreed a scholarship contract with him at Arsenal. Unfortunately Tom suffered shin splints for much of his scholarship and he was subsequently released. His career appeared over before it started but with careful rest he was able to restart his career in Singapore's S. League, in which he scored 15 goals for perennial strugglers Marine Castle.

In 2001, Tom was due to sign for Queens Park Rangers when he returned from a holiday in Tenerife with his friends. Tragedy struck when his phone was stolen and, in his determination to catch the thief, he jumped over a wall only to find a 40ft drop beneath him. He subsequently spent ten days in a coma but mercifully survived. Professional football though was out of the question although remarkably he later went on to play at a high non-league level with, among others, Hendon. Only when he was 29 did he finally stop playing.

* * *

I was a PE teacher from 1971 to 1994 and during this time I worked with many pupils, some of whom I remain in contact with. On learning that I was writing this book, I received the following comments from some of them.

Jonathan Clark: 'Roy, Mr Massey, probably to this day doesn't realise the huge effect he and his coaching and his teaching had on my life.

'As a kid I spent a lot of time in hospital with bad legs and when I got out all I wanted to do was play sports. I wasn't good and I knew it but I was a battler. I tried and I know he saw that in me and he always encouraged me and pushed me to do my best. If you did something good he let you know it and the same if you didn't.

'I have never forgotten the first time I saw my name on the A team sheet. I was a sub but it was a huge achievement for me and when I was picked to start, it was even bigger and he knew that.

'I look back on my school years with great fondness and Roy was a massive part of that. I was the fat kid with the bowl haircut and the hand-me-down clothes and dodgy legs. The class clown that kids picked on. But he gave me something to strive for and made me feel like I mattered, I am forever grateful to him, a great man and a great teacher who I always think of with much love and huge respect.

'Congratulations to you, Roy, on the book. I can't wait to read it.'

Paul Nevard, a pupil from Stanway School: 'Roy would always want to join in the games. He would start refereeing and then he would get the ball and start dribbling. He just couldn't appear to resist doing it. It was like a scene from the movie *Kes*, our very own Bobby Charlton but with more hair. Then we had to rush back to shower and get to our next class. But, of course, we were late.

'He was always there for me. When my dad passed away he was the first person I turned to as he was more than a teacher as he went that extra mile for me.'

Carl Fletcher, also from Stanway School: 'Who could forget the school cup finals, training sessions with the great man – we used to call the Gaffa "Royston Platini" as we could never get the ball off him in training. Without a doubt the best coach I ever played under as he gave so much confidence to express yourself. Not only a great man but one that I still speak to every month, but a lovely family. The biggest highlight: 2-0 down half-time in a cup final for Stanway School and winning 5-2 with Roy's son Paul scoring an absolute rocket to get us back in the game. This just spurred us on to win. So many great memories.'

Chapter 20

Managing in non-league football

MY PROFESSIONAL career had ended disappointingly but I still loved football, so when, following a poor season, Tiptree United sacked manager Peter Aitchison and asked me to take charge for 1971/72, when they would compete in the inaugural Essex Senior League, I readily agreed.

Tiptree, ten miles south-west of Colchester, is a little village with a population of around 10,000. The club's Jam Makers nickname referred to the Wilkin and Sons business formed by a local farming family in 1885 and internationally recognised today as a brand of preserves. United had played at Chapel Road, capacity 2,000, since their formation in 1933.

I was going to be very busy as, by the time the new season began in August 1971, I was a full-time teacher at Gilberd School and I also had responsibility for Colchester United's youth team.

Amateur players must strike a balance between playing football, work commitments and family responsibilities. Football could take up a lot of time. Training, which was always done on the Chapel Road pitch whatever the weather, took place two evenings a week. There was then a Saturday game that would occupy most of the day, especially if the match was away.

Training had to be varied and enjoyable to ensure players attended. I employed the fitness ideas of Alf Willey from

Rotherham United, and many of the coaching sessions I organised came directly from the imaginative ideas of Jack Mansell, my manager at Millmoor in the mid-1960s.

No Tiptree player got paid; they played for pure enjoyment. Yet many were more dedicated than some professional players I knew.

In a year where the average weekly wage was £28, I was paid £5 a week from which I covered my travel expenses. The club could not afford to appoint an assistant, who would have been invaluable in searching for players who might come to Tiptree in order to improve the squad standard. It meant that as I lacked the time to seek new recruits then I had to rely on looking at players in opposition teams.

When I did seek to persuade anyone to switch to play for Tiptree, some requested money. While the thought of turning them down for £2 each week seems ridiculous today, I was also conscious that if I paid some players, then this would cause resentment in the side, particularly when a paid player did not subsequently contribute so well.

Even at amateur level it was traditional to lose some of our best players to bigger clubs. Who could blame these lads?

With Colchester not running a youth team between 1970 and 1973, then my U's connections helped me recruit U's youngsters Neil Partner, Nigel Trovell and Richard Bourne, who made his first-team debut for the club on 3 April 1972 against Chester City. He went on to make a further three appearances.

It was a great experience for them to play at Chapel Road. Older players warmed to them as they could see they were talented.

During my first season, Bobby Cram, who returned to North America in 1972 to become player-coach for Vancouver Spartans, enquired if I knew two young players good enough to play for his new club and who would be willing to venture out to British Columbia. I recommended Neil Partner and Adrian Webster, a talented youngster who was frustrated at his limited first-team opportunities at Colchester. Within days both players had agreed to move to Canada. Neil subsequently missed his family and girlfriend and stayed for only a year but Adrian had a successful career for many seasons. He played for the Spartans for two seasons in the British Columbia Premier League. When the NASL awarded a franchise to Seattle Sounders for the 1974 season, Seattle coach John Best spotted Webster playing in a cup final for the Spartans and signed him immediately. He made over 100 Seattle appearances before later playing for Pittsburgh Spirit and Pittsburgh Inferno.

Sounders reached the 1977 Soccer Bowl – the NASL championship final – where they faced New York Cosmos. Adrian, who was comfortable playing at full-back or in the centre of the pitch, played in midfield that day and had the task of marking the world's greatest footballer, Pelé, who was playing his final competitive match. The pair had previously played against one another on several occasions.

Although his side lost 1-0, Adrian did well and was thrilled at the end when the two players embraced and swapped shirts. Adrian has the photograph to prove it! He also played against George Best when the Manchester United legend was at Los Angeles Aztecs in the late 1970s. Adrian played for six seasons with the Sounders but such has been the ebbs and flows of football in the USA over the decades that the club later went bust. Adrian stayed in the game in a coaching role over many years and in 2016 he wrote a successful book on his career.

Between 100 and 150 spectators would attend Tiptree home matches. Many were passionate about the club. They certainly wanted to see promotion gained and progress made up through the league structure.

Committee members were all village residents and each had their own responsibilities, from fundraising, ground maintenance, laundering the playing kit and matchday organisation.

The committee built a clubhouse adjacent to the changing rooms. Supporters could socialise and enjoy a drink together and it was a very good way to make money to keep the club afloat.

Tiptree merged in September 2009 with Maldon Town to form Maldon & Tiptree, who play in the Isthmian League North division at the Wallace Binder Ground, Maldon. They reached the FA Cup first round in 2019/20 and 2020/21 and Colchester have invested in them to use as a nursery club to give some of their youngsters the opportunity to play in a very competitive league.

Clacton Town, who I joined in 1973, could pay players £2 a week each, which also covered travel expenses. They already had a clubhouse when I arrived and combined with other fundraising activities they were able to attract more talented players.

Players at non-league levels tend to socialise with team-mates more than in the professional game.

After training and home matches, the players would gather in the clubhouse and have a couple of beers together, possibly more after a victory. No one back then thought this would be detrimental to their fitness in an era when professional players enjoyed a drink.

Arsène Wenger was key to changing attitudes. On his first day at the Colney training ground, Arsène had the Coca-Cola machine removed and instructed the players to drink water after coaching. There was to be no eating Mars bars.

I had five enjoyable years in non-league football.

Tiptree and Clacton

Neil Partner, whose son Andy later made three substitute appearances for Colchester United, Nigel Trovell and Richard Bourne quickly established themselves as first-team players. I told the *Maldon and Burnham Standard*, 'The standard is better than I anticipated ... the lads are all giving 100 per cent. I can see no reason why we should not do well ... I have thought of playing but don't think I would be doing myself, or the team, justice if I did.'

The thrill of playing proved too much and despite never being fully fit, I put my books back on. I was ambitious, stating, 'I would like to become a full-time youth-team coach with a professional side. I enjoy seeing youngsters develop their skills and it is good to feel you are responsible, at least partly, for their development.'

The new Essex Senior League consisted of eight other teams in Basildon United, Billericay Town, Heybridge Swifts, Pegasus Athletic, Saffron Walden Town, Southend United A, Stansted and Witham Town. It took time to build the team and we finished fourth in 1971/72. Scoring was a problem and we netted just 21 goals in our 16 league matches as we finished six points behind champions Witham Town.

In 1972/73 I enjoyed scoring three times as we beat Heybridge Swift 4-2. The best goal came from Kelvin Llewellyn who hit a fine 25-yard shot. I had dropped several senior players and replaced them with four youngsters in Stewart Green, Gary Kemp, Graham Coe and Danny Hipton and they responded well. The *Maldon and Burnham Standard* reported that a 'golden hat-trick from Roy Massey' boosted the team.

We ended the season a disappointing seventh, although I had departed before then. In early 1973 I was offered the player-manager's post at Eastern Counties League side Clacton Town, who had just sacked their player-manager Clive Brock. A spokesperson said a series of poor results combined with the bad conduct of some players had led to Brock leaving.

Local papers reported me saying I was moving on because, 'It's an opportunity to further myself. It's a bigger club and a bigger league. They've also got better facilities.'

Nicknamed the Seasiders, Clacton also had an active youth policy and this interested me. Tiptree chairman Bill Horsey understood why I was leaving, telling the press, 'Roy has got a good offer and it is a good opportunity, I don't blame him for taking it and the club certainly bears no grudges.'

Brock, the longest-serving player at Clacton, was good enough to agree to stay on just as a member of the team.

Clacton's population was over 25,000 and it continued growing to reach over 45,000 by 1991. The town's most notable structure was the 360m-long pier, opened in 1871, when Clacton, which is 83 miles from London, began developing as a seaside resort.

In 1936, Billy Butlin bought and refurbished the West Clacton Estate, into an amusement park to the west. On 11 June 1938, Butlin opened the second of his local holiday camps. This location remained open until 1983 when, due to more people choosing to holiday abroad, Butlin's closed the facility due to a lack of visitors.

During my time in charge at Clacton Town, the club sought to persuade holidaymakers to watch their matches.

The first time I saw my new first XI – there was also a reserve team – they lost 3-1 at home to Haverhill Rovers. Clacton controlled the match and hit the woodwork on several occasions.

I added my name to the squad for the visit of Wisbech Town, the reigning league champions. I wanted to help end a run of four consecutive defeats but we lost 4-2, although it was, according to the *East Essex Gazette*, 'an improvement ... inspired by the infectious enthusiasm and skilled prompting of manager Roy Massey ... Clacton showed more purpose and aggression'.

I scored against Great Yarmouth Town but we lost 2-1 and had not won since November, so new blood was needed. I persuaded Colchester to let me have 18-year-old Martin Harvey on loan.

Our first victory in a long time saw us beat March Town United 1-0 when our attacking persistence paid off thanks to a fine Eddie Devaux header.

Our finest performance was a 3-2 home defeat of Ely City, and against Thetford Town I scored a good goal with a low drive from 35 yards finding the net. The game finished 1-1 and we ended in 15th place at the end of the season.

On 5 May 1973, I watched the FA Cup Final and was delighted when my former Orient colleague Vic Halom helped Second Division Sunderland capture the famous trophy when the Wearsiders defied all the odds to beat holders Leeds United 1-0 at Wembley. Watching the final that afternoon and over the years has always brought back memories of my grandad Jimmy and his success in 1896 with the Wednesday. When I was later employed at Arsenal, one of the highlights was watching the Gunners in the FA Cup finals.

I re-fashioned the Clacton first team over the summer of 1973. I persuaded Colchester to send their reserve team and Ipswich their Football Combination championship side to play pre-season friendlies. I scored the fourth goal in a 4-2 victory against the U's and while Ipswich deservedly won 2-1, I was pleased that my side battled all the way.

Ron Cooledge scored three against Colchester and I was pleased with the displays of my new signings, the versatile Neil Partner, who had moved from Tiptree United, and centre-half Alan Dennis, a former professional with our opponents.

Dennis appeared to strike up an immediate rapport with keeper Bob Catchpool and I was quietly confident of a good season. After eight games we had lost once and won six including at Great Yarmouth, whose Wellesley Road ground has the world's oldest football stand, opened on 11 June 1892.

We made it through to the fourth qualifying round of the FA Amateur Cup, which was inaugurated in 1893 in response to football splitting at the time into professional and amateur. The 1973/74 season was going to be the last competition as the FA was scrapping amateur status. Among the famous trophy-winning sides are Bishop Auckland with ten victories, Clapton and Crook Town with five each, and Dulwich Hamlet with four. When the annual final was moved to Wembley in 1949 the place was generally full at 100,000.

In the FA Cup, I struck twice late as Clacton overcame a tough challenge in the first qualifying round to beat Lowestoft Town 2-1 at Old Road. We then lost the services for several months of Alan Cracknell, who had broken his leg playing for the Mason's Arms pub in an Ipswich and District Sunday League match. In the FA Amateur Cup fourth qualifying round we beat Coggleshall 5-1 at home.

We hit a new peak when we beat CNS Old Boys 3-2 at Britannia Barracks, Norwich. This put Clacton into the first round proper of the FA Amateur Cup for the first time. Graham Fletcher, Ricky Robinson and Bobby Davidson scored our goals but it was an all-round team effort that took us through, and everyone associated with the club was overjoyed.

We played very well against Horsham in the first round. A waterlogged pitch meant a wasted 250-mile trip one weekend and when we returned the following weekend to face the Sussex Isthmian League side we lost narrowly 2-1 after taking an early lead through Davidson.

In the Eastern Counties League, we were six points behind leaders Thetford Town with three games in hand. Towards the end of March we won 2-1 at title rivals Lowestoft Town to go top. Unfortunately, I was troubled by an old knee injury and missed a match that was won by a cracking effort by skipper Andy Hillier. I was, however, able to play in the 2-0 defeat of Histon.

I missed out at home against Great Yarmouth who won 2-1, and at March we missed a late penalty to only draw and the loss of three points from these two games left us needing a late run to capture the title after Sudbury Town won their three Easter fixtures.

Cup success

We ended the season tied in second place with Wisbech Town, three points behind Sudbury Town, and then faced the league champions in the two-legged Eastern Counties League Cup. After losing the first leg 2-1 at Sudbury, we roared back to take the trophy by winning 3-1 at home. I was very happy when Robinson received a pass of mine to score the cup-winning goal late on. We had the trophy and medals presented to us by the Norwich City secretary Bert Westwood, the match secretary of the Norfolk FA and chairman of our league.

In partnership with the supporters and social club, we held the club dinner at the Royal Hotel on the seafront. Our club-produced document, the *News Sheet*, contained a few wisecracks and an ode to Clacton Town from Massey's Minstrels. It ended with:

Thanks to Roy, we really started to play,
The directors even watched when we played away
They brought us lots of sherry and champagne
And our league title projects vanished right down the drain.

The occasion marked the end to a first full season at Clacton and I believed we could go one better in the league the following season.

In fact we again finished second, although this time we occupied the runners-up spot on our own with 58 points, two behind Sudbury, who retained the title and did so again in 1975/76. We entertained the fans by scoring 110 league goals in our 38 games but our total conceded, of 44, was 12 more than Sudbury's.

The season's highlight was facing neighbours Harwich & Parkeston of the Isthmian League in the FA Cup first qualifying round. Our opponents had reached the first round proper of the competition five times and had twice reached the FA Amateur Cup Final, losing 1-0 to Stockton in 1898 and 6-0 to Pegasus in 1953 before a 100,000 Wembley crowd.

I had signed Eddie Shaw, who I knew well as he was head of PE at St Benedict's School in Colchester. He had played at a decent level in non-league football and after receiving good reports concerning his reserve appearances, I selected him for the big game. I chose to leave out Clive Brock, who had always given maximum effort in training and games. He was a good midfield player but I felt Shaw would give me extra strength in that department.

After Thursday's training I pinned up the team sheet that listed Brock as substitute. Nothing was said and Clive did not show any malice, but come Saturday he did not turn up. However, as Shaw scored the only goal just before the final whistle I felt justified by my team selection. I was, though, angry at Brock's deliberate absence and I told the local press he would never again play for Clacton.

Clive had been a good player and had given Clacton good service. He was a fans' favourite. Yet, due to my outburst, he subsequently left to play for our defeated opponents that day.

Looking back, I think it would have been better if I had spoken to him after training on the Thursday to explain why he was being made the substitute. I mistakenly followed the traditional professional procedure of pinning up the team sheet on the noticeboard after the final training session. All the players would gather round to see if they had been selected. There were cries of delight and groans of disappointment and the latter players had two options: to sulk, or play in the reserves to the best of one's abilities in order to get back in the first team.

We beat Lowestoft Town 3-0 and Sudbury in the following rounds. Meanwhile, I was being increasingly bothered by my old knee injury and needed to miss games.

We were desperate to know our opponents in the fourth and final qualifying round of the FA Cup, victory in which would put Clacton in the first round proper. We were favoured with the luck of draw, at home to Romford. Clacton had made the first round in 1960/61, losing a memorable match with Southend United 3-1.

Romford and Clacton had played each other many times, including once in the FA Cup in 1952 before a crowd of 3,505.

Romford were experiencing a bad patch, but nevertheless they were in a much higher league than us – the Premier Division of the Southern League. Romford entertained hopes of being elected into the Football League and they made several applications to do so. They also improved their home ground, Brooklands. This proved a poor decision when they were relegated at the end of the 1974/75 season and their large debts ultimately led to them folding in 1978. A new club was formed 14 years later.

A crowd of 700 was inside Old Road. We hoped for more but Colchester and Ipswich were also both at home that afternoon. I was also upset that we did not show our best form for those who had turned up for the first time in a while. I was disappointed at my own performance. I said so afterwards when I also argued that Romford's first goal was two yards offside and their winner – with the game level at 1-1 – was harsh as I felt that Tony Talty had earlier been tripped. Romford, though, were the better team.

The following week brought the shock news that I had been sent off for the first time in my career. I had only once previously been booked! Wisbech referee Kelvin Morton had reported myself and two other players, John Elden and Andy Hillier, after the game at Chatteris Town where we had lost 3-2 and had Robinson dismissed. I was dumbfounded and said to the papers that I had been informed I had been sent off because of a remark I had made to the referee although I had never approached him. There were fines and suspensions for all four players.

Despite our setbacks, Clacton had a very successful Christmas. Against bottom-of-the-table Gothic, I hit four in a 7-0 victory and we then beat Sudbury 2-1 at home on New Year's Day.

At one stage we took 17 points from a possible 18 and amassed a goals record of 33 scored and nine conceded in the games. At Saffron Walden we notched four in the final ten minutes to snatch a 4-2 victory. With 11 matches remaining we were fourth, five points behind leaders Lowestoft Town with five games in hand.

One concern was our poor pitch; while winning 1-0 at home to Wisbech, the game was called off after 40 minutes as the ground was a quagmire. Meanwhile, Sudbury Town moved within two points of us and had two matches in hand.

We then lost badly 4-1 away to Soham Town Rangers. The side was weakened due to injuries and I was forced to make a substitute appearance when Nigel Box limped off.

With the fixtures piling up we managed to thrash March 6-0. In an attempt to do everything possible to win the title for the first time, director Frank Bailey promised the first team a £1,000 holiday.

Thanks to a very good goal by Talty, his 26th of the campaign, we beat table-toppers Lowestoft Town 1-0 as local papers reported that we were speeding towards the championship. It was not so, however, as the following day we lost badly, 4-1 away to Soham, a result which ultimately cost us the number-one spot. We took 18 points from our final 22 but with Sudbury taking 22 from 26 we lost out by two points.

Sudbury scored 82 goals and conceded 32, making their goal average 2.565, and by scoring 110 and conceding 44 then our goal average was 2.5 exactly. If we had beaten Soham, the additional two points would have tied the teams and our goal average would have been better.

After the successes of the previous two campaigns, I remained hopeful of a third good year in a row in 1975/76. It was never going to be the case, though, when Ricky Robinson left the club for Harwich and Hillier moved to Parkeston. Robinson's combination with Tony Talty had produced 70 goals in 1974/75.

My playing career ends

My knee injury meant I had stopped playing for a year after being forced to quit professional football. I was pleased to have had the chance to play again but it was clearly now time to stop doing so as there was the risk of a serious injury that might have made walking a problem. I had a wife and children to consider.

We did quite well when the season started and, although I was frustrated at not being able to direct play by appearing in the matches, it did afford me the opportunity to enjoy a New Year's Eve party at home with my parents who had travelled down from Mexborough to enjoy the festive period with their grandchildren.

It was 3am before my dad and I finished our last whiskies and went to bed. I have never been a heavy drinker and after skipping breakfast I was not feeling great when I journeyed to collect two players before driving the 80 miles to Lowestoft Town. The rest of the players were making their own way there.

I felt sick and when I pulled the car over to the verge and began vomiting my embarrassment was doubled as three cars went past tooting their horns as the players in them were having a laugh at my expense. I had set a bad example. We lost 2-0 and no words were spoken afterwards.

We completed the 1975/76 season in seventh place with 46 points from 36 matches, scoring 66 goals and conceding 43.

I left Clacton in April 1976 saying, 'I have enjoyed my four years ... the players have always given me 100 per cent. I could not have worked with a nicer bunch of lads.' It was reported that the directors had accepted my resignation with regret.

I had told the papers that I had nothing lined up, would not be looking for a new managerial post and would be concentrating on my involvement with schoolboy football. Reserve-team manager Colin Henson took over in my post.

This chapter is dedicated to Vivian John Woodward, the greatest player to play for Clacton Town and one of football's greatest centre-forwards.

Chapter 21

Tragedy

IN 1988, I was thoroughly enjoying the challenge of working as a PE teacher and with the young players at Colchester United. At home, Christine and I continued to work together to bring up three children, including two teenagers.

In September, Christine, with the children at school, applied for a secretarial job at a local school for boys who had difficulty in adjusting to society's rules and regulations. When she was interviewed, the headteacher asked what she would do if a boy came up and said you are 'a f**king old bag'. Instantaneously her reply was open, 'Hey you, less of the old!' She got the job.

Our whole lives, though, were due to take a turn for the worse. I was in the office at Layer Road organising the youth team for the following Saturday when I received a phone call from Christine. She urged me to come home as she had something she needed to tell me. The sound of her voice told me that it wasn't good news. When I arrived, Christine said she had a lump on her breast and the hospital had diagnosed breast cancer. Within a week she was in hospital having surgery to remove her breast.

Christine was 42 years old. We hoped all was well over the next two years and that she was cancer-free. One evening at home, Christine, though, collapsed with back pain. The following day we visited our local doctor, Peter Snell, who I knew well as he was the

U's club doctor for many years. Peter arranged for immediate tests at the local hospital.

His practice was close to our home and when we got back from there he telephoned and asked me to come and meet him. When we again met up, he told me that he feared the cancer had gone into the liver. I walked back home in a daze.

Christine went for the tests and the following week we were sitting outside the cancer specialist's room waiting for his diagnosis. It was like waiting for the death sentence. The specialist eventually called us into the room where he told us the cancer had spread to such an extent that there was no cure. Christine, being a strong woman, indignantly sat up in her chair and replied that she wanted to see her grandchildren before she passed away. She didn't ever see her grandchildren as she died within two months of seeing the specialist.

I have often thought how difficult it must be for a specialist to tell someone that they only have a few weeks to live. I often tried to put this in perspective when, at the end of each season, I had to sit down with some boys and their parents to tell them they were being released as they had not reached the required club standard. The boys would range from ten to 16 years old. I had developed a relationship with them and their parents. It was a difficult task that did not come easy to me, but it was nothing compared with the task of the cancer specialist that Christine and I met that fateful night.

I was asking the specialist how long Christine might hope to live. 'Two or three years?' The specialist did not answer as he knew it was only two or three months. We had booked a holiday in Tenerife for the following week and the specialist said we should go. We went with friends and our youngest child Richard, aged 11. One of the worst moments of my life was telling Richard that his mum had only a few weeks to live.

We had a marvellous first week. During the second week, Christine became ill due to the heat. We had to leave Richard with our friends and go to a cooler climate in a clinic in the mountains.

It was unbearable watching my wife endure increasing pain. The medical staff doctors did their best to make her as comfortable as possible. I was forced to leave Christine at the end of the holiday in order to go home with Richard, and the air ambulance was used to fly her home to the UK.

At 44 years old, Christine died peacefully in the Colchester hospital on 27 October 1990. My whole life was shattered. Some say that genes control our destiny; Christine died in exactly the same way and at the same age as her mum. Her funeral at Colchester Crematorium was packed with over 200 people present.

Life was very difficult for me and my children Justine, Paul and Richard. Justine had begun her college course in Northampton. Paul was working and living in London, and I faced a big challenge looking after Richard, especially as both of us were grieving. I had to carry on working at Thomas Lord Audley School but I gave up my part-time youth role with Colchester United as we needed to adjust to life without Christine.

I was very fortunate that Christine's dad, Eric, and his wife, Vi, came down to Colchester regularly, especially at holiday times and when I was away with Norwich boys at tournaments abroad, to support Richard and myself. I would collect them by car from Doncaster. I was 47 years old and my tiny comfortable world had come to an end. Close families that can support each other when there is tragedy are a godsend.

I was also lucky to have good friends in Mick and Kay Pirnie, teachers at Stanway School and who often looked after Richard.

In the 16 years I worked for the Arsenal youth development department, my door was always open for parents to come in for a chat. It might be about a lack of progress by their son or problems he may be experiencing at school. On three occasions a dad had tears in his eyes as he told me of the death of their wife. We discussed how to help his son deal with the tragic loss of his mother. I could draw on my own experience but it was never an easy task.

In the years following Christine's death, I cried on numerous occasions when I was alone. On my 50th birthday I took the children to a Chinese restaurant in Colchester. After a very enjoyable evening I walked home alone while the youngsters went to meet up with friends. On reaching home I slumped on the wall, felt despair and wanted to cry. Tears would not come. I looked at myself and a voice in my head said 'get over it', 'get on with your life' and 'think of the happy memories that you shared with Christine'. I did my best from then on to live my life.

The U's were playing a big part in my life. The youth programme was expanding and more scouts were being taken on to look for the best young players in the area. We targeted the east London area and Suffolk. The standard was improving and Steve Foley, one of the club's ex-players, was appointed as full-time coach for the under-18s who were now playing in the South East Counties League. I was coaching the under-15s and under-16s sides two nights a week.

Chapter 22

Working full-time in the sport I love

IN 1989, Gordon Bennett was named head of youth development at Norwich City. It would prove to be a pivotal appointment for me too.

Gordon knew of my work at Colchester United and in September 1991 he invited me to work part-time as the Canaries' assistant youth coach. He did not feel that there were sufficient numbers of talented youngsters in East Anglia for a club as ambitious as Norwich and my role would be to construct a network of scouts to discover talented youngsters, in the under-nine to under-12 age brackets, in the Essex, Hertfordshire and London areas. This was a radical move by Norwich. At the time, professional clubs had schools of excellence to which they sought to attract players who were at least 13.

With my life drifting along after the death of Christine, this opportunity gave me a fresh challenge and a feeling of self-worth. I had enjoyed every minute of my time with Colchester but the lure of such a big new role soon seemed irresistible. I looked forward to working for a club at the highest level and to introducing myself to parents on the touchline as a Norwich City scout.

When the job offer arrived, I was still teaching PE at Thomas Lord Audley School and my injured knee was becoming increasingly painful, making it difficult to participate in sporting activities. At the same time, I did have a regular job which offered me security.

But accepting the Norwich role proved a good decision as I was fortunate enough to stay in the game for more than 20 years by initially continuing in my part-time role until Gordon asked me to start work full-time for the club at the start of the 1994/95 season, which marked the third season of the Premier League.

In 1971, when I took charge at Tiptree United, I had said, 'I would like to become a full-time youth-team coach with a professional side.' It took me over two decades of hard work to fulfil my dreams.

I must, though, stress that none of this meant I spent my career as a teacher resenting my situation. To the contrary; I gained so much from working with so many good teachers and pupils, a healthy number of whom I have met regularly and stayed in touch with over the years. I am always delighted when I receive news of former students and they phone me, very often, to keep me informed of how their own sons are doing when playing football.

I began my work at Norwich by organising coaching sessions in Colchester and at a centre I established at Potters Bar. When I became full-time – and by which time I was living with Julia in Upminster – I also helped establish a centre at Brentwood.

Accepting the Norwich offer meant that I had to turn down an approach by Ipswich Town manager George Burley, asking me to work in their youth development department. I was naturally disappointed, recalling how, in the late 1960s and early 70s, Ipswich, with Bobby Robson in charge, had developed a wonderful youth setup, including a very profitable centre in north-east England, which produced such great players as Kevin Beattie, John Wark, Eric Gates and Burley himself.

Under new FA rules introduced in 1994, professional clubs were allowed to run schoolboy teams on Sundays of all ages. Initially, many couldn't see any benefits to recruiting youngsters under 13 and at first only five clubs embraced the FA recommendation regarding recruiting, coaching and running teams for children that young. The enlightened few were Norwich, Peterborough, Lincoln City, Nottingham Forest and Notts County. I certainly did some travelling, taking the boys from London to these clubs for our away games and to Norwich for the home games.

On one memorable Sunday in September 1994, Norwich had seven teams in action – the under-15s and 13s at home to Cambridge United at the University of East Anglia (UEA) Sports Grounds, the under-16s and 14s at Cambridge, and the under-12s, under-11s and under-tens played away to Nottingham Forest. Norwich hired the UEA pitches for youth matches.

The previous month the under-14s had stormed to success in a youth tournament in Sunderland. After brushing aside Manchester United 7-0 in the semi-final, they cruised to a 4-0 win over Celtic to lift the trophy. The boys also won all three group games and Barrington Belgrave claimed the Golden Boot as the tournament's top scorer. The Norwich matchday programme for an upcoming match against Arsenal carried a feature on the work of the youth development department including the Sunderland tournament in which Sammy Morgan, who had just taken over Gordon Bennett's role, said, 'There's enormous competition these days for the best schoolboys, so it must be reassuring to Norwich City that their lads measure up well against the boys at the other leading clubs – and that's a feather in the cap of Roy Massey, who has been largely responsible for the scouting that has brought these boys together.'

Before the 1994/95 season started, Gordon arranged a meeting in Norwich for the youth development staff. Soon there was a knock on the door and Chris Sutton walked in. He thanked Gordon for all that he had done for him and explained that he was going to Blackburn Rovers. The fee was £5m, breaking the British transfer record.

Chris had been a marvellous player for Norwich, equally at home at centre-half as he was up front, and he wasted no time in showing Blackburn they had spent their money wisely. Rovers won the 1994/95 Premier League, with Sutton and Alan Shearer being the main goalscorers, Sutton hitting 15 and Shearer 34 out of a total of 80 league goals. The pair were a brilliant combination up front.

Norwich also spent the transfer fee wisely by investing much of it on land just outside the city where they developed their Colney training centre.

When I was working at Colchester I met Tony Head, who organised a schoolboy team in Brentwood, and Eddie Clayton, who was managing a Redbridge district team. Eddie had been a well-known professional footballer with Tottenham Hotspur in the 1960s, then after retirement he went into teaching. I recruited them both to do scouting and coaching for Norwich City.

My first assignment scouting in my full-time post was at a Colchester schoolboy match against Newham schoolboys. The boys were in year seven at school. As the game started the number nine for Newham caught my eye. He looked a natural young footballer and showed good technique and pace. He also had an eye for goals as he scored three. I was excited about the prospect of introducing myself to his parents. Fortunately, there were no other scouts in attendance so I faced no competition from other clubs.

Once the final whistle sounded I made my way to the boy's parents. 'Your boy had a very good game,' I said. 'What is his name?'

'Bobby,' the father replied, 'Bobby Zamora.' 'Would he like to have a trial with Norwich?' I asked. His dad told me that he had recently signed for West Ham. I was gutted, but tried not to show my disappointment to Mr Zamora. I gave him my card and said that if things did not work out at West Ham, he could give me a ring. Two years later when the phone rang, I found Mr Zamora on the end of the line. He told me that Bobby had been released by

West Ham and asked if Norwich would still be interested in him. It was one of those calls that made you jump in the air with delight.

Bobby trained and played with the Norwich school of excellence for two years until the end of his under-16 season, his final school year. This was the time when decisions would be made about which young players would be offered scholarships.

Gordon Bennett had just left the club to become Aberdeen chief executive and was replaced by Sammy Morgan, who had a very successful career as a centre-forward with Aston Villa and Northern Ireland. Sammy had coached the Norwich youngsters for several years and now the first task in his new role was to discuss the issue of scholarships with his youth staff.

Among the boys being considered were some very good players including two strong and quick forwards. Sean Carr and Barrington Belgrave had served the Norwich schoolboys well, having scored plenty of goals at that level. They were obvious candidates for a scholarship and I had a feeling that young Zamora would miss out because of the competition he faced. Bobby had good technique and intelligence but he was still going through puberty and thus lacked some strength and pace. He was not offered a scholarship.

The next day, Richard Everson, a friend of Gordon's who had been a scout for Norwich in the Bristol and South Wales area, got in touch. Now employed by Bristol Rovers, he wanted to know which boys had not been offered a scholarship. I told him that Bobby was unlucky to have been released and that he would be a good player with the Pirates. The phone call must have been the best call Richard made in his scouting career. He invited Bobby and another Norwich youngster, **Luke Williams,** for trials at Rovers.

Both boys were taken on and while Luke did not quite make the grade as a professional footballer, he put this disappointment behind him. Years later he came to the Arsenal academy as coach for the Leyton Orient under-15 squad. I have since followed his career with interest. It has included being manager at Swindon Town in 2016/17, and in 2022 he was appointed at Notts County.

Bobby went on to have a wonderful career, next joining Brighton & Hove Albion before moving into the Premier League and scoring goals for Tottenham, West Ham, Fulham and Queens Park Rangers. At the height of his career he played for England. Scouts naturally take great pride when their prospective players do go on to play at the highest level and I am sure that Richard Everson is no exception.

As I found out over several years when working with talented young players, the boys who reach puberty in the early years and gain success through physical strength may find it particularly difficult coping with professional football in the years to come. Several, such as Bobby, who were released due to a lack of physical strength at 16, have pleased me and gone on to have great careers in the professional game.

When I set up centres in the London area, the boys were coached there one evening each week and we arranged games for them at the weekend. During the holidays I hired a minibus and took the London-based youngsters to Norwich. We stayed in a local hotel and the boys had coaching sessions during the day while in the evening we visited Great Yarmouth. We went to the funfair on the pier and met the owner, Jimmy Jones, who happened to be the Norwich vice-chairman. He allowed free rides for the youngsters who were 11 and 12 years of age. I feel sure that they would look back fondly on their time with the Canaries.

I worked hard in the north London area to bring the best young players to Norwich. One notable player was a 12-year-old goalkeeper called **Robert Green** who went on to have a fabulous career. At his peak he was the best goalkeeper in England and he won 12 caps for the national team.

My colleague Gordon Lawrence picked him out as a potential prospect when his team from west London was competing in the

Canary Cup, a tournament held annually in Great Yarmouth over the Easter holiday. I went along to watch Robert and was very impressed with his physical presence, agility and handling skills. His parents told me that he wasn't with a club, so we invited him in for trials during the following pre-season.

Robert impressed and signed schoolboy forms. He trained locally and played games for Norwich on Sundays. Near the end of his under-14 season, Robert was selected to go to Lilleshall for the last two years of his school education.

At this time, the mid-1990s, the FA ran the England schoolboys under-15 and under-16 squad at Lilleshall. The 15-year-old elite players from English clubs were invited to live at the sports centre there. They were provided with all their education and had football coaching sessions daily to enhance their abilities. They would also play English representation matches. Robert was very excited at going to Lilleshall, but he was soon left devastated after a medical examination showed he had a stress fracture of his spine and needed an operation.

Gordon Bennett now had a dilemma. Should he release Robert or should he sanction payment for an operation on the stress fracture knowing that it would take him at least 18 months to recover full fitness?

Gordon didn't think twice. He promised Robert a scholarship, got him in hospital within weeks and stood by him until he could play again. Robert repaid Gordon and Norwich by later establishing himself in the first team before eventually being sold to West Ham for £3m. He finished his career with Leeds United when he was 38. I am sure Gordon still gets great satisfaction when he is reminded of the wonderful career that Robert had.

It was prior to taking a training session at Potters Bar that I saw **Henri Lansbury** training with his under-eights Sunday team. He was a cut above everyone else and I approached his manager who told me the player was only six. I spoke to his mum and dad about him coming to Norwich at academy level and he agreed. When I left to go to Arsenal, I got Henri to come training with the Gunners and he subsequently got himself a scholarship and a professional contract. He has had a great career and was playing for Luton Town in the Championship at the time of writing.

Craig Bellamy was also spotted by Richard Everson. He was a chirpy, confident and competitive young boy. More importantly, he was always capable of scoring goals. He moved from Cardiff to Norwich at the age of 15 and was very homesick initially, but the birth of his first child helped him to settle down and he went on to have a first-class career during which he won the League Cup with Liverpool in 2011/12 and the Scottish Cup with Celtic in 2003/04. He played 78 times for Wales.

Darel Russell lived in Gants Hill and was, along with Luke Williams, seen playing for his district school team. They both played in midfield and showed good skills when in possession of the ball. Darel had a competitive edge to his game whereas Luke wasn't as aggressive but showed more composure on the ball. Darel went on to be a regular Norwich first-team player with two spells at the club in which he made more than 250 appearances. He played regularly for Stoke City between 2003 and 2007 and in total made more than 500 domestic league appearances and collected League One championship medals with both Norwich and Charlton Athletic.

John Sutton was Chris Sutton's brother and the son of Mike Sutton, who was a coach with the Norwich schoolboy players when I began working with the Norfolk club. Mike had played in the lower tiers of the Football League, and it was only natural for John to come along to the training sessions. He did not have the pace or physique of Chris but he showed football intelligence, good ability on the ball and like his brother he was capable of scoring goals.

John started his career as a youth trainee at White Hart Lane but failed to make the first team. After a handful of matches with

Carlisle United and Swindon Town, he moved to Scotland and, with the exception of a short spell with Millwall in 2004/05, Wycombe Wanderers in 2007/08 and Australian side Central Coast Mariners in 2012, he played there with distinction, especially for Motherwell, from 2003 to 2019. At the start of the 2022/23 season, John was the assistant manager at Greenock Morton.

At 15, **Ade Akinbiyi** was persuaded by Gordon Bennett to leave his London home and join Norwich. At the time, several big London clubs were keen on signing the teenager but his mum told Gordon that she felt it would be best for him to live in the countryside of Norfolk as there would be fewer distractions to divert his attentions and restrict his opportunities to forge a professional footballing career. Ade was a strong, physical player and through determination and desire he became a regular Norwich first-teamer, making his debut as a 19-year-old substitute in the second leg against Bayern Munich in the UEFA Cup match on 3 November 1993. This ended 1-1 and Norwich thus progressed 3-2 on aggregate to face Inter Milan in the following round. Ade had a much-travelled career and played once for Nigeria, from where his parents originated. He scored more than 100 league goals in English football.

Another young player who came to my attention was **Anthony McFarland.** He was playing for South London Schoolboys against the Colchester Schools team. I invited him to Norwich and he asked me if he could bring his friend along with him. 'Who is your friend?' I asked. 'They call him **Rio Ferdinand,**' I was told.

Rio came along and played a game against Luton Town. Rio showed real ability. Gordon and myself looked at one another. We didn't have to say a word and were both marvelling at the talent of this young player. On his 14th birthday we went to Peckham to visit Rio and his mum to ask if he would like to sign schoolboy forms for Norwich. Unfortunately for us, a few days later, his mum rang to thank us for our visit but told us that Rio had decided to sign for his local club West Ham, so we missed the chance to sign one of the best players of his generation.

Some years later, when Rio was playing for Manchester United, my son Paul, then a photographer with *FourFourTwo*, telephoned to say that he had been commissioned to photograph Rio at a Hertfordshire hotel the day before United played Arsenal.

I asked Paul to give him my best wishes, but I wasn't sure that he would remember me. When Paul met Rio, he mentioned my name and Norwich City. Rio's reply was, 'Gordon Bennett and Kentucky Fried Chicken.' Gordon used to wait at Norwich railway station for boys travelling up from London on Saturday afternoons, staying in a hotel on the evening and then being transported to the game the following morning. Apparently the weekend always began the same way. When the boys arrived at the station, Gordon would buy them all a KFC. Rio's comments put football in perspective for a 13-year-old. He respected Gordon and thoroughly enjoyed his food.

While I was working for Norwich, the London clubs eventually started following our example by looking at the 12- and 13-year-old players. Liam Brady, I heard on the news, had rejoined Arsenal in July 1996, as head of youth development and academy director. Very soon he had a team of scouts who were telling him that several good young players from the London area had been signed by Norwich. How was this happening, he wondered.

A few weeks after his appointment, Liam asked if Arsenal could play against our under-nines, tens and 11s at Potters Bar. Arsenal had only just got a group of boys together. The Norwich players had been handpicked and had been training and playing with us for some time. Unsurprisingly, the Norwich teams won these games fairly comfortably. A few weeks later we received a letter from Liam stating that he would be approaching six of the boys and offering them trials with Arsenal.

We also played Arsenal in an under-14 match, foolishly putting Ross Flitney, a trialist goalkeeper from Potters Bar, in the Norwich goal. Ross had a very good game and the following day I rang his father saying I was pleased to offer him schoolboy forms on the strength of his performance against Arsenal. There was an embarrassed silence at the end of the telephone before Mr Flitney said that an Arsenal scout had been to his house that morning and Ross had signed for the club. No doubt my future colleague, Steve Leonard, had been up to his tricks again. I was beginning to realise the competitive nature of recruiting talent for professional clubs in London. Ross later played for Brighton & Hove Albion, Barnet and Gillingham plus several non-league clubs.

* * *

Although England reached the semi-final at the European Championship in 1996, defeat against Germany meant that 30 years had passed since they had last won a major tournament. Even worse, there had been a failure to qualify for the World Cup finals in 1974, 1978 and 1994 plus the European Championship finals in 1992.

Something had to be done to improve our game and in 1997 the Football Association appointed Howard Wilkinson to revamp youth development.

Howard introduced the FA's 'Charter for Quality', which revolutionised youth football in England. Youth players were to be inducted into professional club academies rather than youth-club football itself. One of the aims of the academies was to produce players for the first team. Rather than signing players from other clubs, it is cheaper to produce homegrown players, who are also aware of the club's philosophy and culture. Each academy does have a slightly different philosophy, aim and objective.

For an academy to stand any chance of success, clubs needed to improve their facilities significantly, especially as Wilkinson proposed that clubs – as had been the case in Europe for decades – should recruit and develop young players from the age of eight.

The regulations for the academies were duly drawn up and clubs were frantically trying to get ready to start their first season of academy football in September 1998. In early February that year I was at home looking through the rules that Howard had established.

I came across a passage that stated all boys that could be signed should live within one hour of their academy. I was taking boys to Norwich from London which was a minimum two-hour journey. I was left stunned. I knew immediately that I would not be able to continue to work for Norwich in the London area and would be out of a job for the following season.

Having worked so hard to get back into full-time employment in football and enjoying life as a married man in Upminster, then, at the age 54, I was more than a little anxious about what the future might hold.

Just as the disappointment was beginning to sink in, the telephone rang. I answered and heard the words in a strong Irish accent, 'Roy, it's Liam Brady. Would you come over to see me? I am looking for someone to work with the youngsters of the Arsenal academy.'

I met Liam at Highbury the following week. My head was buzzing with the thought of working for him, and within days of thinking I would be out of work for the following season, I had a two-year contract starting on 1 March 1998 at Arsenal. Norwich were very pleased for me and I departed with their best wishes.

Chapter 23

Exiting Arsenal to become a scout

IN JANUARY 2013 it was announced that Liam Brady had decided to leave his post at the end of the following season as head of youth development and the academy. A year later I was still thoroughly enjoying myself overseeing the academy when Liam walked into my office with news that rocked me to the core.

Arsenal had decided to appoint, as Liam's replacement, Andries Jonker, a Dutch coach then working as the assistant manager at German side VfL Wolfsburg.

Liam explained that Andries, who would start work on 1 July 2014, wanted to appoint two of his colleagues as his assistants and so there was no need for David Court and myself to remain in post. Both of us were deeply disappointed and did not feel in a retirement mood as we still felt we had plenty to offer the academy for, at least, another two years.

It was agreed that David and I would help ensure a smooth transition for the new team by continuing to work for Arsenal until September 2014. On our final day the academy organised for a barbecue where speeches were made and gifts and mementos were presented to us as reminders of our time at one of the greatest football clubs in the world.

There were many tributes paid to us. They included these words from director Richard Carr, 'Many congratulations and thanks on the establishment [from scratch] and the development of the Arsenal academy. The club and scores of young professionals are deeply in your debt.'

Arsène Wenger, meanwhile, penned a letter, 'Can I take this opportunity to thank you for your fantastic commitment, loyalty and quality of work during your time at Arsenal Football Club.

'After working here for so many years, your personality and day-to-day contribution will be sorely missed by so many people at the club.

'You have played such an important role towards the youth development at Arsenal Football Club, and I know for sure that your positive legacy will remain here for many years to come. For that, we owe you a huge debt of gratitude and sincere thanks. There are so many footballers out there today who have so much to thank you for. You have played such a positive role in the lives of so many young people, and for this, you should be deeply proud.

'Thanks for your immense contribution, you will be sorely missed.'

While it was a great occasion, I still could not help but feel a little bit depressed as I really did not want to leave a job where I so enjoyed getting out of bed each morning to go to work. In fact, it had taken me six weeks to tell Julia, whose response was of delight, as she hardly saw me at times, that I was leaving the Gunners for good.

However, at the end of the evening as I drove out of the academy gates for the final time, my thoughts drifted back to my first day on 1 March 1998 when I drove down the road leading to Highbury before walking up the steps to enter the famous marble halls. That was a very exciting moment and there were to be many more. I had no idea that I was to be at Arsenal for probably the finest period in the club's illustrious history under the guidance of Arsène Wenger. It had proved difficult to produce players from the academy to replace players of the calibre of Tony Adams, Dennis Bergkamp, Thierry Henry and Patrick Vieira.

Nevertheless, I had enjoyed the challenge of finding youngsters good enough to represent Arsenal at academy level, then develop relationships with these children and young people, help them as they matured into adults, improve their footballing ability and bringing along the best of them to become professionals at the very top level. So I felt proud of my efforts, including the joint work I had undertaken with many scouts and coaches. I had also enjoyed some great, fun times and visited many exciting places along the way.

Arsenal bought their academy training ground in 2000. Today, it has been totally transformed into a wonderful facility for the development of young players from eight years of age onwards.

When he heard that I had retired, my old colleague Colin Watts, the Norwich City youth development officer, rang and asked me to consider doing some scouting for the Norfolk club on Saturdays and Sundays and also work with Gregg Broughton who had been appointed as the Canaries' academy manager in 2014.

The work would entail visiting other academies in the London area and sending in reports of any players that impressed me. Keen to remain in the game, I accepted the invitation.

I had left Norwich 16 years earlier when the new rules regarding academies restricted clubs' rights to sign young players under 14 years of age who lived over an hour away. Norwich had established centres for coaching talented youngsters not only in the East Anglia catchment area but also in Bristol, which could take in the south-west and Wales area and he also had the north and east of London covered.

After 1998 there was a dismantlement of the centres outside East Anglia, which has not traditionally been a hotbed for talented young players. Like other clubs based in rural and, in particular, coastal locations, where one half of their area is in the sea, Norwich felt aggrieved at the new rules. The Canaries and clubs in similar situations complained bitterly when the academy structure first began and the Football Association subsequently rectified this situation by allowing the coastal clubs to have a centre in another part of the country. Southampton established a Bristol centre that has been very successful for them and through which Gareth Bale came to the Saints.

Norwich had returned to London in 2012 and had set up centres in Brentwood, Walthamstow and west London.

I thus found myself returning to my role of the previous century, in scouting and looking for talented young players for the club in the London area. When I began by visiting the centres and watched the 12 to 15-year-olds, I could see they showed ability but the really talented players were few and far between. All the best talent was being recruited by the numerous professional London clubs and I could see it was going to be difficult to reverse this process.

On Saturday mornings I would watch youngsters playing district football and on Sundays I would watch games at grassroots level. I found this very unrewarding as the standard of play was well below academy football. The great majority of players who are now professionals started out as under-nines with an academy.

After 18 months in his post, Gregg, who had, between 2012 and 2014, been head of recruitment at the Norwich academy before taking full charge, lost his job. Wholesale changes were made, with the Canaries particularly cutting down on the scouting scheme in the London area. So I was again out of a job, although it was not unexpected.

When Martin Waldron, the head of academy recruitment at Everton, heard what had happened, he asked me if I would scout for Everton in the London area. In my time at Arsenal, Martin would bring his under-six, under-seven and under-eight teams down to play the Arsenal youngsters. I had developed a good relationship with him and was pleased to accept his offer and still be involved with professional football in some capacity.

Scouting in London for a Liverpool club was difficult as it is almost impossible to attract top young players when they are already with one of the Premier League clubs in the capital. There are only two successful deals I can think of in this regard. One was the transfer in 2010 of Raheem Sterling at 16 years of age to Liverpool from Queens Park Rangers for around £1m. Fortunately for Liverpool the move paid off as Raheem established himself in their first team before moving to Manchester City where he proved himself to be a world-class player. In June 2015, meanwhile, Liverpool took Joe Gomez from Charlton Athletic and he has proved to be a wonderful player for the Reds and England.

As I felt that I was unlikely to ever get the most talented young players to go all the way to Liverpool for trial, I resigned after two years of scouting for Everton.

I was very disappointed when I later heard that Martin Waldron had been suspended in September 2018 pending an investigation into tapping up a schoolboy player. Everton subsequently admitted to a Premier League charge that they 'offered inducements to a player and his family to encourage the player to register with the club'. An internal investigation by the club revealed six similar breaches. Everton were hit with a two-year academy transfer ban and fined £500,000.

Martin left the club after 30 years of loyal service during which he produced such players as Wayne Rooney and Ross Barkley. It was a sad end to his time at Goodison Park.

Joe Monks had been appointed as the new lead nation academy recruitment officer for Wolverhampton Wanderers in September 2017. When he heard that I had left Everton, Joe asked me if I would look at young players in the London area for the Black Country club. After two months in my new role, Joe resigned, so I didn't bring much luck to any of the guys who appointed me as a scout.

In the four years since I had left Arsenal, I had worked for three clubs. At the end of the 2018/19 season I decided to retire altogether from professional football. I never envisaged finishing my life in football scouting with Wolverhampton Wanderers, the club that my grandad's Wednesday team beat 2-1 in the 1896 FA Cup Final.

Scouting and recruitment is a vital part of academy football and probably, a view that will be hotly contested by more than a few coaches I have worked with, more important than the coaching provided to boys to help their development as young players.

What is without question is that without enthusiastic scouts who are prepared to go out whatever the weather to watch matches in anticipation of finding a young diamond, then an academy is doomed to fail. Whereas many coaches have played football at a decent professional level and where they have studied the game, that is not generally the case with scouts. They tend to have had limited footballing ability but have always possessed a real love of the game and enjoy watching matches at all levels. They are happy to travel on Saturdays and Sundays and do a report on any player who might catch their eye. In return they claim expenses only.

At times it must seem a thankless task to go to so many games without the scout seeing a player to recommend to his club. However, it is very satisfying when a player put forward is signed by the academy. Some clubs give the scout an incentive of a fee if the player subsequently signs as a scholar at the age of 16, plus a further bonus payment might be expected if the young man then signs as a professional. Extra money might be awarded if the player represents the first team. However, most scouts don't do their job because of the financial benefits. How can they! He has just taken a child of say eight years of age to a club and it will be another eight years before he can be signed as a scholar and even more years before a first-team opportunity might be on the horizon. No, scouts are not in the game for money, but they do have a real pride in representing their club, often the one they have supported over the years.

Before the introduction of academies, scouts would watch school, district and Sunday league matches in their search for any outstanding young footballers aged 14 to 16. Scouts might watch as many as five games in a day or ten to 12 a week on school, amateur and parkland pitches. Very often they might be checking on just one player and rarely would they stay for the whole 80 or 90 minutes. Sometimes ten minutes might be sufficient to see if someone is worth checking again. Leads to good players might come in from schoolteachers, former players, friends, boys' clubs and parents and keen observers of local junior football.

Finding a good player as a scout then and now was only half the battle; you then have to persuade them to sign for your employers and clearly the bigger the club you are working for the greater the likely attraction to a youngster and his parents. Once they are signed up comes the long haul to ensure the initial skills and attributes that have been identified are given the opportunities to be fully developed so that the player has a chance of becoming a professional footballer in due course.

Steve Rowley, who gave Arsenal great service as their chief scout over many years, scouting for the club at all age levels, was one day reminiscing about scouting in the pre-academy days. He remembered David Beckham as a 14-year-old who could only get on the subs' bench for the Essex Schoolboys under-14 team. David was small but it was noted that he showed good technique in striking the ball. All the London scouts knew about him but did not feel confident enough to give him a trial at their club. Malcolm Fidgeon, a retired headmaster who scouted for Manchester United, decided to take David north for a longer period.

The London scouts joked behind Malcolm's back as they were thinking David was nowhere near good enough to have a trial at Manchester United. How wrong could they be? The story makes me feel better when I recall not seeing the future potential of, for example, Harry Kane.

Before his United trial, Beckham went to a Bobby Charlton coaching school and I understand that Sir Bobby had recommended him to Alex Ferguson, so besides being a great footballer, the United and England great also had an eye for spotting young talent.

The scout of today is sent by his employers to watch other academy players on Saturdays, where he watches the under-16 and under-18 teams, while on Sundays he views the under-nine to under-15 age groups. The scout who works for a Premier League or Championship club is welcomed with open arms if they are visiting a team in League One or League Two, known in my playing days as the Third and Fourth Divisions, as this means that the staff at the smaller club know they are interested in one of their boys. If there is then a transfer, much-needed revenue can be injected into the lower-league club as compensation will be paid for the loss of their young player.

The attitude is very different when a scout from a Premier League club visits another Premier League or Championship club. They will be asked to wait at the entrance gate to the academy until five minutes before kick-off. I have been in the company of five or six scouts waiting to be escorted by a club official to the corner flag of the pitch where they have to watch the game, as an official of the home club will make sure they stay in their allocated place. If a scout needs to go to the toilet, he is escorted by another club official.

This is designed to make sure they do not make contact with any parents. It is only natural that clubs do not want to lose their top players to a rival. After all, they have worked hard to identify their players and spend time, effort and finance into developing the boy's skills. Understandably, clubs are very protective of their own players and are not keen on bigger, richer clubs coming in to check over their best players, as these youngsters can be worth an extraordinary amount of money if they can break into the first team.

Severe penalties have been introduced by the FA to stop club officials making an illegal approach for another club's player by, for example, making contact with the parents or the boy.

Alan Knowles, a valued Arsenal scout whose many discoveries include Folarin Balogun, who the Gunners turned down a £5m bid from Brentford for in January 2020, was in hot water when he was accused of making an approach to a boy signed with another London Premier League club. The hearing for this misdemeanour was set up and cost many thousands of pounds. Alan was found not guilty. A guilty verdict would have seen him lose his job.

Chapter 24

My life today

AS I move towards my 80th birthday, I am happily married and living in Upminster. It was in 1993, three years after Christine died, that my cousin Pat, who lives in Upminster, introduced me to Julia, a local reflexologist and aromatherapist with her own business in complementary therapies. She was divorced and had two young daughters – 11-year-old Verity and 16-year-old Elizabeth.

Julia, by a strange coincidence, was a fan of Norwich City, for whom I was then working. Pat, who went to Julia's for reflexology, encouraged me to take her to a Norwich game. Along with Pat and my teaching colleague Mick Pirnie, who had also encouraged myself and Julia to meet up, we attended Norwich versus Bayern Munich, possibly the biggest match ever at Carrow Road. Norwich progressed from this tie into the last 16 of the 1993/94 UEFA Cup, which was a tremendous achievement for a club of their size. We sat next to each other and immediately got on very well and when Norwich scored we wanted to hug each other.

Another event I organised proved not to be so successful. I invited Julia to come over to Colchester for an evening out, and arranged to go to the gym where I was a member and where we could swim in the pool and relax in the Jacuzzi. Afterwards I cooked a steak dinner. Julia confessed later that she was not a fan of working out in a gym, had never liked the thought of sitting in a Jacuzzi and was a vegetarian. Nevertheless, our relationship blossomed and after two years we married and I moved into Julia's Upminster home. We held the ceremony in Kenya and I am delighted that we are still very happily together despite the considerable amount of time I spent working in professional football.

Eight years after Julia and I first visited Kenya, we returned to Mombasa and we booked another safari trip. This was a wonderful experience, seeing animals in Africa in their natural habitat.

As we were making the six-hour journey back to our hotel in Mombasa, we stopped at a petrol station where there was a shop, café and toilet. Julia made her way to the shop in order to look at some souvenirs. I went on to the café to buy a coffee. Julia bought a carved wooden elephant and the young man who was attending her asked if she would like to buy another wooden carving to go with the elephant. She declined and the salesman asked her if I might like to buy something. She laughed, telling him the only thing I thought about was football, which is almost true. I am, of course, not unusual in that regard.

Five minutes later the salesman tapped me on the shoulder while I was drinking my coffee and asked me which English team I supported. I was working for Arsenal and told him Arsenal. His eyes lit up and he said that he was an Arsenal fan and the young man who worked with him had a football team in which most of the players supported Arsenal. He asked me if I could send them a ball when I returned to England as their match ball had seen better days.

I asked him to show me the ball. It was in a poor state, only fit for the rubbish bin. It looked as if it had been kicked about every day for the last five years. It was split with the bladder peeping out of the casing and it did not look as though it would see through many more games.

I asked to be shown the pitch where they played. I felt so sorry for this young man who loved playing football, but could only play on a barren stretch of land behind his workplace. There was no grass, no nets, there were potholes on the pitch and while the touchline was faintly marked out there were no markings indicating a penalty area.

I asked him for his address and said that I would see if I could send him a football from England. He was delighted with my response and he introduced me to the rest of his colleagues and football team-mates. We had a brief chat about football and I was impressed at their knowledge of teams and players in England. Julia and I walked to our minibus waiting for us in the car park.

The young men came over to wave us off. I smiled thinking that I was very fortunate to work for the Arsenal Football Club while Julia was also touched when we heard a voice saying, 'You have got a beautiful wife and if you don't want her then she can stay here with me!'

When we got back to England, I put four new footballs in a box and sent the parcel to the address the young man had given me in Kenya. I hoped the parcel would get to its destination. Several weeks later I received a letter from him to say his team were delighted with the presents.

The experience helped me not to take anything for granted. I was working at the Arsenal academy with fantastic facilities and it showed me how lucky our young players were. It also revealed just how extra difficult it is for youngsters in Africa and, no doubt, many parts of the world, to become professional footballers as they don't have the facilities to practise on and refine their skills.

Victor Wanyama is, of course, possibly the finest Kenyan footballer to have played in the Premier League, doing so with Southampton and Tottenham Hotspur. Let's hope his success inspires future generations of Kenyan youngsters to match and beat his achievements.

This might be easier in the future as just before the coronavirus pandemic there were reports that top-flight English teams were close to striking a deal with the FA to ease work permit regulations for overseas players. Many talented Kenyans, such as Michael Olunga, Ayub Timbe and Eric 'Marcelo' Ouma, were hoping to take advantage of any changes in the rules at the time of writing.

I was, of course, happy to see the World Cup take place for the first time in Africa in 2010 when it was hosted by South Africa. Arsenal legend Thierry Henry, a French World Cup winner in 1998, had long called for the competition to be played in Africa.

Dennis Kucinich

I was at a tournament in Belgium with the Arsenal under-13 team. The boys were asleep and the staff were sitting outside in the warm evening discussing the performances of the young players. The week before we left for Belgium, Julia and I said goodbye to her daughter Elizabeth who was to spend six months in America working alongside Stephen Zarlenga, a researcher and author in the field of monetary theory, trader in stock and financial markets, and advocate of monetary reform. Stephen was also the founder in 1996 of the American Monetary Institute in New York.

My mobile phone rang and Julia was on the line. She blurted out that Elizabeth had just spoken to her from the USA to say that she had visited a politician, Ohio Congressman Dennis Kucinich, regarding her work on monetary reform plans. They had got on very well and after a second meeting he invited her to spend the weekend with him at the home of actress Shirley MacLaine, who was a friend of his. Over the course of the weekend, they got on so well that they decided to get married.

I was as initially surprised as Julia on hearing this news but this soon turned to great joy when we found out more about Dennis and his outstanding qualities as a man and a political activist who shares many similar values with Julia. They did get married and we subsequently met Dennis and he has visited us on many occasions. He is an integral, much-loved part of our family.

Elizabeth, who has degrees in Theology and International Conflict, supported her husband on his campaign to rival Barack Obama as the Democratic presidential candidate in 2008 but, as in 2004, when Dennis stood against John Kerry, he was unsuccessful.

Dennis was the youngest mayor in the US when he secured the post in Cleveland at the age of 30 in 1977. He was a target of the mafia in Cleveland and he survived three murder attempts. There is a film on YouTube when a member of the mafia was asked by the television interviewer about the attempts on his life. The answer came back, 'Kucinich can't be bought.'

Dennis remains politically very active and he and Elizabeth are doing good works in tackling climate change and improving the environment. Dennis is keen for the war in Ukraine to end as soon as possible.

Julia was born out of wedlock on 1 October 1949. Her mum, Joyce, found out that the father was married with three children. Joyce was naturally distraught but was determined to keep her baby. Joyce was a highly regarded midwife for 40 years, delivering over 1,200 babies, and passed away at Julia's house aged 86.

Life was very difficult in Julia's early years, not just financially but also because this was a period when there was a stigma to not having a father. Things have improved significantly since then.

Julia had spent half a century wondering who her dad was. On the rare occasions when Joyce spoke about him, she said his name was Horatio Sandhurst and he worked as a pilot. Julia searched the name of Sandhurst in the Royal Air Force archives but found no records.

Julia is a very spiritual lady and when she was in her 50s, she decided to go to a medium and see if she could be helped to communicate with him and pass on a message. Joyce had no problems with Julia doing this.

When Julia came out of the meeting, she was very excited. The medium had told her that her father had said that he was sorry for taking advantage of her mum and that Julia should find and meet his other children, who would now be in their 50s.

At the time of seeing the medium each Wednesday morning, Julia attended a breakfast club for local businesspeople. At one of these meetings she was in conversation with a private detective. She asked him if he could find her father's other children but she only had the name Sandhurst to help him. He accepted the challenge and within two days the detective rang to say that he had found a Stanley Sandhurst who lived in Crowborough, a small Sussex town. He said that he had telephoned Mr Sandhurst and after telling him Julia's situation the detective asked if he could visit him at his home.

This was agreed and later the detective knocked on the door of Mr Sandhurst. On entering the house, the detective saw a photograph of Stanley's dad on the mantlepiece. His first words to Stanley were that the man in the photograph was the father of his client. The facial likeness to Julia was so significant. Some weeks later a meeting was set up with Julia and her half-brother and it was proved they had the same dad, Horatio Carl Sandhurst. This meeting was in 2008 and for the next 12 years Julia and Stanley built up a special relationship of brother and sister.

Julia's dad had died some years before she met Stanley and she was now able to find out the missing part of her life, which she had been longing to do.

She now has a good understanding of her father and herself and she wears with pride his watch that was given to her by Stanley, who died in March 2020. Julia, together with Shirley, Stanley's partner, was at his bedside. As he was dying, Stanley called out 'Dad, Dad' and it was amazing for Julia to be with her brother knowing that her father had come to take Stanley to the spirit world.

I'm personally not inclined to believe in a spiritual world, but a story like this does make you wonder. Julia also found out that she had two half-sisters and has made friends with Michelle and Deirdre.

Julia, who is a very compassionate person, believes that her upbringing proved advantageous in later years as it has made her very understanding of people who can themselves be victims of prejudicial behaviour.

Julia is still running her business and I am only too happy to help out by answering the phone when there is no receptionist. We have two dogs and a massive garden with a pond. I make most of the meals and have become a good cook. Julia and I have a wide circle of friends and when we have time we visit the theatre.

I am in regular contact with my three children, Justine, Richard and Paul, and my grandchildren Ethan, Isaac and Ivy, plus Justine's husband Keith and Paul's wife Dagmara. I am very proud of all of them.

I continue to enjoy receiving many calls from former pupils, players and their parents. I keep a regular eye out for the results of my former teams, and players who I had under my wing at Colchester, Norwich and, of course, Arsenal. I am delighted to have been helped to write this autobiography by Mark Metcalf.

Tributes

Alex Iwobi: 'Roy was a father figure at the Arsenal academy. He has an infectious laugh and made everyone feel welcome. He gave all of us equal opportunities to get on to the pitch during matches. He gave us belief and freedom to enjoy our football and to express ourselves.

'Roy used to tell me to enjoy my football, apply myself and to always give my best. He encouraged me to do my tricks when appropriate and did not tell us off if the trick did not come off. He told me to always work hard and made it clear that talent alone does not get you to the top but talent combined with hard work does.

'Everyone respected, loved and adored Roy, he was the nicest person at the academy. There was no negativity about Roy, he concentrated on the positives and constructively told us areas he would like us to work on. His role was sometimes to let people go but people understood that this was a difficult part of his job and never held it against him.

'Roy lived not too far from my parents' house. I remember a time Roy had problems with his car and my dad gave him lifts back to his house. Roy used to make us laugh with stories about his football-playing days at Rotherham, Leyton Orient and Colchester. He just couldn't stop talking – I certainly miss his stories.

'We were very young at the time and part of the banter was to try and imitate Roy's voice – we had so much fun doing this. Roy nearly caught us a few times doing this but knowing Roy, then I am sure he would not have minded.

'Roy played a significant role in my development as a footballer. He imbibed in me the discipline to succeed. He taught me fair play, respect for team-mates and opponents. If I were to describe Roy in two words it would be – "Perfect Gentleman".

'Roy gave me hope and confidence that one day I would become a professional footballer. I will remain forever grateful to him for all he did for me.'

Chuka Iwobi, father of Alex: 'Roy is a perfect gentleman and I have never heard anyone have an unkind word to say about him. He was a father figure to the boys and loved by all the parents.

'He told me the hardest part of his job was to look a boy in the face and say, "Unfortunately we won't be offering you a contract." On the converse you could see the absolute joy in his face when he offered a contract extension to a boy.

'Roy loved watching the kids expressing themselves on the pitch. You could see him jumping about excitedly on the touchline when the boys did a trick or two and he would never chastise a boy for losing the ball while attempting to be expressive of his skills.

'We did have a difficult decision when Alex was offered a scholarship only, rather than also be asked to sign professionally as was the usual practice at the time for players who had represented England and which Alex had at under-16 level and he also later played at under-17 and under-18 levels.

'I encouraged Alex to remain strong and prove why he deserved a professional contract. The rest is history as Arsène Wenger took him under his wings.

'I remember an occasion when I was passing by Roy's house and decided to pop in for a five-minute chat. We spent a lot of time reminiscing about the good old days – Roy has the habit of making you feel at home – when I eventually looked at my watch three hours had gone. Roy is compassionate and kind.

'We have great memories of Arsenal and a lot to be grateful to Roy for.'

Charles and Sarah Willock, parents of Chris, Joe and Matthew: 'When we think back to those exciting but uncertain times as our boys were trying to make it through the academy system at Arsenal FC, we encountered a father figure at the helm with knowledge, insight, patience, encouragement, and a hearty spirit. That man was Roy Massey.'

Joe Willock: 'I remember crying because I wanted to join in with the older boys in a game in the dome. I was around five years of age at the time.

'My dad was a bit hesitant because of the age difference and I wasn't wearing shin pads. Roy went away and came back with a pair of enormous pads, shoved them down my socks and allowed me to play.

'He always believed in my ability and encouraged and nurtured my progression.'

Chris Willock: 'I was allowed to start my development at the Arsenal academy at five years of age. I didn't know at the time that it was rare to do so; however, Roy Massey made it possible for me to participate.

'With that initial early start, it developed in me a football education second to none; it also gave me a platform to showcase my ability.'

Matthew Willock: 'I was given my opportunity at the Arsenal academy by Roy Massey. He understood me as a player and saw a potential in me and for that I will be forever grateful.'

Rob Dipple, emerging talent scouting manager in Europe for the Manchester City Football Group; Arsenal academy coach/ development centre co-ordinator: 'Roy Massey was the most important person in my career. He gave me an opportunity that probably nobody else would have. He was an innovator in his use of younger coaches with younger elite players and saw the need to have coaches that were teachers in the foundation phase.

'He was the best manager of people I have seen and simply a genius at managing the most difficult situations. Everybody looked up to Roy – players, coaches, medical staff and parents. He is without doubt one of the most unselfish people I have ever met and he had time for absolutely everybody.

'You could talk to Roy about anything, football or otherwise and no matter how bad anything was he would always leave people feeling a little bit better. His room was always open for everyone that came to the Hale End training ground. He is one of the most supportive and caring people I have ever met.'

Jack Wilshere

When I think back to my time in the academy, he was the guy who I remember the most.

Roy was good in so many ways. Not just for me but for all of the Academy as he had great experience and he always kept everyone to a high standard and he demanded that right across Hale End. That rubbed off on me and eventually as I grew up a little bit then he was a bit like a father figure. He was the one that I trusted most in in terms of getting feedback and what I needed to do and what I needed to work on and we just developed that relationship overtime.

Has some of Roy's skills and personality helped you in your current coaching role at Arsenal?

I went to Arsenal when I was aged 9 and you're working out what type of person you are. Your family naturally has a major impact has but I also regarded the academy as my family and Roy was the one who drove things forward and he had a strong work ethic. That rubbed off on me and helps now when I'm doing my day-to-day coaching stuff.

Someone said to me recently that players do not always remember what the coach says. I do remember a few things Roy said but it was the way he made us comfortable whilst also holding us to high standards that I especially recall.

Career Statistics

Rotherham United (Division 2) 18/1 subs 6 goals
Orient (Division 3) 68/5 subs 17 goals
Colchester (Division 4) 35/6 subs 15 goals

Overall total first team appearances in League, FA and League Cup
121/12 subs 38 goals

Bibliography

Numerous Club Who's Who, Official History and Complete Record books and *Rothmans Football Year Books* and, of which the most important were: *Arsenal: The Complete Record* by Josh James, Mark Andrews and Andy Kelly, *Who's Who of Arsenal* by Tony Matthews, *Leyton Orient* by Neil Kaufman and Alan Ravenhill, *The Who's Who of Colchester United: The Layer Road Years* by Jeff Whitehead and Kevin Drury, *Still United: The History of Rotherham United* by Gerry Somerton, *The Definitive Rotherham United* by Pendragon Books, *Sheffield Wednesday: The Complete Record* by John Brodie and Jason Dickinson and *The Wednesday Boys* by Jason Dickinson and John Brodie.

Arsene Wenger: An autobiography
Scouting for Moyes by Les Padfield.
The Nowhere Men: The Unknown Story of Football's True Talent Spotters by Michael Calvin.
Flying Over An Olive Grove: The remarkable story of Fred Spiksley, a flawed football hero by Clive and Ralph Nicholson and Mark Metcalf
Football's Black Pioneers: The stories of the First Black Players to represent the 92 League Clubs by Bill Hern and David Gleave
The Golden Boot: Football's Top Scorers by Mark Metcalf and Tony Matthews
The Hamlyn Book Of World Soccer A Pictorial History Of World Soccer by Dennis Signy
Purnell's Encyclopedia of Association Football
Mexborough, Conisbrough, Denaby and Swinton by Peter Tuffrey
Backpass magazine

Index